# Encyclopedia
## — of —
# LIFE SCIENCES

Second Edition

# 7

## Hands – Larvae and pupae

Marshall Cavendish
New York • London • Toronto • Sydney

**Marshall Cavendish**
99 White Plains Road
Tarrytown, New York 10591-9001

www.marshallcavendish.com

© 1996, 2004 Marshall Cavendish Corporation

Created by **The Brown Reference Group plc**

**Library of Congress Cataloging-in-Publication Data**

Encyclopedia of life sciences / [edited by] Anne O'Daly.—2nd ed.
    p.    cm.
Summary: An illustrated encyclopedia with articles on
agriculture, anatomy, biochemistry, biology, genetics,
medicine, and molecular biology.
Includes bibliographical references (p.   ).
    ISBN 0-7614-7442-0 (set)
    ISBN 0-7614-7449-8 (vol. 7)
    1. Life sciences—Encyclopedias. 2. Biology—Encyclopedias. [1.
Biology—Encyclopedias. 2. Life sciences—Encyclopedias.] I. O'Daly,
Anne, 1966–
    QH302.5 .E53    2003
    570'.3—dc21
                                            2002031157

Printed in Malaysia
Bound in the United States of America

07 06 05 04 03  6 5 4 3 2 1

**Artworks by:**
Darren Awuah, Bill Botten, Jennie Dooge, Dax Fullbrook,
and Mark Walker.

**For The Brown Reference Group:**
Project Editors: Caroline Beattie and Lesley Campbell-Wright
Editors: Richard Beatty, Robert Cave, Simon Hall, Rob Houston,
Jim Martin, and Ben Morgan
Designer: Joan Curtis
Picture Researcher: Rebecca Cox
Managing Editor: Bridget Giles
Design Manager: Lynne Ross
Indexer: Kay Ollerenshaw

**For Marshall Cavendish:**
Project Editor: Joyce Tavolacci
Editorial Director: Paul Bernabeo
Production Manager: Michael Esposito

**Title page:** holdfasts of giant kelp (Frank Lane Picture Agency)

# CONTENTS

# USEFUL INFORMATION

Use this table to convert the English system (or the imperial system), the system of units common in the United States (e.g., inches, miles, quarts), to the metric system (e.g., meters, kilometers, liters) or to convert the metric system to the English system. You can convert one measurement into another by multiplying. For example, to convert centimeters into inches, multiply the number of centimeters by 0.3937. To convert inches into centimeters, multiply the number of inches by 2.54.

| To convert | into | multiply by |
|---|---|---|
| **Acres** | Square feet | 43,560 |
| | Square yards | 4840 |
| | Square miles | 0.00156 |
| | Square meters | 4046.856 |
| | Hectares | 0.40468 |
| **Celsius** | Fahrenheit | First multiply by 1.8 then add 32 |
| **Centimeters** | Inches | 0.3937 |
| | Feet | 0.0328 |
| **Cubic cm** | Cubic inches | 0.06102 |
| **Cubic feet** | Cubic inches | 1728 |
| | Cubic yards | 0.037037 |
| | Gallons | 7.48 |
| | Cubic meters | 0.028317 |
| | Liters | 28.32 |
| **Cubic inches** | Fluid ounces | 0.554113 |
| | Cups | 0.069264 |
| | Quarts | 0.017316 |
| | Gallons | 0.004329 |
| | Liters | 0.016387 |
| | Milliliters | 16.387064 |
| **Cubic meters** | Cubic feet | 35.3145 |
| | Cubic yards | 1.30795 |
| **Cubic yards** | Cubic feet | 27 |
| | Cubic meters | 0.76456 |
| **Cups, fluid** | Quarts | 0.25 |
| | Pints | 0.5 |
| | Ounces | 8 |
| | Milliliters | 237 |
| | Tablespoons | 16 |
| | Teaspoons | 48 |
| **Fahrenheit** | Celsius | First subtract 32 then divide by 1.8 |
| **Feet** | Centimeters | 30.48 |
| | Meters | 0.3048 |
| | Kilometers | 0.0003 |
| | Inches | 12 |
| | Yards | 0.3333 |
| | Miles | 0.00019 |
| **Gallons** | Quarts | 4 |
| | Pints | 8 |
| | Cups | 16 |
| | Ounces | 128 |
| | Liters | 3.785 |
| | Milliliters | 3785 |
| | Cubic inches | 231 |
| | Cubic feet | 0.1337 |
| | Cubic yards | 0.00495 |
| | Cubic meters | 0.00379 |
| | British gallons | 0.8327 |
| **Grams** | Ounces | 0.03527 |
| | Pounds | 0.0022 |
| **Hectares** | Square meters | 10,000 |
| | Acres | 2.471 |
| **Horsepower** | Foot-pounds per minute | 33,000 |
| | British thermal units (Btu) per minute | 42.42 |
| | British thermal units (Btu) per hour | 2546 |
| | Kilowatts | 0.7457 |
| | Metric horsepower | 1.014 |
| **Inches** | Feet | 0.08333 |

| To convert | into | multiply by |
|---|---|---|
| **Inches (continued)** | Yards | 0.02778 |
| | Centimeters | 2.54 |
| | Meters | 0.0254 |
| **Kilograms** | Grams | 1000 |
| | Ounces | 35.274 |
| | Pounds | 2.2046 |
| | Short tons | 0.0011 |
| | Long tons | 0.00098 |
| | Metric tons (tonnes) | 0.001 |
| **Kilometers** | Meters | 1000 |
| | Miles | 0.62137 |
| | Yards | 1093.6 |
| | Feet | 3280.8 |
| **Kilowatts** | British thermal units (Btu) per minute | 56.9 |
| | Horsepower | 1.341 |
| | Metric horsepower | 1.397 |
| **Kilowatt-hours** | British thermal units (Btu) | 3413 |
| **Knots** | Statute miles per hour | 1.1508 |
| **Leagues** | Miles | 3 |
| **Liters** | Milliliters | 1000 |
| | Fluid ounces | 33.814 |
| | Quarts | 1.05669 |
| | British gallons | 0.21998 |
| | Cubic inches | 61.02374 |
| | Cubic feet | 0.13531 |
| **Meters** | Inches | 39.37 |
| | Feet | 3.28083 |
| | Yards | 1.09361 |
| | Miles | 0.000621 |
| | Kilometers | 0.001 |
| | Centimeters | 100 |
| | Millimeters | 1000 |
| **Miles** | Inches | 63,360 |
| | Feet | 5280 |
| | Yards | 1760 |
| | Meters | 1609.34 |
| | Kilometers | 1.60934 |
| | Nautical miles | 0.8684 |
| **Miles nautical, U.S. and International** | Statute miles | 1.1508 |
| | Feet | 6076.115 |
| | Meters | 1852 |
| **Miles per minute** | Feet per second | 88 |
| | Knots | 52.104 |
| **Milliliters** | Fluid ounces | 0.0338 |
| | Cubic inches | 0.061 |
| | Liters | 0.001 |
| **Millimeters** | Centimeters | 0.1 |
| | Meters | 0.001 |
| | Inches | 0.03937 |
| **Ounces, avoirdupois** | Pounds | 0.0625 |
| | Grams | 28.34952 |
| | Kilograms | 0.0283495 |
| **Ounces, fluid** | Pints | 0.0625 |
| | Quarts | 0.03125 |
| | Cubic inches | 1.80469 |
| | Cubic feet | 0.00104 |
| | Milliliters | 29.57353 |
| | Liters | 0.02957 |
| **Pints, fluid** | Ounces, fluid | 16 |
| | Quarts, fluid | 0.5 |

| To convert | into | multiply by |
|---|---|---|
| **Pints, fluid (continued)** | Cubic inches | 28.8745 |
| | Cubic feet | 0.01671 |
| | Milliliters | 473.17647 |
| | Liters | 0.473176 |
| **Pounds** | Ounces | 16 |
| | Grams | 453.59237 |
| | Kilograms | 0.45359 |
| | Tons | 0.0005 |
| | Tons, long | 0.000446 |
| | Metric tons (tonnes) | 0.0004536 |
| **Quarts, fluid** | Ounces, fluid | 32 |
| | Pints, fluid | 2 |
| | Gallons | 0.25 |
| | Cubic inches | 57.749 |
| | Cubic feet | 0.033421 |
| | Liters | 0.946358 |
| | Milliliters | 946.358 |
| **Square centimeters** | Square inches | 0.155 |
| **Square feet** | Square inches | 144 |
| | Square meters | 0.093 |
| | Square yards | 0.111 |
| **Square inches** | Square centimeters | 6.452 |
| | Square feet | 0.0069 |
| **Square kilometers** | Hectares | 100 |
| | Square meters | 1,000,000 |
| | Square miles | 0.3861 |
| **Square meters** | Square feet | 10.758 |
| | Square yards | 1.196 |
| **Square miles** | Acres | 640 |
| | Square kilometers | 2.59 |
| **Square yards** | Square feet | 9 |
| | Square inches | 1296 |
| | Square meters | 0.836 |
| **Tablespoons** | Ounces, fluid | 0.5 |
| | Teaspoons | 3 |
| | Milliliters | 14.7868 |
| **Teaspoons** | Ounces, fluid | 0.16667 |
| | Tablespoons | 0.3333 |
| | Milliliters | 4.9289 |
| **Tons, long** | Pounds | 2240 |
| | Kilograms | 1016.047 |
| | Short tons | 1.12 |
| | Metric tons (tonnes) | 1.016 |
| **Tons, short** | Pounds | 2000 |
| | Kilograms | 907.185 |
| | Long tons | 0.89286 |
| | Metric tonnes | 0.907 |
| **Tons, metric (tonnes)** | Pounds | 2204.62 |
| | Kilograms | 1000 |
| | Long tons | 0.984206 |
| | Short tons | 1.10231 |
| **Watts** | British thermal units (Btu) per hour | 3.415 |
| | Horsepower | 0.00134 |
| **Yards** | Inches | 36 |
| | Feet | 3 |
| | Miles | 0.0005681 |
| | Centimeters | 91.44 |
| | Meters | 0.9144 |

# HANDS

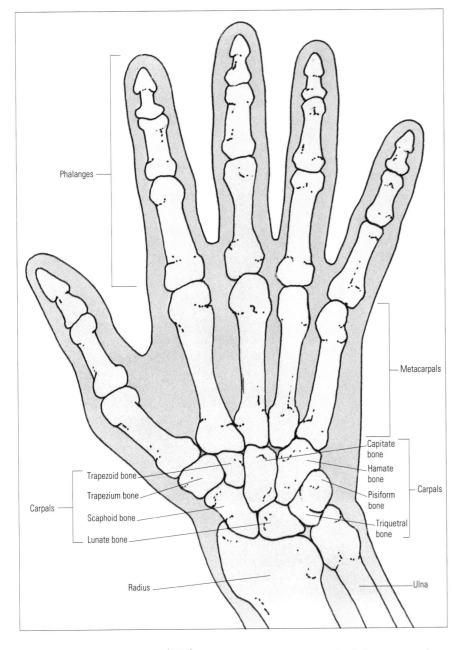

*The human hand's flexibility is partly due to its many bones and joints.*

Phalanges

Carpals

Trapezoid bone
Trapezium bone
Scaphoid bone
Lunate bone

Radius

Metacarpals

Capitate bone
Hamate bone
Pisiform bone
Triquetral bone

Carpals

Ulna

## CONNECTIONS

● Rheumatoid **ARTHRITIS** can cause joint immobilities, hand deformities, pain, and loss of mobility.

● A **CALCIUM**-rich diet is essential for strong **BONES**.

The human hand has been called the most sophisticated tool on Earth. It enables people to perform delicate tasks, such as embroidery, piano playing, and engraving. This highly maneuverable part of the body has played a vital role in the evolution of human cultures.

### Maneuverability unmatched

Although modern monkeys, gorillas, and chimpanzees all have hands, theirs can never match the maneuverability of human hands. The reason lies partly in a human's highly flexible saddle joint, which links the thumb to the wrist and allows humans to rotate their thumb and grasp objects.

Another factor is the length of a human's thumb in relation to the fingers. Other primates have shorter thumbs and longer fingers; thus, it is harder

for them to press the tips of their thumb and fingers together as a human can. This opposable capability of human thumbs is unique. With their relatively long fingers, apes have a clear edge over humans in grasping branches, but they would have a tough time competing against humans in a game of darts.

Humans can perform prehensile, or grasping, movements that involve holding an object between the palm and the thumb. A hand's grip is both precise and powerful. In using the precision grip, humans can hold an object between the pads of their thumb and one or more fingertips (for example, when picking up a pen from the floor). The power grip is performed by the pads of the fingers and the palm, with the thumb serving only as reinforcement (as in a golf club grip). Apes, gorillas, orangutans, chimpanzees, and most monkeys can also use both types of grips, although their precision grip is weak and awkward.

Both humans and apes share an aptitude for nonprehensile hand movements. These movements do not involve grasping. They include pushing, lifting, and punching and tapping the keys of a typewriter or piano.

### Structure of the human hand

The hand is made up of 27 bones comprising the wrist, palm, and fingers. Eight small bones, packed together in two rows, make up the wrist. These bones, called the carpals, are joined to the radius and ulna of the arm at one end and to the metacarpals at the other. The five metacarpals are the bones of the palm. They connect the fingers and the wrist. Each finger contains three bones: the proximal, middle, and distal phalanges. Thumbs lack the middle phalanges.

Between the bones are cartilage joints that are lined with thin membranes called synovia. The joints in the fingers are hinge joints; they enable the finger segments to move up and down like the hinged lid of a trunk. Biaxial joints between the phalanges and metacarpals move the fingers not only up and down but also sideways. The carpals are joined by plane joints, which allow sliding movements. The most mobile joint is the one between the thumb's metacarpal and the wrist. This saddle joint, named for its shape, gives the thumb a wide range of movements, including rotation inward and outward. The long,

### CORE FACTS

■ The hand of humans and some primates is unique in that it has an opposable thumb (modified for grasping).

■ The human hand is made up of 27 bones—carpals, metacarpals, and phalanges.

■ Left-handedness is thought to be inherited, although it is possible to learn right-handedness.

*Orangutans have long fingers that can be securely wrapped around branches. This ability allows the animal to swing easily through trees of its native rain forest.*

thin cords that stand out when the fingers are spread apart are called tendons. They connect the muscles of the forearm to the bones of the hand and thus help move the hands (see BONE).

The skin on the surface of the hand aids grasping. For example, the skin of the palm is tightly connected to the underlying tissue to help protect it from being torn away (see SKIN). This tight connection also causes deep, permanent lines to develop where the palm bends. Tiny ridges called papillary ridges covering the palms and the undersides of the fingers act like tire treads to increase friction and therefore improve the grip. The unique patterns of papillary ridges on human fingertips leave fingerprints on smooth surfaces. Such fingerprints help police identify and convict criminals.

The back of the hand is covered with fine hairs. At the bottom of the hair follicles (the pits that contain the hairs) are sebaceous glands. They secrete an oily substance called sebum that keeps the skin supple and fills the pores in the hand and thus protects the skin from microorganisms and excessive water loss.

On the palm of the hand, there are no hairs and therefore no sebaceous glands. This lack of sebum is the reason why the fingers wrinkle if they are immersed in water for a long time (for example, in the bath). The water enters by osmosis and causes the skin to swell and form into wrinkles.

The skin of the hand is generously supplied with touch receptor organs, called tactile corpuscles. Nerves connected to these microscopic sensors carry impulses to the brain. Up to 200 nerve endings are packed into 1 square inch (6.45 cm$^2$) of skin on the hand and thus it is one of the most sensitive parts of the body. Fingertips are particularly sensitive and have an even higher density of touch receptors.

Blood is supplied to the hand by two arteries (the radial artery on the thumb side of the wrist and the ulnar artery on the side of the little finger) and is carried away by veins that are most visible on the back of the hand.

Fingernails are made of keratin, the tough protein that is also the main constituent of hair (see HAIR). A fingernail takes about six months to grow

## DISORDERS OF THE HAND

Hands are susceptible to injuries, such as cuts, bruises, and fractures because they are frequently used to manipulate a large variety of tools and other objects. Dry skin conditions, such as dermatitis, are also very common because hands are exposed to many different chemicals and irritants. Inflammatory diseases, such as arthritis, rob some people of their manual dexterity. Osteoarthritis is characterized by the gradual wearing away of the cartilage that covers the articulating ends of bones (see BONE). As the cartilage erodes, new bone builds up around the joints, giving them a knotty appearance. Although painful, osteoarthritis rarely causes crippling deformities. In hands it mainly affects the joint at the base of the

thumb. A more harmful but less common form of arthritis is rheumatoid arthritis. This debilitating disease may appear very early in life and often leads to bone deterioration. *Rheumatism* is a general term, referring to a number of disorders that are marked by discomfort in the joints, ligaments, tendons, bursae, or fibrous tissue. Heberden's rheumatism produces nodes, or knots, in the finger joints. Another potentially disabling ailment is carpal tunnel syndrome—compression of the median nerve in the wrist within the carpal tunnel by inflammation of the tissues. Symptoms may include pain, tingling, or burning in the fingers and hands. Many cases have been linked to repetitive movements in the workplace.

A CLOSER LOOK

from base to tip. In vertebrates claws evolved as traction (gripping) organs, a purpose they still serve in most reptiles, birds, and mammals. Human nails evolved from claws and also serve this purpose. As with many vertebrates, nails may also be used as weapons for scratching and clawing. Humans frequently use their nails as tools for prying, manipulating, and grasping small objects. Fingernails may also act as a barometer of health. Brittle, ridged, concave nails are a sign of iron-deficiency anemia (see IRON), while splinterlike black marks beneath the nail's surface suggest there is bleeding under the skin and may signify a serious bleeding disorder.

## Evolution of the hand

The earliest primates that had nails rather than claws were the Adapidae, which lived in trees and resembled modern-day lemurs. Although they had nails, fossils of the Adapidae provide evidence that these primates had immobile and nonopposable thumbs.

Many scientists believe that the common ancestor between ape and early humans is *Proconsul*, which appeared about 19 million years ago. However, since *Proconsul* was adapted for walking on all fours and had no true hands, the evolution of the hand must have occurred later on. About three to four million years ago, the human ancestor, *Australopithecus afarensis*, had hands. However, these hands had curved fingers and did not appear to have the fine manipulative abilities associated with toolmaking.

Until recently, anthropologists believed that the opposable thumb emerged in the species *Homo erectus* about 1.6 million years ago. However, fossils of the species *Australopithecus robustus*, which lived about two and a half million years ago, suggest it was these primitive humans that first had opposable thumbs and thus hands that were capable of making tools. Their fingertips were also quite broad; this feature is thought to be associated with the abundant supply of blood vessels and nerve endings that give rise to sensitive fingertips.

Three million years ago, primitive humans were bipedal (walking upright on two legs). This shift from using four to two feet, thought to have occurred about four million years ago, marked the first adaptive breakthrough in the development of modern humans. It also allowed early humans to develop manual dexterity. It fostered not only the evolution of a hand better suited for toolmaking than weight bearing but also, and perhaps more important, the development of the portion of the brain that controls hand movements. This region now occupies a far greater portion of the human brain than it does in any other animal.

C. WASHAM

**See also:** BONE; FEET; HAIR; IRON; SKIN.

## Further reading:
Tortora, G. J., et al. 2000. *Principles of Anatomy and Physiology.* 9th ed. Reading, Mass.: Addison-Wesley Educational Publishers.

# LEFT- AND RIGHT-HANDEDNESS

Left-handers make up only 10 to 15 percent of the population, yet there are more left-handers than right-handers among great musicians, mathematicians, artists, actors, engineers, and architects. Gifted left-handers include Albert Einstein and the artists Pablo Picasso and Michelangelo.

Scientists are not sure why left-handers excel in these occupations or even why people are left-handed. They suspect, however, that the key lies in the adaptability of their brains. For 95 percent of all right-handers, speech is controlled by their brain's left hemisphere. The same is true for 60 to 70 percent of all left-handers. About 20 percent, however, have speech control in their right hemisphere. The rest have it in both sides of their brain. This rare ability to control speech through both hemispheres may enhance creativity.

Family trees suggest that left-handedness is hereditary. For example, only 9 percent of children with two right-handed parents are left-handed. Among children born to one right-handed and one left-handed parent, the percentage jumps to 19 percent. Parents who are both left-handed have a 26 percent chance of having a left-handed child. However, a child made to use the right hand despite natural preference may become right-handed. Ambidextrous people are able to use their left and right hands equally.

Handedness may have existed even before the development of hands. Fossil evidence has shown that ancient crustaceans fleeing a predator were inclined to turn to the right. Scientists link this tendency to asymmetrical body parts, including the dominant left brain hemisphere and the larger right hand in right-handed humans. In less-developed animals, this instinct may have helped species survive.

*The great Italian painter Leonardo da Vinci (1452–1519) was left-handed.*

## A CLOSER LOOK

# HEARING

**Hearing is the ability to detect sound waves, convert them to nerve impulses, and perceive them as sounds**

## CONNECTIONS

● The ability to hear declines as part of the **AGING** process.

● **BATS** have specialized forms of vocalizations and hearing, called **ECHOLOCATION**, which enable them to hunt in the dark.

● Some marine **MAMMALS** have become specially adapted for hearing under water, and some of them, namely dolphins, also use echolocation.

*This diagram shows the basic structure of the human ear.*

In humans hearing ability decreases as one ages. Tiny hair cells (with hairlike processes) in the inner ear are gradually damaged by loud noises in the environment, the result being a slow loss of hearing. Hearing, the ability to detect sound waves, occurs in the ears, where the mechanical energy of the sounds entering the ears are changed to the electrical messages of nerves. From birth loud noises begin stiffening the delicate hair cells, which act as tiny transducers to convert sound to nerve impulses. The cells can hold their rigid pose only so long before they die. By age 65, the average human has permanently lost more than 40 percent of the hair cells present at birth.

## Which animals can hear?

Hearing is commonly present in only two major animal groups: vertebrates and arthropods. Scientists believe other groups lack the complex nervous system necessary for hearing. Hearing promotes survival, by enabling an animal to detect a predator or a mate. In more developed vertebrates, hearing also aids communication and expression of emotion.

Of the many orders of insects, only a few are known to be capable of hearing. They include crickets, grasshoppers, katydids, cicadas, butterflies, moths, and flies. Crickets and katydids have ears on their legs; grasshoppers and cicadas have ears on their abdomens.

Hearing reaches its highest level of development in mammals. Most mammals, including humans, have an outer, middle, and inner ear. The outer ear, or pinna, focuses the sound into the auditory canal and helps locate the source of a sound. Many mammals can move their pinnae forward or backward,

toward or away from the sound source. In marine mammals, such as seals and dolphins, the pinna is reduced so the body is more streamlined. These mammals can also close their ear canals when diving. The outer ear opening in whales has been reduced to the size of a pinhole; the animals are unable to hear through these minute holes and instead detect waterborne sound waves that pass through an organ in their head that transmits the sound to their middle and inner ears.

The frequency range of hearing varies greatly among species. Human adults hears tones as low as 100 Hz (hertz, a unit of frequency; 1 Hz = 1 sound pulse per second) and as high as 10,000 Hz, although young people may hear frequencies up to 24,000 Hz.

Bats and dolphins navigate and hunt their prey by a process called echolocation, "seeing" with sound (see

### CORE FACTS
■ Hearing is the conversion of sound waves to nerve impulses, which are recognized as sounds in the brain.
■ The pinna, or outer ear, of many vertebrates has a degree of movement, enabling the direction of the sound to be determined and optimizing hearing.
■ The important sounds in human speech generally fall within the frequency range between 500 and 4,000 hertz.
■ The human ear detects sound through vibration of the eardrum. These vibrations are transferred directly to the inner ear, where their frequencies are analyzed and appropriate nerve messages (action potentials) are sent to the brain via the auditory nerve.

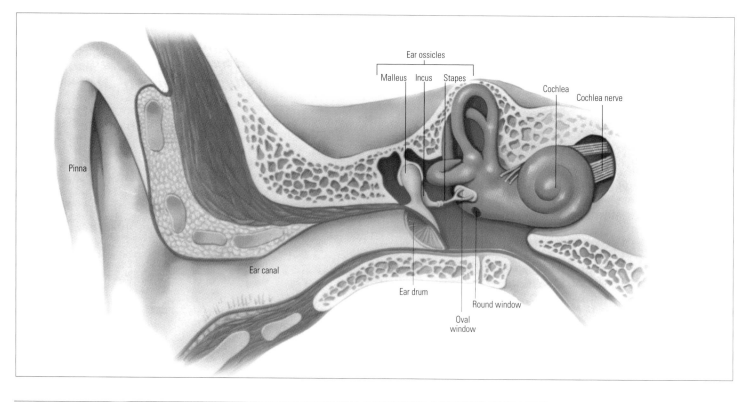

Ear ossicles
Malleus  Incus  Stapes
Cochlea
Cochlea nerve
Pinna
Ear canal
Ear drum
Round window
Oval window

BATS; ECHOLOCATION; WHALES, PORPOISES, AND DOL-PHINS). It involves transmitting a sound pulse and then listening for the echo as it bounces off objects. The echo enables these animals to determine how far they are from an object and what it is made of. Bats emit ultrasonic signals in their search for insects and other prey. Scientists have proved that many of the insects that bats prey on have developed an ability to detect these signals. By putting both earless moths and those with ears into a chamber with bats, the bats ate all the earless moths, while 90 percent of those with ears escaped by diving away from the echolocating bats.

The fossil record shows that green lacewings, tiger beetles, praying mantises, katydids, crickets, and other insects were able to produce sounds long before bats evolved. Therefore, it is thought that these early insects could also hear. When they began to fall prey to bats, evolution operating by natural selection extended their hearing range. Moths, however, most likely developed ears only after the evolution of bats.

## THE HUMAN EAR

Clapping the hands produces a sound, seemingly at the moment the hands meet—but only seemingly. At that moment, the sound wave was just being produced. It had to travel to the eardrum and then through a maze of organs in the ear and be converted into nerve impulses before finally reaching the brain, where the sound is recognized and its location computed. The entire process takes time—albeit a mere fraction of a second.

Sound waves are collected by each pinna, where they are funneled through the auditory canal to the tympanic membrane, or eardrum. The eardrum separates the outer ear from the middle ear. Three tiny bones occupy the middle ear's air-filled chamber.

Sound makes the eardrum vibrate against the malleus, or hammer, setting off a chain reaction. The hammer moves the incus, or anvil, which in turn moves the stapes, or stirrup. The stirrup then vibrates the oval window, transferring the mechanical stimulus from the middle to the inner ear. The three bones of the middle ear amplify sound by focusing the vibration on the tiny oval window. The ear is protected from extremely loud noises: at high sound volumes, two tiny muscles connected to the bones of the middle ear contract by a rapid reflex, diminishing the amount of

*The pipistrelle bat (Pipistrellus pipistrellus) uses echolocation to find insects and other prey while in flight. It sends out sound pulses and then listens for the echo as the pulse bounces off objects.*

## TEACHING THE DEAF TO COMMUNICATE

Through time humans have looked for ways to overcome or reverse the causes of deafness. In the past, tools such as the ear horn were employed to amplify and funnel sound into the outer ear. Such basic early attempts to alleviate the difficulties of deafness have now been replaced by modern electronic equipment. In cases where the individual is irreversibly deaf, the ability to communicate must be achieved in another way.

In the early 19th century, U.S. educator Thomas Hopkins Gallaudet (1787–1851) advocated sign language as communication for the deaf. A deaf child, trained from infancy, can say only about 500 words by age five, compared with the 5,000 to 20,000 words of a child who can hear. Those who are taught sign language can learn to express more ideas at an earlier age. However, opponents of sign language argue that it isolates the deaf from the hearing population. Since the 1970s, many schools for the deaf have incorporated both philosophies, teaching speech, lipreading, and sign language. American sign language (AMSLAN) uses some 6,000 signs for words and word combinations. Deaf students also learn signs representing each letter of the alphabet so that they can spell out words or names.

Because deaf people cannot hear speech, they find it difficult to mimic the sounds in their own speech. Speech instructors begin by teaching deaf students to make sounds of varying volume and pitch. Sound-sensitive lights are often used to provide feedback. Students learn to associate the brightness of the light with the volume and length of the sounds they make. Eventually, they are taught to combine the sounds into words.

## COCHLEAR IMPLANTS

In the 1970s researcher Robert Schindler of the University of California at San Francisco developed a cochlear implant that directly stimulates the auditory nerve. In 1984 the Food and Drug Administration agency gave its approval to his cochlear implant for adults. In 1990 the agency extended the use of these implants to children. Now thousands of people worldwide use them.

A microphone in the patient's ear picks up sounds and transfers them to a sound processor worn on a belt. In the processor, important sound patterns are identified and amplified, making them easier to understand. The processor then transmits the sound signals to a receiver implanted in the patient's skull and then through a fine wire to the cochlea, where they stimulate the auditory nerve fibers.

For some deaf patients, particularly those who lost their hearing after learning to speak, cochlear implants have been a godsend. Yet the overall results of implants have been disappointing. Only one-fifth of people with implants can hear and speak well. Three-fifths can use the implants only as an aid to lipreading. The remaining one-fifth are not helped at all. These failures may be due to the appropriation of brain "processing power" in the deaf person's auditory areas for other brain functions.

Researchers at the House Ear Institute in Los Angeles are also developing a device for patients who have a damaged auditory nerve. This experimental implant sends impulses directly to the part of the brain controlling hearing, called the cochlear nucleus. The implant allows the perception of sound but nothing as distinguishable as human speech. As of 2002 the implant is in clinical trials.

### A CLOSER LOOK

*U.S. lecturer Helen Keller (1880–1968), who became deaf and blind after an illness at age 19 months, regarded her absence of hearing, not sight, as her most isolating factor.*

vibration transmitted from the middle ear bones to the oval window. These contractions also lessen the intensity of one's hearing when one is speaking.

From the oval window, the pressure waves enter the fluid of the inner ear. The piston action of the stirrup against the oval window is transmitted to perilymph fluid in the cochlea, a membrane-covered bony tube the diameter of a pea. The movement of the perilymph causes vibrations in the basilar membrane, a thin sheet of tissue that lies along the base of the middle cochlear chamber.

These vibrations stimulate the 15,000 hair cells lining each organ of Corti, a delicate coiled organ within the cochlea. The hair cells convert the mechanical vibrations into nerve impulses (action potentials), which travel in the neurons of the auditory nerve to the brain, where they are perceived as sounds.

The eustachian tube, running from the middle ear to the end of the nasopharynx (the upper throat area), equalizes pressure in the air-filled middle ear with that of the outside air. It works through a valve that opens and closes at the throat end of the tube. This tube may become clogged during infection; airplane passengers suffering from colds may experience pain and temporary hearing loss during the airplane's descent, which causes an increase in air pressure and painful inward stretching of the eardrum.

In 1824 French neurologist Marie-Jean-Pierre Flourens found that cutting the semicircular canals in the inner ears of pigeons produced abnormal head movements of the birds. This discovery showed that the fluid in the inner ear helps control equilibrium (the sense of balance; see EARS). Diseases of the inner ear and semicircular canals may therefore also cause dizziness, nausea, vomiting, and disorientation.

### Measuring hearing

An electronic device called an audiometer is typically used to measure hearing. Most audiometers test hearing in the range 125 to 10,000 Hz. As tones of different frequencies are produced, sounds the patient can and cannot hear are plotted on a graph. The shape of the graph helps doctors diagnose the cause of hearing loss. When an audiometer shows impaired hearing, the doctor may also test for bone conduction (vibrations through the skull), which involves only the inner ear. A patient with a weak performance on the audiometer and a strong one in the bone conduction test most likely has a middle-ear problem.

Children too young to indicate whether they hear a tone may be tested using an audiometer coupled with an electroencephalogram (EEG). Electrodes placed on the scalp record the nerve activity in the brain's auditory areas when a sound is heard. Cochlear function may be tested through an electrocochleogram: doctors thread a fine needle through the eardrum to the cochlea to measure its nerve impulses.

### Hearing loss and deafness

The most common form of hearing loss is conductive deafness, which most people eventually develop as they get older. It stems from problems in the

*This section of the inner ear shows the organ of Corti (at center), the delicate coiled organ within the cochlea.*

outer ear or middle ear and can often be corrected with a hearing aid worn on the ear. Sensorineural, or nerve, deafness results from damage in the inner ear or along the nerve pathway to the brain.

A common cause of conductive deafness is otosclerosis. This condition occurs when bony growths on the stirrup diminish its ability to transmit sound waves to the inner ear. An estimated 10 percent of the adult population (twice as many females as males) has otosclerosis, although many do not notice its effects until their senior years.

Loud noises in the environment cause hearing loss. Overamplified music, noisy cars, and loud machines have all been blamed. Surveys have shown that most dentists, truck drivers, machinists, and miners have substandard hearing. Loud noise damages hearing by making the ear's delicate hair cells stiffen and ultimately die. Unlike other cells, they are not replaced. Such damage may come from a single exposure to an exceptionally loud noise or from repeated exposure to lower levels of sound. Sounds of 90 decibels (a unit for expressing the relative intensity of sounds), a level common in many workplaces, can produce long-range hearing loss. Sound levels at rock concerts commonly exceed 120 decibels. People living in unusually quiet environments often have keen hearing. Members of a central African tribe have been known to hear a soft murmur from a distance the width of a football field.

Certain drugs cause hearing disturbances. Large doses of aspirin may cause temporary ringing in the ears (tinnitus). Quinine sometimes leads to permanent hearing loss. Several antibiotics, including streptomycin and kanamycin, may also diminish hearing. Concussions and skull fractures can also impair hearing, particularly if the fracture runs through the labyrinth of the inner ear. Hearing loss is sometimes related to viral infections, particularly mumps.

Congenital nerve deafness is present at birth or occurs shortly afterward. It results from a defect in the auditory nerve in the cochlea and in most cases severely limits hearing in both ears. Congenital nerve deafness often develops if the mother contracts rubella (German measles) during her first three months of pregnancy. Other cases occur when a baby receives too little oxygen during a particularly long and difficult delivery. Sometimes the condition is hereditary.

C. WASHAM

**See also:** BATS; BRAIN; COMMUNICATION; CONDITIONING; EARS; ECHOLOCATION; LEARNING; WHALES, PORPOISES, AND DOLPHINS

**Further reading:**

Bellis, J. 2002. *When the Brain Can't Hear: Unraveling the Mystery of the Auditory Processing Disorder.* New York: Atria Books.
Geisler, C. 1998. *From Sound to Synapse: Physiology of the Mammalian Ear.* New York: Oxford University Press.

## RESTORING HEARING

Modern hearing aids work by amplifying sounds. These battery-operated devices consist of a microphone to capture sounds, an amplifier to magnify them, and an earphone/speaker to channel them into the ear. Traditional hearing aids fit between the back of the outer ear and the skull. They send sounds through a rounded tube leading into the ear canal. Newer, button-shaped models fit onto the hollow just outside the ear canal and are so small they can barely be seen. Doctor and patient may experiment with several models before finding one that provides just enough amplification without making sounds painfully loud.

A breakthrough in the treatment of hearing loss caused by otosclerosis (growth of spongy bone in the inner ear) came in the 1950s, when doctors developed a plastic stirrup. This prosthesis can be implanted in a 20-minute operation that requires only a local aesthetic. The procedure permanently improves hearing in 80 percent of cases. In 1985 researchers Doug Cotanche at the University of South Carolina and Ed Rubel at the University of Washington discovered that chickens could regenerate dead hair cells inside the cochlea. Later experiments proved that these new cells functioned normally. Now researchers at several laboratories are searching for the molecule that stimulates hair-cell growth in birds in the hope that a drug can be developed to restore hearing. Other workers are attempting to culture and implant hair cells in the cochlea.

Yet other researchers are seeking a cure for hearing loss by examining the human genetic code. Scientists now believe that most deafness is hereditary, even if it is hastened by other factors, such as infections and exposure to loud noise.

# HEART

The heart is the organ of the body that pumps blood to other organs

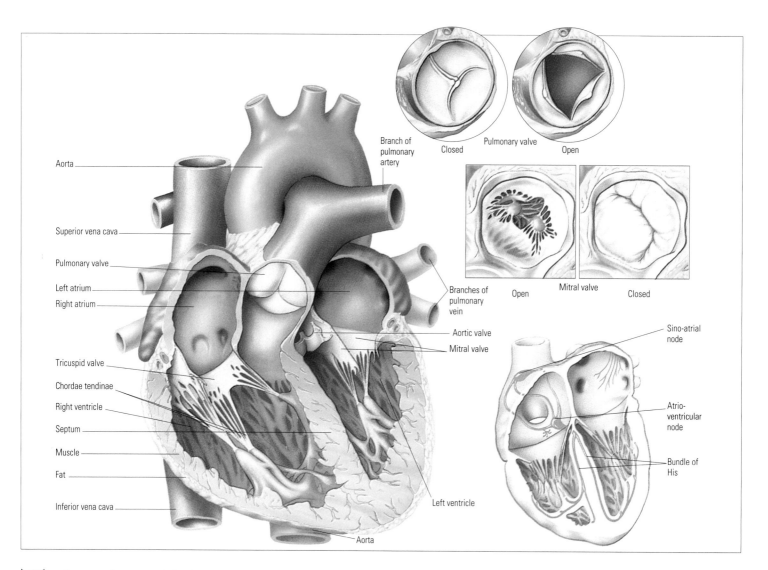

Aorta

Superior vena cava

Pulmonary valve

Left atrium

Right atrium

Tricuspid valve

Chordae tendinae

Right ventricle

Septum

Muscle

Fat

Inferior vena cava

Aorta

Branch of pulmonary artery

Closed    Pulmonary valve    Open

Branches of pulmonary vein

Open    Mitral valve    Closed

Aortic valve

Mitral valve

Left ventricle

Sino-atrial node

Atrio-ventricular node

Bundle of His

The sheer endurance of the human heart almost defies adequate description. After all, it develops and starts beating weeks after conception and may continue to do so for over 100 years. On average, the adult human heart beats 75 times a minute. In an 80-year lifespan, its tireless muscle will pump 62 million gallons (235 million l) of blood around the body.

## Evolution of the heart

Any structure that can be called a heart must pump blood and must be part of a circulatory system (see

CIRCULATORY SYSTEMS). Like the primitive heart of a human embryo, the first heart, which probably belonged to a distant ancestor of the earthworm, was little more than a pulsating tube. The modern earthworm's so-called heart is still a long way from that of more complex organisms. It consists of five pairs of pulsating tubes that push blood through two major blood vessels, one of which runs along the worm's back and the other along its underside. These major vessels also contract to help pump the worm's blood throughout its body.

The heart of arthropods, such as grasshoppers and crayfish, shows a higher level of complexity. For example, blood flows into the crayfish heart through openings called ostia (Latin for "ports"), which are sealed by a set of valves. This arrangement ensures that when the heart contracts, blood cannot flow backward. It is forced forward into a series of arteries that lead to the creature's other organs. Unlike earthworms, arthropods have open circulatory systems and lack veins that return their blood (called hemolymph) to the heart, and thus, the heart must have ostia.

*Blood flow through the heart is controlled by valves that stop it from flowing in the wrong direction.*

## CONNECTIONS

● The amount of blood pumped by the heart is controlled partly by the need to supply **OXYGEN** to the tissues and to remove **CARBON DIOXIDE**.

● During **STRESS**, the heart beats faster and transports more **BLOOD** to the muscles, so they they can work harder.

### CORE FACTS

■ As the heart pumps blood through the circulatory system and around the body, oxygen, carbon dioxide, nutrients, wastes, and hormones are carried to and from the sites where they are made, used, or eliminated.

■ The most primitive hearts are present in invertebrates.

■ Mammals and birds have four-chambered hearts: two atria (upper chambers) and two ventricles (lower chambers).

The ancestor of vertebrates (including humans) probably looked like the lancelet, or amphioxus, an inch-long creature that lives in marine and estuarine environments. Amphioxus is a chordate: it has a nerve cord and a notochord (flexible rod of cells) running along its back (see CHORDATES), but it is not a vertebrate because it lacks a backbone. Like other chordates, amphioxus has a circulatory system composed of arteries and veins. A number of tiny bulbs, distributed along certain arteries, act as pumping chambers, or miniature hearts. However, other parts of the animal's circulatory system also contract, pushing the blood along. The contractions are very slow (about once every two minutes) and irregular.

Fish, perhaps the simplest of the vertebrates, have a heart that consists of two distinct chambers. One, the atrium, receives blood from the body, while the other, the ventricle, pumps blood through the gills and on to the body. This two-chanbered heart supplies the fish with enough oxygen to stay alive.

Amphibians, such as frogs, have a more complex life cycle than fish, living part of their life out of water. The evolution of lungs has allowed them to do

so, and lungs demand a more complex heart—one with three chambers. In the frog, blood from the body, which is poor in oxygen, enters a small upper chamber called the right atrium (plural, atria) and is pumped into a larger lower chamber, a ventricle. The ventricle contracts, sending some blood to the frog's lungs and skin and to the body. The blood that goes to the lungs and skin picks up oxygen and returns to a second upper chamber, the left atrium. The blood is then pumped into the ventricle to mix with oxygen-poor blood. The ventricle contracts again, sending blood back to the lungs and out to the body.

Sending a mixture of freshly oxygenated blood and used blood to the lungs and body is a waste of energy. The frog at rest can tolerate this waste and when active can more efficiently route oxygenated blood to the tissues and deoxygenated blood to the lungs and skin. In most reptiles, except crocodiles, the heart has four chambers—two atria and two incompletely separated ventricles.

Animals such as birds and mammals, which need greater amounts of energy to move rapidly and to maintain a constant body temperature, require

*Among vertebrates, the heart ranges from the two-chambered heart of fish to the four-chambered heart of mammals and birds.*

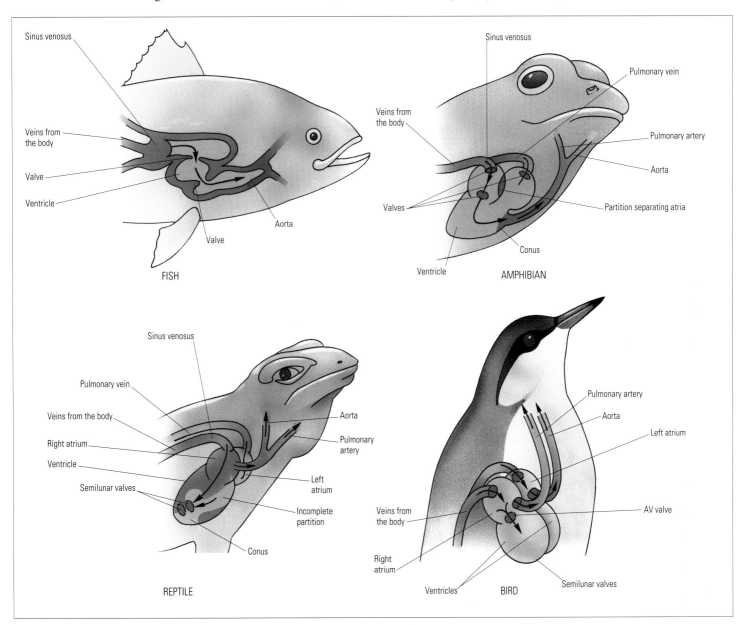

FISH

AMPHIBIAN

REPTILE

BIRD

## THE FETAL CIRCULATION

The circulatory system begins to function early in gestation, but the cardiovascular system (comprising the heart and blood vessels) does not come fully into operation until birth. During gestation—the time developing mammals spend in the womb—the developing fetus does not breathe, so little blood is being carried to and from the lungs. Instead, temporary structures shunt most of the blood from the right side of the fetal heart directly to its left side, into the systemic circulation. The fetus receives its oxygen supply from the placenta, the temporary organ that develops to sustain the unborn young in all placental mammals, including humans. Embedded in the wall of the uterus, the placenta is well supplied with blood vessels. Blood from the mother enters the placenta, and the oxygen and nutrients it carries are passed into the fetal circulation. At the same time, fetal wastes (including carbon dioxide) diffuse into the mother's circulation, to be carried away for disposal.

### A CLOSER LOOK

hearts in which oxygen-rich blood and deoxygenated blood are kept separate. Their hearts—the most efficient in the natural world—consist of four distinct chambers, two atria and two ventricles.

### The mammalian heart

The mammalian heart consists of two thin-walled atria and two thick-walled ventricles. The right atrium receives deoxygenated blood from the body. Blood passes into the right ventricle and is then pumped to the lungs, where it picks up a fresh supply of oxygen and loses carbon dioxide (the pulmonary

*The heart sound is often described as "lubb-dubb." The ventricles fill with blood (1) and contract. Blood presses against the valves, producing the first sound, "lubb" (2). Blood leaves the ventricles (3) and, when they relax, presses back against the valves, producing the "dubb" sound (4). The atria fill up (5), and the cycle repeats.*

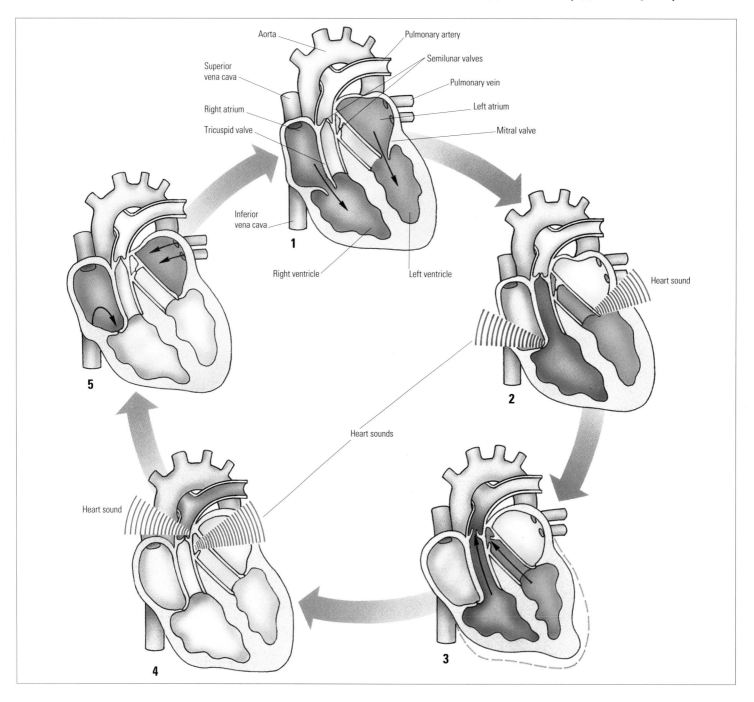

1

Aorta
Pulmonary artery
Superior vena cava
Semilunar valves
Pulmonary vein
Right atrium
Left atrium
Tricuspid valve
Mitral valve
Inferior vena cava
Right ventricle
Left ventricle

2

Heart sound

3

5

4

Heart sound

Heart sounds

circulation). The blood returns to the heart, entering the left atrium. Finally, the oxygenated blood is pumped into the left ventricle and circulated to the rest of the body via the systemic circulation. The wall of the left ventricle is at least three times thicker than that of the right because it pumps blood against the higher pressure of the systemic circuit.

The term *cardiac cycle* is used to describe the events that take place during a single heartbeat—a timescale of about 0.8 seconds. First, the two atria relax and fill with blood. As they distend, two valves (bicuspid and tricuspid) separating the upper and lower chambers are pushed open, and some blood flows into the relaxed ventricles. This resting period is termed diastole. Then both atria contract (atrial systole), forcing more blood into the ventricles. The ventricles then contract (ventricular systole), closing the valves behind them and the atria. Pressure in the ventricles rises, forcing open two further valves (aortic and pulmonary) so that blood can be expelled from the left ventricle into the aorta and from the right ventricle into the pulmonary artery. The heart relaxes, and the cycle repeats itself about 75 times each minute.

Physicians sometimes use the expression "lubb-dubb" to describe normal heart sounds (see the diagram on page 878). The pressure of blood against the closed aortic and pulmonary valves during ventricular systole closes them forcefully and causes the first sound ("lubb"). Ventricular systole is followed by ventricular diastole, when the high pressure in the outgoing vessels (aorta and pulmonary artery) forces blood back toward the ventricles. The aortic and pulmonary valves shut, preventing backflow into the ventricles, and the second heart sound ("dubb") occurs.

The recoil of blood in the large vessels at the beginning of diastole results in a series of pressure pulses in the pulmonary and systemic circuits. These pulses diminish as blood is carried farther from the heart along a vascular network, which, in the adult human, contains some 60,000 miles (97,000 km) of arteries, capillaries, and veins. The pulses can be felt with a finger applied to any artery near the skin surface: the measurement of the pulse is the way heart rate is commonly monitored.

## Maintaining the beat

The resting heart's blood output is usually consistent during a person's lifetime, unless that person has heart disease. However, the heart frequently changes its output and rate of contraction to meet various circumstances, ranging from sleep to vigorous exercise.

The heart can beat on its own. For example, a heart removed from a frog continues to beat for hours if it is placed in a salt solution representative of the frog's body fluids. A human heart also beats (slowly) outside the body if it is given artificial circulation and nutrients and kept at normal body temperature.

The electrical stimulus for contraction originates from within the heart. It comes from the sinoatrial (SA) node, a group of nerves, blood vessels, and muscle cells located at the top of the right atrium,

### TIRELESS MUSCLE

The shape and organization of cardiac muscle cells (see below) differ from those of skeletal and smooth muscle cells. These differences give heart muscle its unique properties. Under the microscope the fibers can be seen to be arranged in patterns of spirals and whirls. These patterns—quite unlike those of other types of muscles—are in part responsible for the great power with which the heart rhythmically contracts. Also, heart muscle responds as a unit to action potentials, whereas only individual cells of skeletal muscles do. This response coordinates and maximizes the power of the heart's contraction.

near the point of entry of the venae cavae (the two large veins returning blood from the body to the heart). The SA node is more commonly called the pacemaker because each wave of heart excitation originates here and spreads throughout the heart.

The SA node usually sends out electrical impulses at a rate of 75 per minute. Within 0.09 seconds, the impulse flashes over both atria, causing them to contract and move blood into both ventricles. In about 0.04 seconds, this same impulse darts through the atria to a group of tissues in the right atrium where it attaches to the septum between the right and left ventricles, the atrioventricular (AV) node.

The impulse received by the AV node is conducted down the septum to the bottom of the heart, delaying the contraction of the ventricles until they are filled with blood. The delay is not long: 0.19

### THE ARTIFICIAL PACEMAKER

Disorders of the conducting mechanism—the heart's natural pacemaker—may result in potentially serious arrhythmias, or disturbances of heart rhythm. Such conditions can sometimes be rectified by implanting an artificial pacemaker. This tiny device—about 2 inches (5 cm) across—is placed under the skin of the chest near one of the shoulders. The wires leading from it are threaded through a vein to one or more regions of the heart. Depending on the particular heart problem, a pacemaker can be programmed to take over the work of the heart's natural pacemaker completely or to go into action only when the heart's own pacemaker undergoes a temporary malfunction. An artificial pacemaker can be reprogrammed from outside the patient's body. The batteries last from 8 to 10 years and can be replaced through minor surgery under local anesthesia.

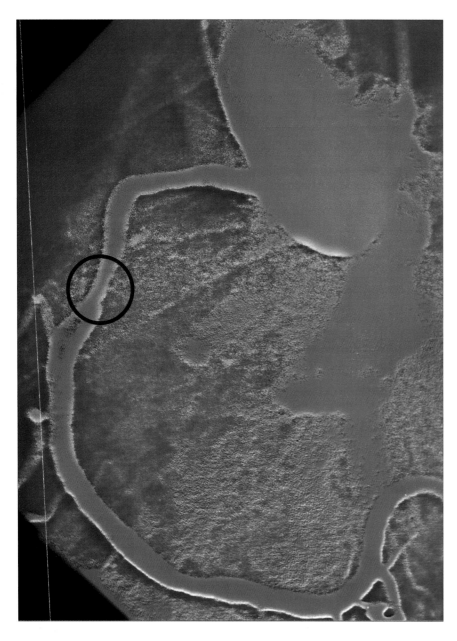

*An angiogram of the right coronary artery, showing how the blood flow has been impaired by the formation of a blood clot (circled).*

## VARIABLE HEART RATES

Among mammals, normal heart rates differ greatly. The average heart rate for a gray shrew, which weighs between 0.1 to 0.2 ounces (3 and 5 g), is about 1,000 beats per minute. That of a golden hamster weighing 4.6 ounces (130 g) is in the neighborhood of 350 beats per minute. The heart of a 66-pound (30 kg) goat beats about 80 times a minute and that of an Asian elephant thumps at perhaps 30 beats a minute.

The pattern that emerges is that heart rate varies inversely with weight: the smaller an animal, the faster its heart beats. One explanation for this pattern relates metabolic rate to heart rate. In simple terms, the smaller an animal is, the greater its metabolic rate (the rate at which energy is produced from food) per gram of body weight. This rate, in turn, depends on the oxygen supply (see METABOLISM). So the faster the heart beats, the more oxygen becomes available.

This explanation is supported by data from animals that hibernate. The metabolic rate of a hibernating animal is much lower than it is when the same animal is fully active. Thus, its heart rate is lower also. For example, the heart rate of a golden hamster – normally about 350 beats a minute – drops to between 4 and 15 beats a minute during hibernation.

seconds after the initial impulse produced in the SA node, the electrical signal has spread through the muscles of both ventricles. In this brief timespan, the impulse races down the tissue between the ventricles, causing them to contract from the bottom up, closing the atrioventricular valves ("lubb" sound) and then pumping blood into the aorta and pulmonary artery.

### Regulating pressure

In addition to pumping blood, the heart helps regulate blood pressure in the arteries. An increase in blood pressure can be caused by several factors, including an increase in blood volume caused, for example, by drinking fluids. As an increasing volume of blood enters the atria, the pressure rises, stretching the chamber walls. Certain cells in the atria respond to this stimulus by secreting a hormone called atrial natriuretic factor (ANF) into the bloodstream. As the ANF reaches the kidneys, it stimulates the excretion of sodium in the urine. Sodium and water excretion are closely associated, and both are excreted, lowering the circulating volume of blood plasma, which in turn lowers blood pressure toward normal.

Changes in other parts of the body produce variations in heart rate. For example, pressure-sensitive sensors, called baroreceptors, are located in major blood vessels such as the aorta (which carries blood away from the heart), the carotid artery (which carries blood through the neck toward the head), and the vena cava (which returns deoxygenated blood to the heart). The sensors detect increases in blood pressure in these vessels and send a signal to a heart-inhibiting center in the brain's medulla. The brain signals a reduction in the rate and force of contraction and so reduces the blood pressure. If the drop in blood pressure is too great, signals to the heart-accelerating center of the brain are increased to increase the blood pressure.

The heart also responds to chemical changes in the body. For example, exercise increases the blood concentrations of waste products of respiration, especially carbon dioxide. When blood carrying a raised level of carbon dioxide reaches the carotid artery, it comes into contact with chemoreceptors (cells that are sensitive to chemicals). These cells send impulses to the brain, causing it to speed up the heart rate. Thus, the rate at which blood is delivered to the lungs increases, and the excess carbon dioxide is more rapidly exchanged and exhaled. Changes in oxygen concentration in the blood also stimulate chemoreceptors, but with the opposite effect on the heart—the more oxygen there is, the slower the heart beats.

Certain hormones also change the rate at which the heart beats. For example, danger causes the heart to race—the result of a release of the hormone epinephrine into the bloodstream from the adrenal glands when one is threatened. The epinephrine reaches the heart muscle, immediately stimulating it to contract faster. Blood carrying oxygen and nutrients speeds to the muscles of the body so that the person can respond to the danger (see EPINEPHRINE AND NOREPINEPHRINE).

## Hearts under attack

A number of diseases interfere with the ability of the heart to pump blood. Coronary artery disease (CAD) is the main cause of death in the United States, claiming about 750,000 lives each year. In CAD, coronary arteries, which carry the heart's own blood supply, narrow owing to a buildup of deposits of fats and cholesterol. The amount of blood—and oxygen—reaching the heart muscle cells is thus limited, and if oxygen supply falls too low, these cells die. If enough cells die, the heart is no longer able to pump enough blood to meet the body's needs.

When people with narrow coronary arteries exercise, or are under emotional stress, the heart tries to compensate by working harder. If the coronary arteries are too narrow to cope, the heart cannot receive enough oxygen-rich blood. The oxygen-starved heart tissues respond by producing chemicals that stimulate pain receptors in the heart. The pain, called angina pectoris, is felt as pain in the chest that may radiate to the left shoulder, arm, or jaw.

This pain can be relieved by taking drugs that temporarily enlarge the coronary arteries or slow the heart so its need for oxygen decreases. However, although the pain may be relieved, the underlying problem—clogged arteries—remains. Anyone with CAD is at increased risk of a heart attack caused by the death of a portion of heart muscle from oxygen starvation. Half of all heart attack victims die within the first two hours; among the remainder, survival is improved by the prompt use of thrombolytic drugs that dissolve blood clots blocking the heart's arteries.

Successful recovery from a heart attack involves mild but regular exercise and avoidance of known risk factors such as undue weight gain, the intake of high cholesterol or fatty foods, and cigarette smoking. If a person has had a heart attack, the physician may prescribe an anticoagulant drug or aspirin to reduce the risk of further clot formation and coronary artery blockage. Various other drugs may be prescribed to reduce or regulate the work of the heart.

Blocked coronary vessels can be treated using coronary artery bypass grafting (CABG), in which the heart is stopped and blood is pumped through the body using a heart-lung machine. In CABG the clogged vessel is bypassed using a length of vein, usually taken from the patient's leg. Another option is balloon angioplasty, which is carried out under local anesthesia. A balloon-tipped catheter is inserted into a large artery in the groin and moved through the aorta until it enters the narrowed coronary vessel. The balloon is then inflated, compressing the fatty deposit against the wall of the artery, increasing its diameter and allowing blood to flow more freely.

If a heart has been irreparably damaged by disease, doctors may recommend a heart transplant, in which most of the heart is removed. Only the rear portion of the atria and the major blood vessels leading to and from it are preserved. It is to these vessels that the ventricles and front portion of the atria from a donor heart are joined.

C. PROUJAN

## ELECTRICAL ACTIVITY

An electrocardiogram, or EKG, can often reveal a heart problem that might otherwise go undetected. The EKG is a machine that monitors the electrical activity (action potentials) of the heart muscle. This activity is printed out in the form of a graph as a series of waves (see below). The procedure is completely safe, takes only a few minutes, and involves nothing more than attaching wires, or electrodes, to the person's chest, wrists, and ankles. The electrodes pick up electrical impulses as they travel through different parts of the heart.

Each part of the waves that are printed out conforms to the activity of a different part of the heart. By studying the shape of the waves, a cardiologist can determine such things as whether the atria and ventricles are contracting normally, whether these chambers are of normal size or enlarged, and whether one or more parts of the heart muscle have been damaged (and to what extent). Moviemakers are much enamored by the dramatic potential of the flat line on the EKG, indicating the absence of the heartbeat (called asystole).

A portable EKG may be worn over a 24-hour period to monitor the heart during a normal day's activity. Called a Holter monitor, this device records electrical impulses from the heart onto the tape of a small cassette recorder. Later the recorder is connected to a computer and printer to produce the EKG graph. A Holter monitor often detects intermittent problems that a regular EKG, which lasts only a few minutes, may miss.

The EKG is also used during a stress test. This diagnostic procedure monitors heart functions during controlled exercise on a treadmill. Under these conditions, the EKG printout may indicate disease that would not otherwise be evident at rest or during normal activities. Stress tests are also used to determine the fitness of a healthy person by measuring how much work the heart does to support different levels of physical activity. The less work it has to do, the fitter the heart.

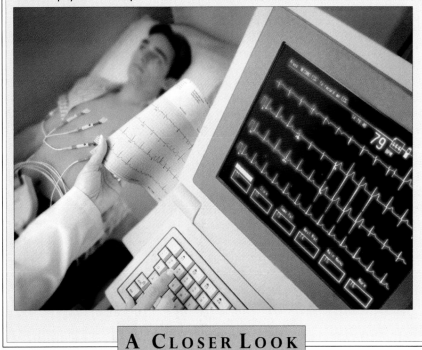

### A CLOSER LOOK

**See also:** CHORDATES; CIRCULATORY SYSTEMS; EPINEPHRINE AND NOREPINEPHRINE; HOMEOSTASIS; RESPIRATORY SYSTEMS.

### Further reading:

Langer, G. 1999. *Understanding Disease: How Your Heart, Lungs, Blood, and Blood Vessels Function and Respond to Treatment.* Fort Bragg, Calif.: QED Press.
Tortora, G. J., and S. R. Grabowski. 2000. *Principles of Anatomy and Physiology.* Reading, Mass.: Addison-Wesley Educational Publishers.

# HEATHS AND MOORLAND HABITATS

**Heaths and moors are open and uncultivated landscapes with poor soils, overgrown mainly by heather**

Heaths and moors, with no trees to break the monotony, may at first sight seem uninteresting and desolate places. To a naturalist, however, they are of interest because of the hardy plants and animals that manage to survive their harsh, exposed conditions: strong winds, wet climate, and nutrient-poor, acidic soil. People who visit moors appreciate the fine, open country and an opportunity to enjoy nature's serenity, away from the closed-in environs of the city. Modern-day heaths and moors were once primeval forests, like those in many parts of North America, Scandinavia, and northern Asia. These forests were destroyed thousands of years ago when humans felled the trees to clear land for agricultural use.

## Heaths

The distinction between heaths and moors is not always clear because gradations of soil quality and moisture content exist between the two. However, a heath can be defined as a large expanse of open wilderness densely overgrown with dwarf shrubs and with a soil composed of sand and gravel, which allows rainwater to drain through freely. The soil may also have a thin layer of peat (partially carbonized and decomposed vegetation) and is poorly supplied with the minerals, especially nitrates, that plants need. The soil is normally acidic and can be as low as pH 3.5. Heaths are found mostly in the central to eastern parts and some of the upland areas of Britain, in northwestern Europe, western Asia, the Mediterranean region, eastern Africa, and Greenland.

## Moors

Moors, although similar to heaths, differ in their climate and soil characteristics. Moors are usually much cooler than heaths and are found on higher ground. Moor soils are acidic and generally wet, with poor drainage, and contain a considerable layer of peat. If the ground is always very wet, the area may be called a bog. Moors exist in the Scottish, Irish, and Welsh highlands and parts of England.

## Heath and moorland vegetation

The most common native plant of European heaths and moors is heather (*Calluna vulgaris*), also called ling or scotch heather. It grows as a low evergreen shrub and varies in size from only a few inches to a height of 3 feet (91 cm) or more.

Heather is able to survive in acidic, nutrient-poor soils because of an association between the roots of the heather and thin filaments of fungi. The fungi send mycelia, or threadlike extensions, into the heather roots and help the plant absorb minerals from the soil. These fungus roots are called mycorrhizae. This association is an example of a symbiotic relationship called mutualism from which both the heather and the fungus benefit (see SYMBIOSIS). The seeds of heather have been found to carry fungal threads, which enable the germinating seedlings to grow effectively on the poor soil.

Other plants commonly found on moors and heaths are gorse, bracken, bilberry, cowberry, crowberry, and cloudberry. In the wetter bog areas of moorland where the ground is too waterlogged for heather, it is replaced as the dominant plant by various bog mosses of the genus *Sphagnum*.

M. BLEIFELD

**See also:** BIOMES AND HABITATS; FUNGI KINGDOM; ROOTS AND ROOT SYSTEMS; SOIL ECOLOGY; SYMBIOSIS.

### Further reading:
Aerts, R., and G. W. Heil., eds. 1993. *Heathlands: Patterns and Processes in a Changing Environment.* Geobotany Series, Volume 20. Boston: Kluwer.

*Native heather and bracken dominate this heathland habitat.*

## CONNECTIONS

● Heath and moorland habitats are a subgroup of shrublands—a biome group that includes the **CHAPARRAL BIOMES** found in the western United States.

● Controlled burning of heaths prevents the introduction of **TREES**.

## FIRE IN MOORLANDS

Most moors are essentially the result of humans clearing ancient forests. Significant clearing began as early as 1000 BCE to make way for cultivation and animal grazing. Modern-day moors support native plant and animal communities and are managed by controlled fire burning every 7 to 12 years. Wild, destructive fire can be a threat to the survival of plants and animals anywhere, but controlled burning has been a standard tool to maintain moorlands since the Middle Ages. Burning prevents the introduction of unwanted trees and woody shrubs and stimulates the production of new shoots, which are more favorable for grazing animals and game birds. Heather has a remarkable ability to regenerate itself by growing shoots from the stem bases, which are buried and protected from the fire by the surface humus.

**A CLOSER LOOK**

# HEMIPTERA

**Hemiptera is an order comprising insects that have distinctive piercing and sucking mouthparts**

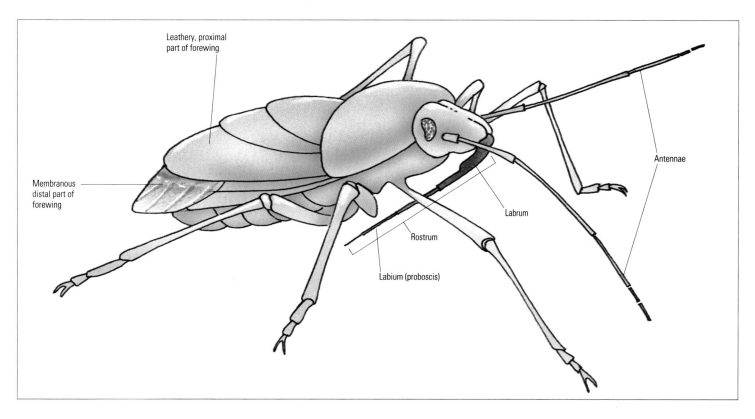

Leathery, proximal part of forewing

Membranous distal part of forewing

Antennae

Labrum

Rostrum

Labium (proboscis)

*The green shield bug, pictured above, shows the distinctive beaklike mouthparts typical of all bugs.*

## CONNECTIONS

● Most species of Hemiptera are oviparous, that is, their **EGGS** mature and hatch after being expelled from the body.

● A type of **SYMBIOSIS** exists between ants and aphids, which are bugs.

● Many species of Hemiptera transmit **VIRUSES** to their hosts.

Hemiptera are a diverse group of insects with distinctive mouthparts. Shield bugs and squash bugs, water striders and water boatmen, froghoppers and spittlebugs, cicadas and aphids, assassin bugs and bedbugs—all of these and more are members of the order Hemiptera. Although most people refer to all "creepy-crawlies" as bugs, biologists reserve the term for insects in this order.

Hemiptera is the fifth largest order of insects, with approximately 150 families and just under 82,000 species. They are distinguished from other insects by their specialized piercing-and-sucking mouthparts. The evolution of these mouthparts has allowed the Hemiptera to occupy an enormous range of habitats—freshwater, marine, and terrestrial.

## CLASSIFICATION

Hemiptera used to be divided into two suborders, Heteroptera and Homoptera, on the basis of their structural features and different feeding habits. However, the three groups that made up the suborder Homoptera are now recognized as distinct suborders. Presently, the order Hemiptera is divided into four suborders: Heteroptera, Auchenorrhyncha, Sternorrhyncha, and Coleorrhyncha.

The suborder Heteroptera are called the "true bugs." This suborder includes many families that are plant feeders (phytophagous), including the plant bugs, stinkbugs or shield bugs, squash bugs, and seed bugs. Heteroptera also contains all the Hemiptera that are insect predators, including the assassin bugs, ambush bugs, damsel bugs, and pirate bugs.

Some Heteroptera, including bedbugs and some assassin bugs, are parasites (see PARASITES) that feed on the blood of vertebrates.

Most freshwater environments and even the brackish marshes at the edge of the sea have been invaded by bugs, including water striders, water boatmen, giant water bugs, and water scorpions. All these bugs are classified as Heteroptera.

The suborder Auchenorrhyncha comprises only phytophagous families, including leafhoppers, plant hoppers, spittlebugs, and cicadas. The wings of the adults are membranous (made of a thin pliable layer of tissue) throughout, and the antennae are all short and bristlelike in appearance.

The suborder Sternorrhyncha also comprises phytophagous (plant-feeding) families, including aphids, scales and mealybugs, whiteflies, and psyllids. The wings of the adults of this suborder are also membranous. However, the antennae of

### CORE FACTS

■ Hemiptera are insects with distinctive piercing and sucking mouthparts.

■ There are more than 150 families and just under 82,000 species of hemipterans, including assassin bugs, aphids, and bed bugs.

■ Hemiptera live in a range of habitats: on land, in fresh water, and on the oceans.

■ Some hemipterans are pests of agricultural crops.

■ Hemiptera reproduce sexually and asexually.

## COLOR FROM INSECTS

Cochineal scale insects, *Dactylopius coccus* (suborder Sternorrhyncha, family Dactylopiidae), feed on cactuses in Mexico and Central America, chiefly the cochineal cactus, *Nopalea cochenillifera*. The female insect contains a red pigment called carminic acid. The pigment can be extracted from the female scale insects by crushing them and then treating them with steam or dry heat. The pigment, called cochineal, has been used as a scarlet-red dye for cosmetics, wool, and food coloring. However, because so many scale insects are required to produce a practical amount of dye, synthetic aniline dyes, which can be manufactured less expensively, have now replaced cochineal in most uses. Cochineal presently is used as a stain for biological tissues.

### SCIENCE AND SOCIETY

the Sternorrhyncha are long and threadlike compared with those of the Auchenorrhyncha.

The suborder Coleorrhyncha is very small, comprising only one family, the Peloridiidae. All species in the suborder feed on mosses and liverworts (see MOSSES AND LIVERWORTS). Together with their particular characteristics and restricted distribution, that the Coleorrhyncha feed only on primitive plants suggests that this suborder may be a survivor from primitive times.

*The assassin bug, seen below feeding on a ladybird beetle, is one of the main predatory bugs.*

## FORM AND FUNCTION
As in all insects, the body structure of Hemiptera consists of three sections, the head, the thorax, and the abdomen (see INSECTS).

### The head
The head bears the beaklike mouthparts, antennae, and eyes. The mouthparts are modified into a narrow, two-channeled piercing tube; one channel carries salivary secretions from the mouth, while the other sucks up food. These specialized mouthparts have evolved from the chewing type of insect mouthparts—the mandibles and maxillae, which are the jaws, and the labrum and labium, which are the structures that enclose the mouth cavity above and below, respectively. The modified mandibles and maxillae are called stylets and form the piercing tube. The modified labrum and labium form a jointed sheath that covers the stylets; this sheath is usually the only visible portion of the mouthparts. The complete structure is called the beak, or rostrum.

The suborders of the Hemiptera are distinguished by the position of the rostrum. In the Heteroptera, the rostrum starts from the front of the head and can be tucked under the body. The rostrum of the Auchenorrhyncha and Coleorrhyncha is clearly connected to the back of the head, while the rostrum of the Sternorryncha appears to be attached to the thorax.

Hemipterans have salivary glands. Blood-feeding and predatory hemipterans inject saliva into the host's tissue, which helps to break it down.

### The thorax
As in all insects, the thorax carries the wings and legs. Generally, two pairs of wings are attached to the thorax of the adult. The forewings are larger than the hind wings, the forewings being the main power for flight. However, some Hemiptera lack wings completely. Adult females of all the scale insects (suborder Sternorrhyncha, superfamily Coccoidea) have no wings, while adult male scale insects have normal forewings, but their hind wings are reduced in size.

### The abdomen
The abdomen in insects generally contains most of the alimentary canal, circulatory vessels, excretory organs, and reproductive system. The Hemiptera have a digestive system that allows efficient uptake and absorption of the liquid food sucked from the plants or animals on which they feed.

Many species in the two suborders, Sternorrhyncha and Auchenorrhyncha (most notably aphids), excrete surplus fluid containing sugars and amino acids. This fluid is called honeydew. Ants often tend and protect aphids to feed on the honeydew. The ants collect aphid eggs and care for them over the winter. When the young aphids hatch, the ants carry them to the roots of plants, particularly corn, where they can feed. Many species of aphids rely so much on the ants that they are called "ants' cows."

## Reproduction

Reproduction in Hemiptera can be sexual or asexual, with several generations produced in a year. Most Hemiptera are oviparous (their eggs mature and hatch after being expelled from the body) and they lay their eggs on or in plant tissue or other surrounding surfaces. In the suborder Sternorrhyncha, reproduction without fertilization, or parthenogenesis, is common. In most Hemiptera, a gradual metamorphosis to the mature adult takes place through several nymphal stages, with external development of the wings occurring in the final stages (see LARVAE AND PUPAE).

## Adaptation

Living in so many different environments, the Hemiptera have adapted in striking ways. Some 1,300 predatory species—water striders or water skippers—live on the surface of ponds, lakes, slow-running rivers, and even on the sea. A number of predatory bugs hunt below the surface of fresh water. Water scorpions have a long siphon at the end of the abdomen through which they breathe the air above the surface. Giant water bugs and backswimmers carry air bubbles as a source of oxygen on the underside of their bodies.

On land, the principal predatory bugs are the assassin and ambush bugs, of which there are some 4,000, mostly tropical, species. Some lie in wait for their prey but most are active hunters. Smaller species feed on mosquitoes and other small flies, but others are big enough to overcome beetles and millipedes. Some of the larger species (genus *Triatoma*), which live in South America, are carriers of Chagas' disease. This disease is an infection caused by a minute protist called a trypanosome (*Trypanosoma cruzi*), which is transmitted in the carrier insect's feces. The carrier insect excretes its feces onto a human before biting to feed on its blood. Humans infect themselves with the disease by stratching the bug's feces into the wound created by the carrier insect's bite.

## Economic effects

Aphids are serious pests of many agricultural and horticultural crops not only because of the direct effects caused by sucking plant fluids but also because many species transmit viruses and other diseases to the host plants. One infamous aphid, the green peach aphid (*Myzus persicae*), can transmit at least 100 different viruses. Scale insects, which feed on the leaves of houseplants and ornamentals and on the branches of fruit and nut crops, cause direct damage to these plants. Several capsid bug or plant bug species (family Miridae) are serious pests, including lygus bugs (especially *Lygus hesperus* and *L. lineolaris*), which cause extensive damage to cotton crops by attacking the leaves and flower buds.

M. GRISWOLD

**See also:** INSECTS; LARVAE AND PUPAE; MOSSES AND LIVERWORTS; PARASITES; PREDATION.

## Further reading:

Hubbell, S. 1993. *Broadsides from the Other Orders: A Book of Bugs.* New York: Random House.
Schuh, R. T., and J. A. Slater. 1995. *True Bugs of the World (Hemiptera: Heteroptera): Classification and Natural History.* New York: Comstock Publishing Associates, Cornell University Press.

*Peach aphids are small insects that form large colonies, their large numbers seriously weakening or killing the plants on which they feed.*

# HEPATITIS

## Hepatitis is an inflammation of the liver, caused by a toxin, virus, bacterium, or autoimmune disease

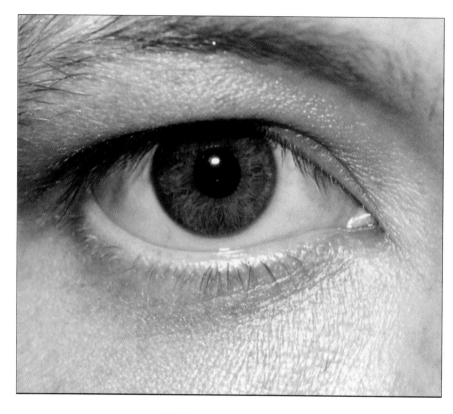

*Closeup of the eye of a patient suffering from jaundice, as a result of hepatitis, showing yellowing of the white of the eye and of the surrounding facial skin.*

## CONNECTIONS

● Hepatitis destroys cells in the **LIVER**. The condition is often treated with **CORTICOSTEROID** drugs.

● **IMMUNIZATION** is possible against the hepatitis A and B viruses.

Hepatitis is a condition in which the liver becomes inflamed. It is most commonly caused by infection by one of five hepatitis viruses (A, B, C, D, and E). Such viruses cause systemic (generalized) infection, although the liver is the primary site of damage. Hepatitis can also be a symptom of other viral diseases such as yellow fever, mononucleosis (Epstein-Barr virus), and cytomegalovirus (giant cell virus).

Early symptoms of hepatitis are nonspecific in that they include symptoms that are typical of many viral diseases: tiredness, muscle and joint pain, and fever. These symptoms give way to the sudden severe onset of the disease (the so-called acute symptoms): loss of appetite, swelling of the liver and spleen, and the characteristic skin color changes typical of jaundice (the yellow discoloration of the skin and the whites of the eyes is due to an increase of bile pigments in the blood). When the liver fails to function properly, the liver cells that normally remove and process bilirubin (a bile pigment) from the blood fail to do so, the result being jaundice as well as pale-colored feces. Patients often become very sick, but with treatment many recover, and the liver gradually repairs itself.

When liver inflammation continues for longer than six months, the condition is called chronic hepatitis, that is, hepatitis of long duration. In addition to the acute, infectious forms of hepatitis, there are also noninfectious forms, resulting from alcohol abuse, acetaminophen poisoning, autoimmune disease (attack by the body's own immune system), and Wilson's disease (in which there is a toxic buildup of copper in the liver).

Effective vaccines against hepatitis A and B viruses are available, although they cannot offer a cure if the disease is contracted. The most effective way to deal with hepatitis is to try to prevent the disease. Prevention involves good hygiene in the home and workplace, testing blood products, and the use of thorough infection-control methods by health workers and others. The sharing of syringes and needles by drug addicts is a major route of hepatitis transmission.

### Hepatitis A virus (HAV)
HAV is an enterovirus that lives in the digestive tract. Outbreaks of disease are frequently traced to sewage-contaminated shellfish. HAV is the most common single cause of viral hepatitis, responsible for up to 40 percent of cases worldwide.

### Hepatitis B virus (HBV)
Hepatitis B is highly contagious—it can be easily spread, especially by contact with body fluids. The HBV virus is a serious problem around the world and is thought to be the ninth leading cause of death worldwide. Hepatitis B can be passed between drug users who share needles, by sexual intercourse, and as a result of transfusions of infected blood.

### Hepatitis C virus (HCV)
At first HCV was called simply "non-A non-B" (NANB) because no antigens (any foreign substance that causes the body to produce antibodies) for either of these viruses could be found. The virus is now recognized as HCV and is related to the viruses that cause yellow fever and dengue fever, both spread by mosquitoes. Hepatitis C can be passed by infected drug users and infected blood transfusions.

### Hepatitis D virus (HDV)
HDV is common in the Mediterranean region and is able to replicate only when HBV is present. Simultaneous infection by the two viruses may explain the severity of some cases of hepatitis B.

### Hepatitis E virus (HEV)
HEV used to be called enteric NANB. It is a waterborne virus of India and South America that usually causes a mild form of hepatitis. In pregnant women, the death rate is close to 20 percent.

E. SAREWITZ

**See also:** LIVER AND GALLBLADDER; VIRUSES.

**Further reading:**
Dolan, M., I. Murray-Lyon, and J. Tindall. 1999. *The Hepatitis C Handbook.* Berkeley, Calif.: North Atlantic Books.

# HERBAL MEDICINE

**In herbal medicine plants with medicinal properties are used to treat or prevent disease**

*Herbal remedies are becoming more readily available in the West thanks to an increase in demand for this type of medicine.*

## CONNECTIONS

● Early North American herbal practices involved the use of **HALLUCINOGENS,** such as **CACTI** and **MUSHROOMS AND TOADSTOOLS.**

● **CHINESE MEDICINE** has relied on herbal practices for thousands of years, and its use continues to be important in modern treatments.

Herbal medicine, sometimes called phyto-therapy (derived from the Greek *phyto*, meaning "plant"), refers to the use of plants with medicinal properties to treat or prevent disease. Many of the herbs people sometimes use in the kitchen—including garlic, sage, rosemary, and mint—are thought to have medicinal properties.

Plants contain an array of compounds that attract beneficial insects, ward off pests and plant diseases, and may benefit humans. Although many conventional medicines prescribed by doctors are made from purified plant compounds—the anti-cancer drugs vincristine and vinblastine are derived from the periwinkle plant, for example—herbal medicine differs in its emphasis on the use of material from the whole plant.

Conventional medical scientists believe that isolated plant compounds have the same effect as the whole plant material and, being in a prescribed dosage, are often safer. Herbalists, however, argue that the herb's effectiveness often relies on several plant compounds present within a single plant—some perhaps not yet identified as having medicinal properties—that work together.

## History of herbal medicine

No one knows when the first person discovered that chewing the leaf of a certain plant soothed an upset stomach or that the root of another helped cure insomnia, but it is safe to say that people have known about the healing properties of plants for a long time. Archaeologists have found pollen grains of herbs in sites more than 60,000 years old—indirect evidence that prehistoric peoples used medicinal plants to treat themselves.

It is not clear how early cultures learned to use herbs; they may have used their own intuition or trial and error or even seen animals eat certain plants. Scientists have observed animals apparently seeking out herbs to treat and even prevent illness.

Other herbs may have been adopted because they resembled the affected part of the body. This practice is called the doctrine of signatures, a belief that has continued for centuries. Walnuts, which look like small brains, were used as headache remedies; lungwort, with its lung-shaped leaves, was a medieval treatment for lung diseases; plants with yellow flowers were believed to be good for treating jaundice; and bryony was thought to be good for gout because it is shaped like a swollen foot.

Herbal medicine originated and continues in a wide variety of cultures. The first peoples in North America were well versed in herbal lore. They used roots, bark, and leaves for almost all their medicines. For example, Native Americans used a poultice made from witch hazel leaves and bark to reduce inflammation—and witch hazel lotion is a remedy that is still used to treat cuts and bruises. Hallucinogenic mushrooms, peyote cacti, and morning glory seeds were used to bring on visions in healing and religious ceremonies. There is also a rich tradition of herbal medicine in South American, Australian, and African cultures.

The Chinese emperor Shên Nung wrote the *P'en Ts'ao*, a book about herbs and their medical properties (called a herbal), around 2700 BCE. Chinese medical treatment, which is based on the belief that illness is caused by an imbalance of natural forces in the body, continues to rely heavily on herbs to restore the natural balance of forces (see CHINESE MEDICINE).

A sacred Hindu book that includes herbal medicines, the *Charaka-samhita*, written by Charaka, the first great Hindu physician, dates back to nearly 1000 BCE. The Hindu system of medicine, called ayurveda (see INDIAN MEDICINE), uses a wide variety of plants.

## CORE FACTS

■ Herbal medicine is the use of plants with medicinal properties to treat or prevent disease.
■ Herbal medicine has been practiced by a number of cultures for thousands of years.
■ Modern herbal medicines are not recognized as drugs and therefore are not required to adhere to the same strict quality control standards as pharmaceutical drugs.

*Feverfew (Tanacetum parthenium) is an example of a herbal remedy that is considerd safe and effective. A few of its leaves taken each day are said to help ward off migraine headaches.*

European medicine has its roots in the ancient Assyrian and Egyptian cultures; both produced detailed herbals from about 2000 to 1500 BCE. Some of their herbs, such as licorice and cassia, are still in common use. When the Greeks and Romans took over the Assyrian and Egyptian cultures, they also adopted many of their herbal remedies. The Greek physician Hippocrates, who lived around 400 BCE, listed some 400 herbs used medically, and Dioscorides (1st century CE) wrote a herbal in which he described around 600 plants.

For more than 1,000 years, throughout the European Middle Ages, the theories of an influential 2nd-century Roman physician named Galen were accepted as truth. Galen believed in the four "humors" of the Greeks (black bile, yellow bile, blood, and phlegm), which were supposed to be balanced in the healthy body, and he placed medicinal herbs into rigid classifications according to the humor they were supposed to affect.

Many herbals were published during the 16th and 17th centuries. In the 17th century, an English apothecary (pharmacist) named Nicholas Culpeper wrote *The English Physician*, commonly called Culpeper's Herbal. Believing that medicines should be available to the common people at low cost, he wrote his herbal in English instead of the more traditional language of learning—Latin.

He also described herbs that could be grown in any English cottage garden. An experienced astrologer, Culpeper believed each herb was influenced by the planets. (Modern research has suggested that the potency of herbs can, indeed, vary according to the time of year and possibly even the time of day that they are picked.)

By the mid-19th century, most medical doctors had begun to abandon treatments such as bleeding and purging in favor of herbal drugs. However, herbs could vary widely in their effectiveness and safe dose. When chemists discovered that they could isolate some of the active compounds in herbs in a controlled manner, many doctors adopted the more predictable purified drugs. In the late 19th century, chemists were able to synthesize many of these same compounds in the laboratory. The modern age of pharmacy was born (see PHARMACOLOGY).

## Modern herbal medicine

The popularity of herbal medicine has been revived in the 20th century. People who had become disillusioned with the high cost of drugs and with the artificial nature of their production wanted a more natural alternative (see ALTERNATIVE MEDICINE). Traditional herbal remedies from the Americas, Europe, and non-Western cultures became easier to obtain as the number of people practicing herbal medicine and available for consultation increased.

While many of these remedies are undoubtedly safe and effective, others are not. Scientific research has not kept pace with the renewed interest in herbal medicine, and the safety and efficacy of many herbs remains unproven. As such, they cannot be sold legally as drugs, and the label accompanying them cannot make any claims about therapeutic uses or dosage. The salespeople in health food stores, where herbs are now most frequently sold, are forbidden to make therapeutic recommendations about the herbs they sell. The consumer must rely instead on the advice given in modern herbals, many of which are inaccurate or misleading.

Some herbal remedies are useless or even dangerous. Comfrey (*Symphytum officinale*), one of the most popular herbs sold in the United States, is said to have remarkable healing properties. However, it is toxic and can cause liver failure if taken in large quantities. Manufacturers of herbal remedies are not required to adhere to the same strict quality control standards required of pharmaceutical drugs because herbs are not classified as drugs. The potency of the herb may vary from one batch to another; unscrupulous herb manufacturers may mix the labeled herb with another (less expensive) product. For example, quality ginseng root is very expensive; many commercial ginseng products contain little or no ginseng at all. Some herbs are quite safe and effective. Anyone interested in herbal medicine should consult a good, reliable herbal or a herbalist and follow directions with caution.

S. LATTA

**See also:** ALTERNATIVE MEDICINE; CHINESE MEDICINE; INDIAN MEDICINE; PHARMACOLOGY.

## Further reading:

Gruenwald, Joerg. 2000. *Physician's Desk Reference for Herbal Medicines.* 2nd ed. Montvale, N.J.: Medical Economics/Thomson Healthcare.
Mills, S., and K. Bone. 1999. *Principles and Practice of Phytotherapy: Modern Herbal Medicine.* London: Churchill Livingstone.

# HERMAPHRODITES

**Hermaphrodites are organisms that possess both male and female reproductive organs**

## CORE FACTS

- When an organism has both male and female reproductive organs, it is called a hermaphrodite.
- Hermaphroditism is present in most plant species and a few animal species.
- Sequential hermaphrodites change sex at certain times in their lives.
- Human hermaphrodites are usually the result of a hormonal imbalance during embryonic development.

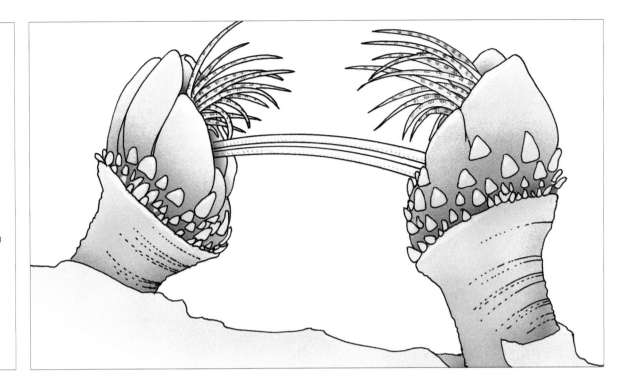

In most animals, individuals exist as separate sexes, either male or female. The scientific term for this condition is *dioecious* (meaning "two houses"). However, most plants and some animals are hermaphrodites; they possess both male and female reproductive organs.

## Reproduction in hermaphrodites

Hermaphroditic organisms have certain advantages when it comes to reproduction. Dioecious animals require members of the opposite sex to reproduce. Hermaphrodites have no need to be so selective. When all members of a species have both male and female sex organs, every individual is a potential mate for every other individual.

Most hermaphrodites are slow-moving or stationary organisms, and it is thought that hermaphroditism probably developed as an adaptation to this way of life. The chances of finding a mate are doubled if an organism is a hermaphrodite; in species where finding a mate is a slow or difficult process, hermaphroditism is a big advantage.

Self-fertilization is also common among hermaphrodites—individuals can fertilize themselves, using their own sex organs. Hermaphrodites can therefore still bear offspring even if they have become isolated from others of their own kind.

## Self-fertilization versus cross-fertilization

Cross-fertilization occurs when an individual is fertilized by another individual. Offspring produced by this method inherit genes from both parents; the resultant genetic mixing gives rise to variation within individuals of the species. Variation is important if a species is to survive changing environmental conditions (see NATURAL SELECTION).

Offspring produced by self-fertilization inherit their genetic material from a single individual. There is much less genetic recombination; the offspring are less genetically diverse than those from cross-fertilization and are less likely to survive changes in the environment. (Self-fertilization differs from cloning, a form of asexual reproduction in which the offspring are genetically identical to the parent.)

## Plant hermaphrodites

The reproductive organs of flowering plants are contained within the flowers. Most plants are hermaphrodites, and their flowers contain both stamens (the male organs) and pistils (the female organs). Hermaphroditic plants have various mechanisms that encourage cross-pollination and prevent or reduce the chances of self-pollination. In some plants the

*Stalked barnacles (Lepas spp.) are hermaphroditic marine crustaceans that reproduce sexually (above), though each individual possesses both male and female sex organs.*

## CONNECTIONS

- The successful reproduction of a species depends on the processes and organs of its **REPRODUCTIVE SYSTEM**.

## HERMAPHRODITISM IN HUMANS

Hermaphroditism in humans is rare and thought to be caused by hormonal imbalances present during the embryonic stage of development. True hermaphrodites have either an ovary and a testis or gonads (sex glands) containing ovarian and testicular structures. The genitals may be male, female, or both.

Another type of hermaphroditism, pseudohermaphroditism, results from a condition called congenital adrenogenital syndrome. People with this condition have a defective adrenal gland, which causes individuals who are genetically female to develop more masculine genitals and males to develop more feminine genitals. Treatment for these conditions usually involves the administration of hormones to correct the hormonal imbalance.

stamens and pistils mature at different times. If the male organs mature first, it is called protandry, and if the female organs mature first, it is called protogyny.

In many plants, such as the grasses, where pollen is carried by the wind, the stamens dangle out of the flower so that the pollen is carried as far away from the plant as possible. Insect-pollinated flowers are usually tubular in shape, and many of these plants have the stigma (opening to the ovary) located higher in the flower than the anthers (pollen-producing structures). When an insect visits the flower, its body comes into contact with the stigma before it reaches the stamens. Any pollen already present on the insect's body will therefore reach the stigma first.

In certain situations, self-pollination might be the only method of reproduction available to a plant. In these situations, some plants are able to overcome the mechanisms that usually prevent self-pollination and fertilize themselves.

*The hoary plantain (Plantago media), which grows on the shores of lakes, seas, or oceans, has separate male and female flowers on each plant.*

## Animal hermaphrodites

Most animal hermaphrodites, such as slugs, flatworms, and earthworms, are invertebrates. Vertebrate hermaphrodites are rare, but some fish fall into this category. Animal hermaphrodites have also developed mechanisms to prevent or at least reduce the chances of self-fertilization. In some animals, sperm and eggs are produced from the same organ, but usually the male and female organs are separate and located in different parts of the body.

Most hermaphroditic animals mate by exchanging spermatozoa, and the male and female sex organs are placed in such a way that self-fertilization is virtually impossible. Self-fertilization is, however, common among animal species in which individuals have very little contact. Certain parasites, such as the tapeworm, usually lead solitary lives, and it is uncommon for a host to be infected by more than one tapeworm. The only method of reproduction possible is self-fertilization.

Most fish species have separate sexes, but a number of hermaphroditic fish do exist. Some species of the family Serranidae (which include the basses of North America and the European coast) and the long belted sandfish (*Serranellus subligarius*) are hermaphrodites. Others include certain species of sea perch, sea breams, and pickerels.

## Sequential hermaphrodites

A few species of plants and animals can change sex at some point in their lives; these organisms are called sequential hermaphrodites. Sequential hermaphrodites cannot self-fertilize because the male and female gametes are not present at the same time. Sex changes are usually triggered by changes in the environment but are sometimes due to a genetic predisposition.

An example of a flower that has the ability to change sex is the jack-in-the-pulpit (*Arisaema*). These plants are male in their first year of life but become female once they have become established.

Animals that begin life as one sex and change sex later in life include the slipper limpet (*Crepidula fornicata*) and the anemone fish (*Amphiprion percula*). In some cases, males and females may secrete different chemicals, which act on individuals to determine their sex. If too many females are present, then males will develop, and vice versa. Thus, a balance between the sexes is maintained, and individuals can continue to reproduce.

P. BARNES-SVARNEY

**See also:** FERTILIZATION; FLOWERS AND FLOWER STRUCTURE; GENETICS; NATURAL SELECTION; REPRODUCTION.

## Further reading:
Mauseth, J. D. 1998. *An Introduction to Plant Biology.* 3rd ed. Sudbury, Mass.: Jones and Bartlett Publishers.
Pechenek, J. 2000. *Biology of the Invertebrates.* Boston: McGraw-Hill.

# HIBERNATION

**Hibernation is a state of lowered metabolism that enables animals to survive periods of extreme cold**

*Dormice are true hibernators. During the winter, they curl up into a tight ball to preserve heat and go into a deep, sleeplike state.*

## CONNECTIONS

● A person's **METABOLISM** varies not only with body temperature but also with age, sex, and the level of certain **HORMONES**.

● Most birds do not hibernate, and **MIGRATION** is the way many escape cold winters. They live in warmer parts of the world for several months at a time.

Hibernation means "winter sleep." A hibernating animal's heartbeat, circulation, metabolism, and body temperature are greatly reduced. Animals that truly hibernate become totally lethargic, seeming to be in a deathlike state.

## Advantages of hibernation

When severe cold threatens an animal, it has two choices for survival. Either it can escape the cold (migrate) or it can counteract it. Some animals, such as the lynx, counteract the cold by growing thick coats. Others have physiological mechanisms adapted for reducing their energy needs during the freezing conditions; they are the hibernators.

Maintaining body temperature demands energy. Homeotherms are animals that maintain a constant internal temperature. Mammals are homeotherms and spend much of their energy keeping warm. If the weather is mild, it does not take much energy for them to maintain their body heat. However, if the external temperature falls below freezing, homeothermic bodies must burn large quantities of food to produce enough energy to generate the heat it needs to survive (see ENERGY).

Poikilotherms (animals in which body temperature fluctuates with the surrounding temperatures), such as lizards, seek outside sources of energy (a sunny rock, a warm hole) to keep their bodies at an optimium tempersture (see THERMOREGULATION).

Homeotherms and poikilotherms are most threatened by cold temperatures—during cold winters—a time when food is also scarce. Hibernation, therefore, is a strategy that helps some animals avoid the scarcities of winter and lower their energy needs.

## Which animals hibernate?

True hibernators include bats, hedgehogs, and some rodents, as well as some fish, amphibians, and reptiles. Ground squirrels are among the animal kingdom's champion hibernators because they can hibernate for eight months of the year. Their torpor (sleepy state) is so deep they do not even stir when handled.

Other mammals, such as bears, chipmunks, and tree squirrels, may sleep for long periods of time during the winter. However, these animals generally do not hibernate because they do not undergo the

### CORE FACTS

■ Hibernation is a physiological mechanism for surviving extremely cold conditions.

■ Hibernating animals have a lowered heart rate and metabolism and use less energy than nonhibernators.

■ Hibernation is triggered by environmental cues, such as the number of hours of daylight or the temperature.

■ Estivation (an aid to survival in hot, dry regions) requires the same physiological adaptations as hibernation.

## SURVIVING HEAT OR DROUGHT

Regions experiencing intolerable heat or drought threaten the survival of animals, just as extreme cold does. Some animals, such as tropical amphibians that live in intensely hot, drought-ridden regions, have adapted a survival strategy akin to hibernation. They estivate ("sleep in the summer"). Estivation involves physiological adjustments similar to those seen in hibernation.

Lungfish (shown below) live in Australia and Africa, and although they are fish, they possess lung pouches. When the Sun evaporates the water in its home stream, the lungfish burrows into the mud. Once buried, it takes infrequent breaths through a small tubelike opening in the surface of the mud. Energy for maintaining its reduced body functions and for arousal comes from the absorption of its own muscle tissue. Lungfish estivate during the dry season, which usually lasts about four months.

Desert-dwelling spadefoot toads dig a burrow beneath the sand with their strong hind feet. When drought strikes, the toads shelter in their hole in the ground and secrete a gel-like substance that lines the burrow and coats their skin and thus reduces water loss from their body. The spadefoot toads estivate for up to 10 months, until a thunderstorm saturates their burrows and arouses them from their torpor.

### A CLOSER LOOK

same metabolic changes that a true hibernator experiences. These false hibernators are more accurately described as being in a "winter lethargy," during which they are drowsy and sluggish. If food is not available close by, a chipmunk may go into a deeper sleep.

The distinction between true and false hibernators is still in debate. The fact that dormant bears do not eat, drink, or eliminate body wastes might qualify them as hibernators. However, a bear's body temperature drops only 10 °F (5.7 °C) during dormancy, compared with a decrease of 50 °F (28.5 °C) in true hibernators. Some scientists point out that the drop in the bear's body temperature is small because the animal is so huge and so easily stores enough fat to maintain a relatively high temperature during dormancy. Most agree that its body temperature during dormancy categorizes the bear as a "light sleeper."

## How hibernation works

Animals that hibernate respond to a variety of environmental cues as winter approaches. Several have a biological clock that triggers the onset of hibernation (see BIORHYTHMS). Some animals enter hibernation when the temperature drops to a specific level. Low temperatures inhibit the appetite of many reptiles, and scientists believe this circumstance prompts them to hibernate. Other animals begin hibernating when the number of daylight hours dwindles or when they experience a certain number of days with a reduced food supply. Hedgehogs enter hibernation any time from the onset of winter, depending on their fat reserves or the available food supplies.

In mammals, these environmental cues provoke the same physiological response: the body of the hibernating mammal begins to produce a substance called hibernation induction trigger (HIT). Only recently discovered and thought to be a type of chemohormone with effects similar to those of opiates, HIT is believed to originate in the area of the brain, called the hypothalamus, that regulates temperature, feeding, and sleep.

Scientists have discovered that HIT's effects can be transferred to nonhibernating mammals. In one experiment, blood serum from hibernating woodchucks was injected into rhesus monkeys. The injections caused the monkeys to lose their appetites and depressed their heart rate and body temperature. The effects lasted for weeks; the lethargic monkeys sat around motionless, as if anesthetized.

Hibernation causes radical changes in an animal's body. When not hibernating, the ground squirrel's body temperature is maintained at about 90 °F (32 °C); during hibernation its body temperature falls to about 40 °F (4 °C). The heart's normal 200 to 400 beats per minute is reduced to a mere 5 beats per minute. When awake and active, a ground squirrel breathes about 200 times per minute; when hibernating, it takes only about four breaths per minute. These drastically slowed body processes can be maintained with far less energy (a lower basal metabolic rate) than a fully active body.

## Stocking up

Nearly all true hibernating species develop voracious appetites before turning in for the winter. Most of the food energy is stored in the body as fat, which the animal burns while it hibernates. In some amphibians, a proportion of the fat reserve goes into gamete production, especially in females, who may store the material in their eggs during hibernation. In newts this fat store is essential for the maintenance of the gonads (reproductive organs) because the destruction of the fat causes the gonads to shrivel up.

Mammals that hibernate have patches of a particular type of fat called brown fat on their backs and shoulders and near the brain, heart, and lungs. Its function is to provide the animal's vital organs with energy during hibernation and also to supply the energy needed for the return to normal functioning following arousal from the dormant state.

Before hibernation, animals prepare their dens or burrows for maximum comfort. Many mammals collect leaves and grass to make a comfortable bed and to provide insulation against the cold. This winter shelter is called a hibernaculum (plural, hibernacula). Many hibernating mammals also collect and store nonperishable food.

The European hedgehog virtually doubles its weight during the summer. As winter approaches, it makes a particularly well-insulated den. Its nest is made of leaves or grass, and the hedgehog molds it into shape so that the material is packed closely together to provide insulation.

Reptiles may hibernate underground because they can metabolize anaerobically (without oxygen). Reptiles and amphibians need moisture so they do not dry out. Hibernation under soils saturated with water solves this problem. Where soils may sometimes freeze, some amphibians secrete cryoprotectants, such as glucose, to prevent the water inside their cells from freezing.

Many hibernating mammals emerge briefly from their torpor several times during the winter. If their body needs additional energy, a mammal may munch sleepily on its food store. Sometimes, hibernating mammals wake to rid themselves of body waste, particularly urine, in designated toilet chambers within their hibernacula.

Hibernating mammals may also wake up temporarily when their body temperature plummets. Although they are adapted to extremely low body temperatures while hibernating, if the external temperature falls precipitously, the mammal may be in danger of freezing to death. In these circumstances, the hibernator may shiver or move about to increase its body temperature. It may refuel by eating some stored food. It is believed that the hypothalamus, a region of the brain that regulates body temperature, sends signals that alert the mammal and impel it to act to raise its body temperature.

Temporary arousal from hibernation is very costly. At least 75 percent of the energy expended and the weight lost during hibernation occurs during these brief awakenings. Thus, it is important not to disturb hibernating animals. Too many arousals may deplete their body stores and reduce their chances of survival through the cold season.

Arousal occurs as spring approaches. It may be triggered by an annual biological clock or by rising external temperatures. Some estivating amphibians respond to heavy rain (see the box on page 892). In mammals the first steps in arousal are dramatic increases in heart rate, blood pressure, and respiration. The brown fat fuels this sudden, enormous increase in energy demand. The body temperature rises slowly. Just before total arousal, the animal shivers. This muscular activity raises the body temperature. Some mammals remain immobile for hours after their body temperature rises while their body readjusts to the dramatic change.

N. GOLDSTEIN

**See also:** BIORHYTHMS; COLD-BLOODED ANIMALS; ENERGY; HOMEOSTASIS; THERMOREGULATION.

**Further reading:**
Perry, P. J. 2001. *Animals That Hibernate* (Watts Library: Animals). New York: Franklin Watts.

*Some amphibians hibernate during the winter. Hibernating frogs live in the mud at the bottom of ponds and rivers.*

## ROYAL PREROGATIVE

When winter approaches, the workers that populate a bumblebee colony in temperate regions succumb to the cold, and only the queen remains alive. She may burrow into a mossy stream bank or find a deep crevice in a rock, where she enters a state of hibernation so deep that it is like suspended animation. When the springtime warmth revives her, the queen searches for a suitable spot to build a nest, and begins to generate a new bumblebee colony. All summer the queen lays eggs to increase the colony population.

# HISTOLOGY

**A histologist studies a tissue sample under a light microscope.**

## CONNECTIONS

● Drug testing in **PHARMACOLOGY** may involve **ANIMAL EXPERIMENTATION** in which the tissues of laboratory animals are examined for signs of side effects or damage.

● Histology is vital in the diagnosis of **CANCER**.

Histology (from the Greek word *histos*, meaning "web") is the study of living tissues and their functions, usually with the aid of a microscope. The basic functional unit of living tissues is the cell. Bacteria and protozoans exist as single cells, but in multicellular organisms, cells become specialized and group together to perform specific functions, such as digestion or respiration. This process is cell differentiation. Cells of one or more types make up the tissues. Vascular plants (those with vessels made of xylem and phloem) consist of seven different types of cells. There are some 200 basic vertebrate cell types, each with a distinctive shape, structure, and function. Cells of similar shape and function act as a cooperative unit within tissues.

Although histologists work in all biological fields, the greatest amount of research, possibly the most valuable, is in vertebrate physiology, particularly the investigation of human disease. Animal organs such as the kidneys, eyes, and ovaries are tissue cooperatives. The different types of cells and tissues present in an

organ work in a coordinated fashion to carry out vital functions. The arrangement of tissues in an organ is called its architecture. For example, the architecture of the stomach comprises a lining layer of acid- and mucus-secreting epithelium (membrane), a layer of loose connective tissue richly supplied with blood vessels, and a triple-layered muscular coat.

In the liver, the architecture is quite different. Rather than layers of different tissues, the four lobes of the liver each contain thousands of hexagonal lobules, their cells radiating outward and surrounding a central vein. At the corner of each lobe are branches of the hepatic artery (bringing oxygenated blood), the portal vein (carrying nutrient-rich blood from the small intestine), and bile ducts (to take bile to the gall bladder).

## Histological investigation

Histologists make valuable contributions to the diagnosis of human disease and the evaluation of disease progression during treatment. Deviation from the normal architecture is a hallmark of disease. Histologists make their diagnosis on the basis of abnormal architecture, identifying specific conditions by the appearance of a tissue sample under the microscope. A diseased tissue is one in which there are variations in or total loss of cell architecture. In liver cirrhosis, for example, normal tissue with its blood supply is replaced by islands of nonfunctioning cells separated by scar tissue. The most serious breakdown of architecture occurs in cancer, when malignant cells from one layer invade the tissues of another layer.

Histologists use microscopes to examine the structure of tissues. With the aid of a powerful light microscope, which magnifies up to 1,500 times, the shape of cells and the appearance of the nucleus can be distinguished. Tissue components can be stained with specific dyes to increase their visibility. However, the resolution of the light microscope is limited. If the microscopist needs to distinguish more detail—for example, the insulating myelin sheath surrounding the axon of a nerve cell or the internal structure of a mitochondrion (the organelle inside the cell that fuels all its chemical activity; see CELL BIOLOGY)—then an electron

### CORE FACTS

■ Histology is the study of the appearance and function of animal and plant tissues.

■ Tissues are made up of cells, which can be of many different types, each of a specific shape and structure.

■ Samples of tissue can be taken from live subjects with an endoscope or by fine-needle aspiration.

■ Tissues are cut in thin sections, stained, and examined by light or electron microscopy.

microscope must be used. This instrument uses a beam of electrons, instead of light rays, to produce an image magnified over one million times. The transmission electron microscope passes a beam of electrons through a thin sample. The scanning microscope, in which the electrons are reflected from a sample coated with gold, makes it possible to study the surface of tissues or individual cells.

## Preparation for microscopy

A tissue sample to be viewed under the microscope must be no more than a single cell layer thick. Samples for histological examination may be taken from a living subject (biopsy) or they may be obtained from a nonliving subject such as a cadaver at postmortem (autopsy). Biopsy material used to be taken by making an incision and cutting away a tiny sample. Now, however, surgeons can use an endoscope (a long, flexible fiberoptic viewing instrument) to access almost every tissue in the body without the need for major surgery. Alternatively, they can perform fine-needle aspiration, in which a long, hollow needle is inserted under ultrasound guidance. Needle aspiration is particularly useful in the investigation of kidney and liver disease.

Once a sample is removed, it must be "fixed" to preserve the cell structure and halt biological detrioration. Chemicals such as formaldehyde and gluteraldehyde cause cross-linking within the cell and fix the tissue structures. Next the fixed sample is embedded in a supporting medium—usually paraffin wax for light microscopy or epoxy resin for electron microscopy—so it can be sliced very finely. Sections are shaved off the hardened block using a knife called a microtome. Just as in a delicatessen meat slicer, the sample is moved toward the blade to give a series of sections. Sections to be viewed by light are cut 3 to 7 micrometers (μm) thick with a highly sharpened metal blade. For electron microscopy, a glass or diamond knife mounted on an ultramicrotome cuts sections 20 to 100 nanometers (nm) thick.

Sections for light microscopy are mounted on glass slides. The supporting wax is dissolved away, and the sections are stained with colored dyes to highlight specific features, such as cell nuclei. For routine examinations, a standard combination of eosin, a negatively charged or acidic dye, and hematoxilin, a positively charged or basic dye, are usually adequate. These dyes color the nuclei blue and the cell's cytoplasm pink. Other staining techniques show up specific substances or certain bacteria.

Stains such as the eosin-hematoxilin mixture react chemically with the tissue. A large number of stains are specific for enzymes and cell products such as fats, sugars, and DNA. These stains are particularly useful to identify tissues under the light microscope. Tissues may also be stained to identify a unique product of the cell. For example, doctors may confirm a diagnosis of the skin cancer melanoma by detecting the enzymes necessary for melanin (skin pigment) formation. Some nontoxic dyes can be used on living tissue samples newly removed from the body.

Sections for electron microscopy are placed on a thin copper mesh grid. Most tissues are transparent to the electron rays and must be "stained" with a heavy metal, such as osmium or lead, which is opaque to electrons and binds in known quantities to different subcellular components.

## Immunohistochemistry

Immunohistochemistry is the technique of identifying a specific cell protein by applying a dye-tagged antibody to the tissue sample. The dye is taken up only by cells that contain the protein. An important diagnostic test for muscular dystrophy (a degenerative disease characterized by progressive muscle weakness) uses this staining technique. Normal muscle consists of bundles of filaments that are bound together in tight networks called myofibrils. These myofibrils are anchored to muscle membranes by a flexible protein called dystrophin, which is missing from the cells of people with the disease. The presence or absence of this protein is shown by using the appropriate stain.

## Autoradiography

Another specialized technique called autoradiography makes use of radioactive markers to study cell function. These markers are usually radioactive metabolic precursors that are taken up by cells. The radioactive cells are then detected by being exposed to a photographic film, which is darkened by any radioactive emissions. The cells literally produce their own image. For example, to study the

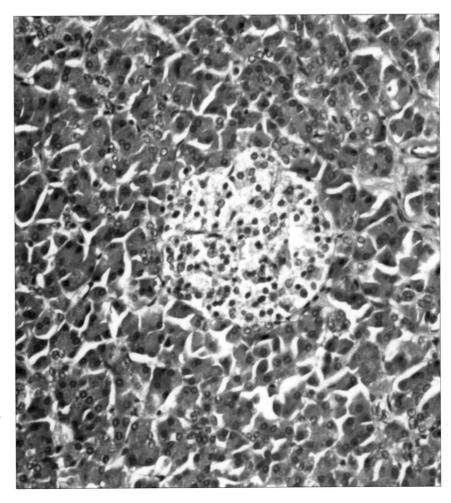

*A sample of tissue from the human pancreas, viewed by light microscopy, showing an islet of Langerhans (center).*

metabolic activity of a cell population, a radioactive nucleotide such as thymidine (a DNA precursor) is added. The cells take up the radioactive nucleotide into newly synthesized DNA, and dark spots on the photographic film indicate which cells are radioactive and thus are actively growing and dividing. This approach is especially useful for studying rapidly multiplying lymphocytes, the cells responsible for the immune system's response to foreign invaders, such as disease microorganisms or transplanted organs (see IMMUNE SYSTEMS; IMMUNOLOGY).

## Histology at work

Histologists use these techniques in a number of ways. They study abnormal tissues and classify them on the basis of variations in cell shape and structure and tissue architecture to diagnose diseases, classify tumors, or ascertain cause of death. They may also help in forensic investigations, by comparing material taken from crime scenes with samples from a suspect.

Thin films of body fluids can also be spread on slides and studied, either in their fresh state or after fixing and staining. This procedure is valuable in the examination of blood, sputum, and vaginal smears for forensic cases as well as for diagnosis of disease.

## Diagnosing cancer

Histology is probably the single most important technique for diagnosing cancer (see CANCER). Cancer is the result of cells growing and spreading uncontrollably.

In the early stages of tumor formation, the newly dividing cells vary in size and lose their uniform appearance. A mass of irregularly dividing cells gives rise to a lump, or neoplasm (new structure). At detection, even the smallest lump contains about 100 million cells. Provided the abnormal cells remain clumped together, the neoplasm is considered to be benign. In some cases, however, cells with new capabilities are produced. These cells fail to adhere to their neighbors, break free, and invade adjacent tissues or enter the bloodstream and are carried to distant sites (metastasis). The tumor is now malignant.

All of these stages are observable under the microscope. A biopsy sample may be obtained during a diagnostic procedure, such as fine-needle aspiration, or during surgery (for example, to remove a breast lump). Even in the middle of an operation, tissue may be sent for histological examination to see whether a lump is benign or malignant and, if malignant, what type of cancer it is and how far it has invaded. Samples taken from the visible margin of the tumor can be flash frozen in liquid nitrogen and then cut with a cryostat (a microtome specially modified to deal with frozen samples), stained, and examined, and the verdict passed to the surgical team within minutes.

## Fertility trials

Fertility assessment routinely utilizes histological techniques. The lining of the uterus (the endometrium) changes throughout the menstrual cycle, depending on hormone levels. A sample of the endometrium can show whether or not the changes associated with ovulation are occurring. Likewise, testicular biopsy allows the state and number of sperm-forming cells to be discovered.

## Postmortem investigation

In the case of sudden, unexplained death, an autopsy may be carried out. Tissue samples from every organ are examined for changes that are diagnostic of known disease. Histological examinations are an important part of an autopsy; they reveal how diseases progress in the body and lead to death. These studies also help maintain standards of medical care by confirming diagnosis and monitoring the effects of treatment. Where death is caused by a criminal act or a criminal act is suspected, the medical examiner requires tests to be performed on all the vital organs, such as the kidneys, liver, and lungs. Histological examination of such tissues sometimes produces conclusive evidence of death by trauma or by poisoning.

S. ABDULLA

See also: CANCER; CELL BIOLOGY; CYTOLOGY; FORENSIC SCIENCE; IMMUNE SYSTEMS; IMMUNOLOGY.

## Further reading:
Fawcett, D. W., and R. P. Jensh. 2002. *Concise Histology.* 2nd ed. Oxford: Oxford University Press.
Gartner, L. P., and J. L. Hiatt. 2001. *Color Textbook of Histology.* Philadelphia: W. B. Saunders.

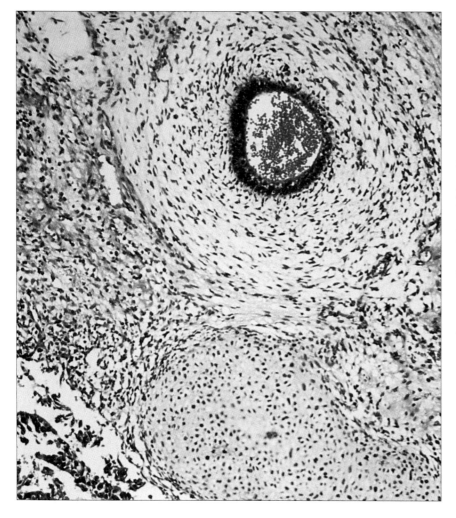

*Tissue from a tumor of the testis. The ability of the cell nucleus to take up more stain than normal is one of the signs for the diagnosis of cancer.*

# HITCHINGS, GEORGE, AND GERTRUDE ELION

**U.S. biochemists George Hitchings (1905–1998) and Gertrude Elion (1918–1999) developed many important drugs**

*Pioneer biochemist George Hitchings carried out his research for over 55 years.*

## CONNECTIONS

● **CHEMOTHERAPY** refers to any treatment using synthesized drugs but is more commonly associated with the treatment of **CANCER**.

● Synthetic drugs are used to prevent organ rejection after **TRANSPLANTS**.

As children, U.S. biochemists George Hitchings (1905–1998) and Gertrude Elion (1918–1999) both experienced the loss of family members after long illnesses, and as a result both wanted to follow careers that would alleviate people's suffering. Hitchings became one of the most successful practitioners of chemotherapy in the 20th century. He also employed Elion at a time when few women could find work doing scientific research. Together they discovered key differences in the biochemistry between normal and abnormal cells and synthesized molecules that were designed to target and attack diseased cells selectively. They and British pharmacologist James Whyte Black (b. 1924) won the Nobel Prize in physiology or medicine in 1988.

### Early life of George Hitchings

George Hitchings was born in Hoquiam, Washington, on April 18, 1905. He attended schools in Berkeley, San Diego, Bellingham, and Seattle before entering the University of Washington as a premedical student in 1923. At the end of the first year, Hitchings switched to major in chemistry, graduating in 1927. He stayed on to earn a master's degree in 1928 but went to Harvard to do doctoral work on nucleic acids. He obtained his degree in 1933; the same year he married Beverley Reimer. For the next nine years, during the Great Depression, Hitchings held a number of temporary appointments, doing research on cancer, electrolytes (substances that conduct ions), and nutrition. In 1942 he joined the Burroughs Wellcome (now Glaxo Wellcome) Research Laboratories in Tuckahoe, New York. He set up a biochemistry department and developed his own program of research. He returned to his work on nucleic acids, and in 1944 he hired Gertrude Elion.

### Early life of Gertrude Elion

Gertrude Elion was born in New York City on January 23, 1918. An excellent student, she gained a degree in chemistry with the highest honors. However, she was unable to attend graduate school because her father had been bankrupted in the stock market crash of 1929 and could not afford to send her. Jobs were scarce, but Elion eventually found work in a laboratory.

In 1939 she finally entered graduate school at New York University. She was the only female taking chemistry, finishing in 1941 with a master of science degree. By this time World War II (1939–1945) had begun, and it was much easier to get industrial laboratory work.

Initially Elion was employed as a quality controller by a food company, but she disliked repetitive work when nothing could be learned from it. She moved to New Jersey to do research work for Johnson and Johnson, but the laboratory was closed after only six months. From here she went to work for George Hitchings.

### The Burroughs Wellcome Laboratories

Hitchings quickly recognized Elion's talent and her intense desire to pursue a scientific career. On his

## CORE FACTS

■ By discovering biochemical differences in healthy and abnormal cells, Hitchings and Elion developed drugs that targeted only diseased cells. This process is called rational drug design.

■ In the 1950s, Hitchings and Elion produced the anticarcinogen 6-mercatopurine and the immunosuppressant azothioprine.

■ Synthetic drugs have been used successfully against a number of diseases, including cancer, malaria, and AIDS.

*Gertrude Elion persevered to make a successful career in science at a time when it was difficult for women to enter research.*

promotion, she moved into the position he had just vacated. Elion started a PhD at Brooklyn Polytechnic Institute, but after several years of part-time study, she was told that to continue she must do full-time research. She withdrew rather than give up her job.

Hitchings was involved in the synthesis of new drugs containing rings of carbon and nitrogen atoms related to the structure of deoxyribonucleic acid (DNA). These purines and pyrimidines interfered with the division of cancer cells. Elion's work focused on the purines, and despite poor working conditions and tedious procedures, she quickly improved the methods for synthesizing drugs and prepared several new compounds. In 1951 Hitchings and Elion produced the anticarcinogen 6-mercatopurine, which is still widely used in the treatment of cancer. In 1953, 40 percent of children with leukemia (a form of blood cancer) who took the drug went into remission.

In 1957 Hitchings and Elion were responsible for a second drug, the immunosupressant azothioprine (Immuran), which slows the division of white blood cells. It was a very important development because it greatly increased the success rate of organ transplants by reducing the likelihood of rejection. Azothioprine is also used to treat rheumatoid arthritis.

By 1977 Hitchings and Elion had developed an antiviral drug acyclovir (Zovirax), used to combat acquired immunodeficiency syndrome (AIDS). It was also the first drug to be used against viral herpes. Their Wellcome Laboratory team, although small, was credited with over 100 drug patents, which were used to treat diseases such as cancer, gout (Zyloprim), malaria (Diaprim) and viral infections (Septra). For this work Hitchings and Elion won the Nobel Prize in physiology or medicine in 1988 along with British pharmacologist James Black (see the box below).

## Later Life

By the time Hitchings officially retired in 1975, the Burroughs Wellcome Research Laboratories had moved to North Carolina. As emeritus professor, he continued his research work and stayed on as president of the Burroughs Wellcome Fund, a charitable organization dedicated to the support of biomedical research, until 1990. Hitchings died in 1998.

Gertrude Elion also received many awards in recognition of her work, but she was most proud of the three honorary doctorates she received, from George Washington University, Duke University, and the University of Washington. On her retirement in 1983, she too became an emeritus professor and continued with her studies and teaching until her death in February 1999.

KIM DENNIS-BRYAN

**See also:** ANALYTICAL TECHNIQUES; BIOCHEMISTRY; PHARMACOLOGY.

## Further Reading

St. Pierre, Stephanie. 1993. *Gertrude Elion: Master Chemist (Masters of Invention)*. Vero Beach, Fla: The Rourke Book Company.

# HOMEOSTASIS

**Homeostasis is the set of processes that maintains and regulates an organism's internal environment**

*The importance of homeostasis was first recognized by French physiologist Claude Bernard (in the white apron above), who wrote in 1857: "All the vital mechanisms, however varied, have only one object, that of preserving constant the conditions of life in the internal environment."*

In the bloody struggle for survival, species must exploit any advantage they have to compete with other species. This advantage may be an external feature, such as larger antlers, longer legs, or more powerful jaws. However, these features would be useless if the organisms were unable to maintain a stable internal environment within the body. For example, a deer would not be able to run on its long legs if it were too cold. Billions of years of evolution have resulted in a remarkable self-adjusting balance called homeostasis (from the Greek, meaning "staying the same"). A homeostatic system has two elements: input and output. Living organisms take in nutrients, air, and water from outside the body, utilizing them in strictly controlled conditions, and get rid of substances, such as water, waste, heat, and chemicals, that would otherwise disrupt normal conditions.

## Help from two systems

Two major control systems help maintain homeostasis in vertebrates: the autonomic nervous system and the endocrine system. Together they influence major vital body functions, such as breathing and temperature control. Certain changes in the environment may trigger a signal to the appropriate organ (the brain or a particular endocrine tissue), called an integrating center, which then signals the target cells to begin their counterbalancing activity.

The autonomic nervous system responds immediately to any stimuli it receives and acts through nerve impulses and chemicals called neurotransmitters (see NERVOUS SYSTEMS). It controls involuntary muscle function, such as heart rate and blood pressure. The endocrine system, using chemical messengers called hormones, acts over a longer time period: the hormones—and the signals to secrete them or inhibit their secretion—have to travel in the bloodstream between target cells and endocrine tissue (see ENDOCRINE SYSTEMS; HORMONES). As well as governing

---

## CORE FACTS

■ Organisms have a variety of homeostatic mechanisms that maintain and regulate their internal environment.

■ In vertebrates, the main control systems that help maintain homeostasis are the autonomic nervous system, via nerve impulses, and the endocrine system, which uses hormones.

■ Homeostatic mechanisms can regulate temperature, fluid balance, blood pressure, and the availability of energy.

---

## CONNECTIONS

● The maintenance or regulation of a particular temperature of the living body is called **THERMO-REGULATION**.

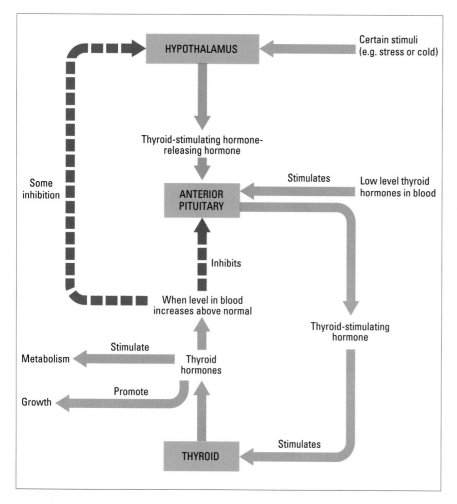

HYPOTHALAMUS

Certain stimuli
(e.g. stress or cold)

Thyroid-stimulating hormone-
releasing hormone

Some
inhibition

ANTERIOR
PITUITARY

Stimulates

Low level thyroid
hormones in blood

Inhibits

When level in blood
increases above normal

Thyroid-stimulating
hormone

Stimulate

Metabolism

Thyroid
hormones

Promote

Growth

Stimulates

THYROID

*This diagram shows the regulation of thyroid hormone secretion in vertebrates, an example of a negative feedback loop between the hypothalamus, the anterior pituitary, and the thyroid gland.*

involuntary processes, such as changes in the volume and content of extracellular fluid, the endocrine system also controls longer-term rhythms, such as the diurnal (daily, or night-day) cycle and women's fertility (menstrual) cycle (see BIORHYTHMS).

Not all chemical messengers are long-distance travelers. Sometimes, a local event triggers a local response. A muscle at work releases chemicals that act on the surrounding blood vessels to cause them to dilate and thus increase the supply of oxygen and nutrients. Neighboring cells communicate by means of paracrines, chemical messengers secreted into the extracellular fluid and absorbed locally.

### Feedback
The balance between input and output in a homeostatic system often depends on a process called feedback. Feedback may be positive or negative (see INFORMATION SCIENCE). Positive feedback reinforces an effect: this type of reinforcement creates a highly unstable situation because the output becomes progressively stronger, increasing an imbalance. On the other hand, negative feedback restores balance by counteracting a change. Negative feedback limits the activity of a system to prevent the output from rising too high. In a negative-feedback loop, the feedback counteracts the output; this effect stabilizes a system near a set point. For example, when a person enters a cold room, the exposed skin temperature of that person drops. Over time, the internal temperature of the person's body also drops if

nothing is done to prevent it. However, the body responds by minimizing heat loss—by narrowing the blood vessels and so reducing the blood supply to the skin and by promoting conscious heat-conserving activity (curling up or putting on a sweater, for example)—and increasing heat production by means of shivering. Thus, heat loss is counterbalanced by heat conservation and gain—a negative feedback mechanism (see THERMOREGULATION).

This example of thermoregulation illustrates the response of the nervous system (causing blood vessel constriction and shivering). An example of action by the endocrine system is the regulation of thyroid hormones, which stimulate metabolism and are essential for normal growth and development (see the diagram at left). When the level of thyroid hormones in the blood drops below normal (or when the body is experiencing stress such as extreme cold), an area of the brain called the hypothalamus stimulates the anterior pituitary gland, also in the brain. The pituitary then releases a hormone called thyroid-stimulating hormone, or TSH. As its name suggests, TSH causes the thyroid gland to produce more hormones and thus raises body temperature by increasing metabolism, as well as promoting growth. As the level of thyroid hormones in the blood increases, the activity of the hypothalamus and the anterior pituitary are inhibited so that metabolism and growth promotion are decreased. Maintaining homeostasis within a complex multi-organ animal, such as a human, demands not only the constant monitoring and regulation of properties such as temperature, water volume, and pH (acidity) but also the coordination of all these activities in the body.

## MAINTAINING THE BODY
The body of an animal may have many homeostatic mechanisms to maintain a constant internal environment, including control of temperature, fluid balance, blood pressure, and the availability of energy.

### Temperature
One of the most important homeostatic mechanisms in so-called warm-blooded animals is the maintenance of constant body temperature. Heat generated during metabolic activity is transferred to the bloodstream (blood temperature equals body temperature) and lost through the skin. The physiological processes involved in keeping the body's temperature at the set point (which differs between species) require the coordination of many biochemical reactions, most of which are controlled by enzymes. Enzymes themselves can catalyze chemical reactions efficiently only within certain temperature ranges (in humans this range is usually around 98.6 °F or 37 °C). Therefore, prolonged changes in the core (internal) temperature disrupt homeostasis.

Mammals and birds are homeotherms, animals that have a relatively constant body temperature. More specifically, they are endotherms; they can maintain a high body temperature by generating their own internal heat metabolically, independent of environmental conditions. The human body usually maintains a constant temperature of between 97.7° and 99.5 °F (36.5° and 37.5 °C) by means of an automatic thermostatic system in the hypothalamus. Thermoreceptors in the hypothalamus detect changes in body temperature by comparing the temperature of the blood flowing through it with an internal set point. The hypothalamus also receives information from cold and heat receptors in the skin. With a change in body heat, responses are triggered to correct the imbalance.

Homeostatic changes occur in response to changes in environmental temperatures. Surface warming causes blood vessels in the skin to dilate (increasing the skin's blood supply) and glands in the skin to secrete a dilute salt solution (sweat). Heat is lost through radiation and by evaporation of sweat. During cold weather, blood vessels constrict, so less heat is lost through blood flowing close to the surface of the skin.

A fever (elevated core temperature) is part of the inflammatory response launched by the immune system in response to infection (see IMMUNE SYSTEMS). It may be caused by the toxins produced by a bacterium or virus. Whatever the cause, a fever creates a hostile environment for disease-causing microorganisms. The thermostatic mechanism in the hypothalamus is temporarily set at a higher point until the infection is resolved. Localized inflammation, which results in redness and warmth in the skin, is also produced by the cells of the immune system fighting an infection.

## Fluid balance

Maintenance of water volume and its ionic content (positive and negative charge) is an essential homeostatic mechanism. The kidneys are the principal

### COLD TEMPERATURES, COLD FEET

Mammals and birds that live in cold conditions are well insulated by fur, feathers, or fat to conserve heat in the core area of the body, where all the important temperature-sensitive organs are located. However, body extremities such as the legs, ears, tail, and nose are "uneconomic" to insulate because of their high surface-to-volume ratio. To prevent these parts of the body from becoming costly sites of heat loss, they are allowed to cool to temperatures close to the surrounding temperature using a countercurrent heat-exchange system. For example, while a duck swims in cold water, heat enters its legs from the core of its body via the arteries. This heat is then transferred directly to the adjacent veins leaving the leg and reentering the core of the body; thus, the blood within the rest of the legs is allowed to remain cool, close to the temperature of the surrounding water. This mechanism prevents the loss of valuable body heat.

organs of homeostasis: they regulate extracellular fluid within narrow limits (see KIDNEYS). Many other tissues, including the lungs, digestive tract, and skin, are also involved with the input and output of fluids.

Body fluids are affected by sodium levels, which are kept within tightly controlled limits by negative feedback. Regulatory cells in the kidney are sensitive to changes in sodium levels. If the sodium concentration in the plasma (the liquid in which blood cells float) drops below the set point, specialized kidney cells secrete an enzyme called renin, which combines with a liver protein to form angiotensin. Angiotensin, in turn, stimulates the adrenal glands to secrete the hormone aldosterone. Aldosterone then acts on the kidney to stop sodium excretion. As the salt concentration of body fluids increases, blood volume increases and blood pressure rises.

*In response to low air temperatures, warm-blooded animals raise the hair or feather shafts in their skin to trap an insulating layer of warm air. In humans, this produces the characteristic goose bumps shown below. With a lack of dense body hair, humans benefit little from this response and usually compensate by putting on warm clothing.*

*Sharks have a much higher concentration of urea in their tissues than have other marine fish. However, they still need to excrete excess sodium, which is discharged in their urine and in a concentrated solution from a gland near the rectum.*

Through the process of osmosis, water has a tendency to move from an area of high concentration to an area of low concentration. Saltwater fish have a particular problem in maintaining the correct sodium level in their body because the surrounding water is much saltier than that in their tissues. As a result, water has a tendency to leave a fish's body and salt has a tendency to enter. To cope with this imbalance, fish drink sea water to replace the lost water and secrete salt ions in a small amount of concentrated urine. The excess sodium and chlorine is then pumped out by salt-secreting cells on their gills (see EXCRETORY SYSTEMS). Sharks, on the other hand, by reabsorbing their urea, keep their body fluids the same concentration as the surrounding water.

Protozoans, such as the amoeba, also have a mechanism for regulating water levels. Water enters the amoeba's body by osmosis and fills numerous small vesicles, which then empty into a central vacuole (see CELL BIOLOGY). This vacuole then releases its water content into the surrounding environment.

## Blood pressure

A highly complex negative feedback system involving the nervous, circulatory, and endocrine systems controls blood pressure, the pressure caused by the blood flowing through the main arteries. Any change in blood pressure is counterbalanced by a change in the system to restore pressure to the set point.

Most organs also have some control over their own blood pressure to meet the demands of metabolic activity. The brain and kidneys are particularly vulnerable to changes in blood pressure. For example, a sudden drop may cause acute renal (kidney) shutdown. A stroke (rupture or obstruction of an artery of the brain, causing loss of consciousness, sensation, and voluntary motion) may result from a sudden surge in blood pressure. These organs have built-in autoregulation mechanisms to stabilize their own blood supply regardless of blood pressure elsewhere in the body.

## Availability of energy

Cells need a continuous supply of energy to drive their nonstop metabolic activity (see METABOLISM). Fuel, in the form of glucose (sugar), must always be available. In vertebrates, it is transported throughout the body in the blood and is ready to be taken up as required. Insufficient supply or ability to use glucose, especially in vital organs such as the brain, may seriously impair tissue function. Too much circulating glucose, however, may also be dangerous. The negative feedback mechanism for glucose levels regulates both storage and release, primarily under the control of the hormones insulin and glucagon (see DIABETES; INSULIN).

Nutrients absorbed from the small intestine are carried to the liver in the bloodstream. This process pushes blood glucose levels above the set point and triggers the release of insulin by specialized cells in the pancreas. Enzymes in liver cells are activated by insulin to convert excess glucose to glycogen, which is stored for future use. Decreasing blood glucose levels stimulate the secretion of the hormone glucagon, also from the pancreas. Glucagon controls the reconversion of glycogen to glucose. When blood glucose levels return to normal, glucagon secretion is inhibited. Other hormones that regulate blood sugar include growth hormone, cortisol, epinephrine, and norepinephrine.

P. BARNES-SVARNEY

**See also:** BIORHYTHMS; CELL BIOLOGY; DIABETES; ENDOCRINE SYSTEMS; EXCRETORY SYSTEMS; HORMONES; IMMUNE SYSTEMS; INFORMATION SCIENCE; INSULIN; KIDNEYS; METABOLISM; NERVOUS SYSTEMS; TRANSPIRATION AND TRANSLOCATION.

**Further reading:**
Bradshaw, S. D. 1997. *Homeostasis in Desert Reptiles (Adaptations of Desert Organisms)*. New York: Springer Verlag.

## PLANT HOMEOSTASIS

Plants also have homeostatic mechanisms, although not to the same degree as animals. One example is the process of transpiration, the loss of water from plant surfaces (see TRANSPIRATION AND TRANSLOCATION), which is regulated by means of pores, called stomata, on the surfaces of leaves. These stomata are made up of guard cells, which open when the level of water inside them is high and close when the water level is low and so preserve moisture.

## A CLOSER LOOK

# HORMONES

## Hormones are chemical messengers in both plants and animals

Chemical messengers produced in plants and animals are called hormones. They usually act away from the site of production to bring about profound and diverse effects. The familiar fight-or-flight reaction to danger is a dramatic example of a hormonal response. Other hormonal actions, such as control of body growth, development to sexual maturity, and regulation of metabolic rate, are less obvious when they are working correctly but are easily noticed when they are not: giantism, dwarfism, and cretinism are developmental problems that have a hormonal origin (see GROWTH DISORDERS).

The word *hormone* is derived from a Greek word meaning "to excite" or "to set in motion." In humans an most animals, hormones are produced by endocrine glands in extremely minute amounts and are usually carried through the circulatory system (see CIRCULATORY SYSTEMS; ENDOCRINE SYSTEMS). Receptive cells in other parts of the organism react to the passing hormones to regulate a variety of physiological processes. Hormones control reproduction, growth, maturation, and the maintenance of a biologically stable internal environment (see HOMEOSTASIS). All hormones, in precise amounts, are vital to the health of the animals and plants that produce them. Too much or too little of particular hormones can cause disease (see the box on page 905).

Animals produce many different hormones. In vertebrates, most hormones are produced in organs called endocrine glands and are carried by the bloodstream. They have specific actions on certain target tissues only. By contrast, plants produce few hormones, but their production is widespread, and their actions are far less specific.

### Classifying hormones

Hormones have been studied in many forms of life, so they can be categorized using traditional classifications (for example, plant, invertebrate, or vertebrate hormones). The hormones of mammals have been studied extensively. Different mammals

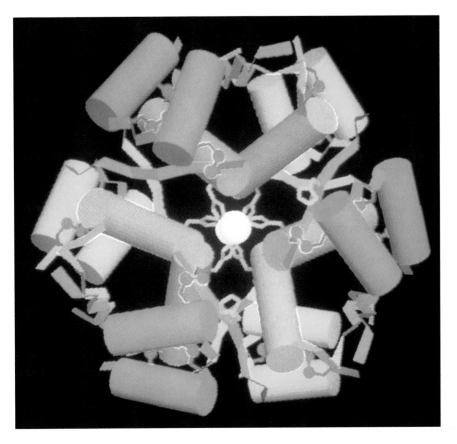

*A computer graphic of an insulin molecule. Insulin is a hormone that plays an important role in regulating blood sugar levels.*

produce hormones that have very similar chemical structures. All hormones are chemical regulators: trophic hormones regulate the production of other hormones and nontrophic hormones have other specific functions. All hormones have specific names, but are often referred to by names that reflect their function. For example, somatotropin is often called growth hormone. Alternatively, hormones are often grouped under headings that refer to the organs or cells that produce them, such as pituitary hormones.

### Where hormones come from

The pituitary gland, at the base of the brain, has anterior (front) and posterior (back) lobes, which each play different roles in hormone production and release. Closely associated with the pituitary gland is the hypothalamus, an aggregation of nerve cells at the base of the brain, which controls hormone production in the anterior lobe and produces two further hormones, oxytocin and antidiuretic hormone, for release from the posterior lobe.

Another important endocrine gland is the thyroid, located in the neck. It is a source of the iodine-containing hormones, thyroxine and tri-iodothyronine, that control metabolic rate.

Four tiny parathyroid glands are located by the thyroid gland. They secrete parathyroid hormone, which helps regulate blood calcium levels. The thymus gland, located below the thyroid in the lower part of the neck, first increases, and then decreases in

## CORE FACTS

- Hormones are chemical messengers produced by one part of the body that travel to another part of the body to produce a response.
- Hormones are produced by plants and animals.
- Hormones can be divided into two groups: steroid and peptide.
- In animals hormones are secreted by the endocrine system.
- Hormones affect growth, metabolism, molting, and the development of sexual characteristics in animals.
- In plants hormones control growth and the ripening of fruit.

## CONNECTIONS

● Knowing how hormones work has applications in **BIOTECHNOLOGY**. By understanding which hormones cause fruit to ripen, farmers can pick unripe fruits, transport them, and then artificially ripen them just before they reach the market.

● When the body's hormonal control goes wrong, **GROWTH DISORDERS** may result.

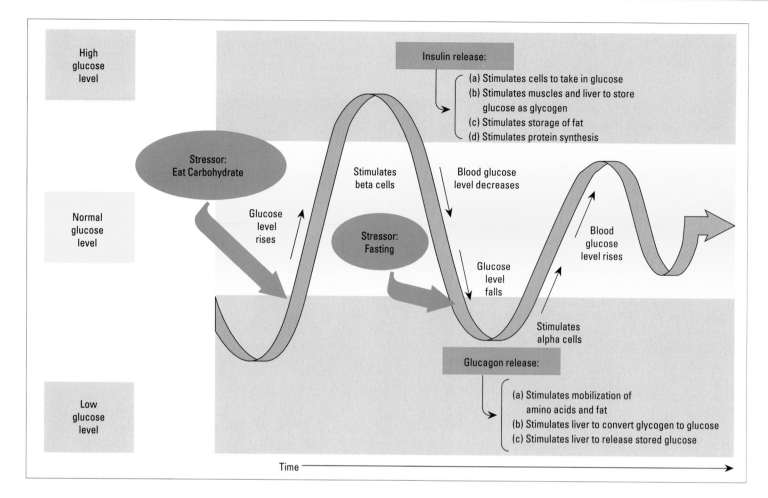

High
glucose
level

Normal
glucose
level

Low
glucose
level

Insulin release:
(a) Stimulates cells to take in glucose
(b) Stimulates muscles and liver to store
    glucose as glycogen
(c) Stimulates storage of fat
(d) Stimulates protein synthesis

Stressor:
Eat Carbohydrate

Stimulates
beta cells

Blood glucose
level decreases

Glucose
level
rises

Stressor:
Fasting

Glucose
level
falls

Blood
glucose
level rises

Stimulates
alpha cells

Glucagon release:
(a) Stimulates mobilization of
    amino acids and fat
(b) Stimulates liver to convert glycogen to glucose
(c) Stimulates liver to release stored glucose

Time

**The diagram above shows
how the hormones insulin
and glucagon act to
regulate blood sugar
levels.**

size with maturity. Its main function is as a source of white blood cells (see BLOOD). It may also produce the hormone thymosin, which is important in the development and maintenance of a healthy immune system.

Just above each kidney is an adrenal gland, each comprising an outer cortex and inner medulla. Cortisol is one of the hormones produced by the adrenal cortex under the influence of the hypothalamus and the pituitary gland. Epinephrine (also called adrenalin) is one of the hormones produced by the adrenal medulla, which is part of the adrenal gland (see EPINEPHRINE AND NOREPINEPHRINE; KIDNEYS).

Between the stomach and the lower intestine is the pancreas (see PANCREAS). Within a very small region of the pancreas are clusters of cells called the islets of Langerhans, after their discoverer, German physician Paul Langerhans (1847–1888). Two major hormones are produced by the islet cells: insulin, which acts to lower blood sugar (glucose); and glucagon, which acts to raise it (see INSULIN).

The sex glands, or gonads, produce hormones that govern sperm or egg production and the development and maintenance of male or female secondary sexual characteristics, such as body hair and enlarged breasts. The major male hormone is testosterone, produced mainly in the testes. The principal female hormones are estrogen and progesterone.

## Hormone regulation of blood sugar level

One example of the action of hormones is the regulation of blood sugar level. Glucose is the main source of energy for all cell functions and is derived

from food. For example, brain cells need a constant supply of glucose to function normally. After a meal has been eaten, the sugars in it are absorbed quickly. Carbohydrates are broken down into glucose and absorbed. The rising level of glucose in the blood and possibly the presence of food in the intestine trigger cells, called beta cells, in the islets of Langerhans to release insulin into the bloodstream.

Insulin stimulates the liver and skeletal muscles to use more glucose and to store excess glucose as glycogen, a starch. Fatty tissues in the body are prevented from releasing their fat stores. Insulin stimulates protein synthesis, using amino acids derived from the protein component of the food consumed. These actions of insulin and the gradual fall in the nutrient influx as food digestion proceeds cause the blood sugar level to fall.

The response to a falling concentration of sugar in the blood is that the beta islet cells become less active and alpha islet cells, also in the islets of Langerhans, begin producing glucagon. This hormone reverses most of the glucose storage and some of the fat storage to raise the blood sugar concentration. Glucagon does not reverse insulin's action on muscle.

Glycogen in the liver is converted back to glucose to satisfy the brain's immediate energy requirements. In normal circumstances the muscles' own glycogen stores are not mobilized, but in prolonged fasting, muscle glycogen, then fat, and eventually protein are broken down to maintain the blood sugar level demanded by the brain.

A sudden high energy demand when blood sugar levels are low can cause the adrenal glands to produce epinephrine, which mobilizes the body's reserves of glycogen.

## The fight-or-flight response

Another example of hormonal action occurs if an individual senses danger. The body enters a state of readiness for physical exertion to allow it to confront the threat or to escape from it. This state is called the fight-or-flight response. Some aspects of the response will be familiar to anyone who has had a fright: heart rate and breathing rate increase, and blood is diverted to the muscles, where it is needed most, so the skin becomes pale. Other aspects are hidden: blood pressure rises; glycogen in the liver is converted rapidly to glucose, which raises the blood sugar level; and muscle strength increases.

The response is brought about in the following way. The brain signals to the hypothalamus to secrete corticotropin releasing factor (CRF), which works directly on the pituitary gland, triggering the release of adrenocorticotropic hormone (ACTH) into the bloodstream. ACTH reaches the adrenal cortex in seconds, where it stimulates the secretion of cortisol. Cortisol stimulates the formation of glucose by reducing the effects of insulin and increasing the effects of glucagon. The net result is a rise in blood sugar. In addition, nerve impulses stimulate the adrenal medulla to pump epinephrine and norepinephrine into the bloodstream. When the response ends, insulin levels begin to rise, and glycogen storage resumes.

## Hormones and growth

Heredity provides the blueprint, and nutrition supplies the substances, but hormones control growth. How tall an individual will be at maturity can vary considerably, depending on the availability of the right hormones at the right time and the right cell structure where the hormones are received. The hypothalamus produces releasing factors to turn on

## HORMONAL DISEASES

Hormonal diseases are caused by the over- or underproduction of particular hormones. If the pituitary in youth produces excessive growth hormone, then a giant adult results. Underproduction of growth hormone can produce a dwarf adult. If excessive growth hormone appears after maturity, when the long bones of the body have stopped growing in length, a condition called acromegaly results: it is characterized by coarsening overgrowth of the jaw, head, tongue, hands, and feet. The disease progresses extremely gradually and can be halted with suitable hormone treatment.

Addison's disease, characterized by a variety of symptoms including extreme weakness, low blood pressure, and pigmentation of the skin, was discovered in the 1800s, when Thomas Addison found diseased adrenal glands in sufferers when performing autopsies after they had died. Doctors now know Addison's disease results from an insufficiency of secretions of cortisol by the adrenal cortex.

The thyroid gland regulates metabolism and growth by releasing the iodine-containing hormones thyroxine and triodothyronine. Hormonal disorders result when too little or too much thyroxine is released. Hypothyroidism is a deficiency disease (*hypo-* comes from the Greek word for "under"). It can occur in a developing fetus and continue in the newborn infant. If the condition is not treated promptly, the child will have stunted growth and mental retardation, a condition called cretinism. Severe adult hypothyroidism is called myxedema. The main symptoms are swollen lips and a thickened nose.

Hyperthyroidism, the production of too much thyroxine (*hyper* is derived from the Greek word for "over") causes rapid heartbeat, weakness, weight loss, nervousness, and protruding eyes. As with hypothyroidism, it can be treated successfully.

If the diet contains insufficient iodine for thyroxine production, the thyroid gland becomes hyperactive and the resulting enlargement of the gland is called a goiter. The ailment can be treated by adding iodine to the diet.

The most common hormonal disease is diabetes, of which there are two kinds. Type I diabetes, or insulin-dependent diabetes, is the result of underproduction of insulin. Type II diabetes is caused by the inability of the body to use insulin (see DIABETES; INSULIN).

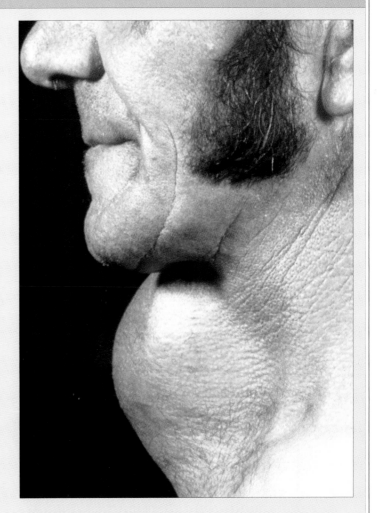

*Hyperthyroidism can lead to a condition called goiter, in which the thyroid gland enlarges and can be seen as a swelling in the neck.*

AT RISK

the anterior pituitary's production of somatotropin, or growth hormone (GH). GH boosts the building of proteins from amino acids and promotes the use of fat rather than carbohydrate to provide energy. The thyroid hormones are also important in metabolism and stimulating growth.

## Hormones, sex, and reproduction

In many animals, including humans, the sex of each new individual is determined at conception by the sperm cell that enters the ovum (female reproductive cell, or egg). If the sperm carries a Y chromosome, the fetus will normally develop as a male; if it carries an X chromosome, the fetus will be a female (see FERTILIZATION). Early in the development of a male human embryo, the hormone testosterone is produced by the fetal testes. After birth the production of testosterone is very low. For testosterone to be produced, the hypothalamus must stimulate the anterior pituitary to release a gonadotropin called follicle stimulating hormone (FSH), which will activate the testes. The onset of puberty in boys at about the age of 12 is triggered by increased production of luteinizing hormones (LH) by the pituitary gland. LH causes testosterone secretion to increase 60-fold. Testosterone and hormones from the adrenal cortex called androgens cause rapid growth and the development of secondary sexual characteristics, such as a deep-

ening voice and the growth of body hair. Testosterone production remains fairly constant at this level until late in life (see ADOLESCENCE; CHILD DEVELOPMENT).

The female fetus develops sexually a few weeks later than the male but still early in the pregnancy. As with males, the hormone level drops at birth and is very low throughout childhood. Puberty begins about two years earlier in the female than in the male. The hypothalamus becomes active, stimulating first the adrenal cortex to produce androgens and the anterior pituitary to secrete FSH and LH. These hormones stimulate the ovaries to produce estrogen and progesterone. The secondary sexual characteristics appear. In females the development of the breasts and the change in distribution of fat are obvious signs of advancing maturity.

Unlike the male hormone testosterone, female hormones are secreted cyclically over about a 28-day period called the menstrual cycle. The first menstrual cycle is called menarche and starts with puberty. Female hormones are secreted in this cycle only to late middle age, when a stage of shutdown called menopause begins (see MENSTRUAL CYCLE).

At the start of the menstrual cycle, there is an increase in the production of FSH and LH, which promotes development in the ovaries and increased secretion of estrogen and progesterone. The uterus lining thickens. Shortly before midcycle, the production of LH increases again, stimulating the release of the ovum. If conception occurs, the uterus is ready; if it does not occur, the progesterone level drops, the excess cells lining the uterus are shed in menstruation, and the cycle starts over.

## Chemical composition of hormones

Chemically, hormones fall into two general classes: steroidal compounds have a characteristic structure containing four interlocking rings of carbon atoms; nonsteroidal compounds consist of single amino acids, short chains of amino acids (peptides), or very complex structures built from hundreds or thousands of amino acids (proteins). The adrenal cortex and gonads (ovaries and testes) produce steroids. The rest of the endocrine glands produce protein, peptide, or amino acid-based hormones.

Alpha amino acids are relatively small molecules containing carbon, hydrogen, oxygen, nitrogen, and occasionally sulfur (see AMINO ACIDS). All have similar structures, differing only in what is attached to one carbon atom in the molecule. They always link with a nitrogen atom from one joined to a particular carbon atom of another. The linkage is called an amide or peptide bond. There are just over 20 alpha amino acids that combine in specific and repeating patterns to make small chains, or rings, called peptides, or larger combinations called proteins.

A chain of two amino acids is called a dipeptide. Three linked amino acids form a tripeptide, and many are called a polypeptide. Oxytocin, a hormone produced in the hypothalamus that stimulates milk secretion in mammals, is a nonapeptide, that is, it has nine amino acids.

*This diagram shows how steroid hormones activate genes. The hormones are transported to the target cell (1). They pass through the cell membrane (2) and the cytoplasm into the nucleus (3). Here the hormone binds with a receptor (4) and forms a hormone-receptor complex, which combines with a protein associated with DNA and thus activates certain genes (5) to synthesize proteins (6). The hormone has altered the cell's activity (7).*

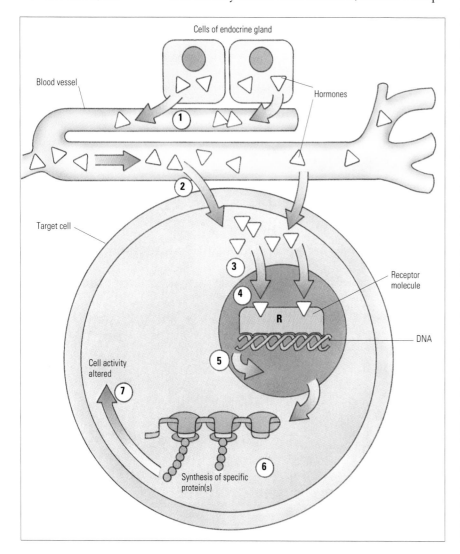

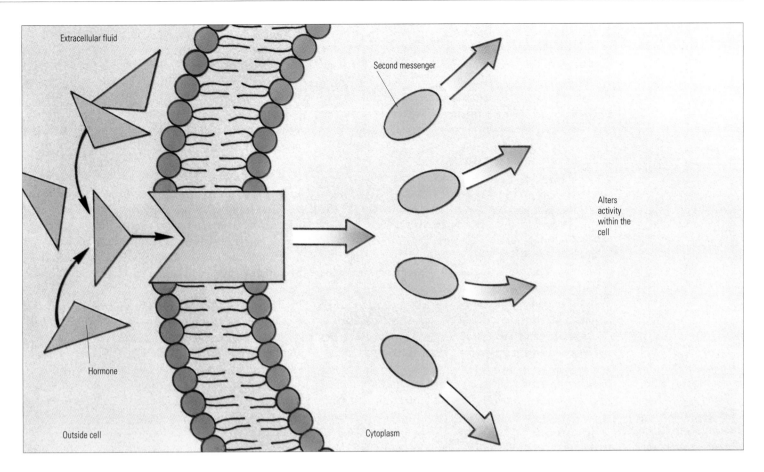

Extracellular fluid

Second messenger

Alters activity within the cell

Hormone

Outside cell

Cytoplasm

ACTH, which is produced in the anterior lobe of the pituitary gland, is a peptide with 39 amino acids. Insulin has two peptide chains, one of 21 amino acids, the other of 30 amino acids. Thyroxine is a complex amino acid shaped like a steroid. It has four iodine atoms, which are bonded to carbon atoms in two-ring structures on the molecule.

## How hormones act on cells

Only target cells with receptors that can respond to the unique chemical structure of a particular hormone will be influenced by that hormone as it circulates through the bloodstream. Although each hormone has a unique chemical structure, there are two general chemical types and two mechanisms for hormones to affect cells.

Steroid hormones are soluble in lipids (fats). This characteristic allows them to diffuse through cell membranes to bond with receptors inside target cells. Thyroid hormones are not steroids, but their chemical structures make them react much as steroids do. Within the cytoplasm of the cell, the hormone-receptor complex enters the nucleus, where it affects protein synthesis.

Protein and peptide hormones act by a different mechanism: these "first messengers" bond to receptors on or within the membranes of target cells. The formation of a hormone-receptor complex causes a "second messenger" to act within the cell, producing a large number of sequential reactions. Calcium ions and cyclic AMP (adenosine monophosphate) are common second messengers, sometimes working in combination. Cyclic AMP, which has a phosphate group attached in a ring-shaped structure, is formed

from ATP (adenosine triphosphate). ATP is the main energy carrier for all metabolic pathways (see ATP PRODUCTION; ENERGY; METABOLISM).

## Controlling hormones

The amount of each hormone in the bloodstream is regulated by a negative-feedback control system: too high a level of a hormone in the bloodstream causes the hormone's own release rate to be slowed. Circadian, or daily, rhythms also have some influence on the production of hormones over about a 24-hour cycle and are regulated by complex inputs from the environment, which are received by the brain and passed on to the autonomic nervous system and the endocrine system (see BIORHYTHMS).

Negative-feedback loops that control the level of hormones in the blood are part of the body's homeostatic regulation system, which maintains a stable internal environment (see HOMEOSTASIS).

## Vertebrate hormones

Vertebrate hormonal systems have much in common: reproduction is stimulated by gonadotrophins produced in the pituitary gland; blood sugar level is mainly controlled by the opposing actions of insulin and glucagon; thyroid hormones regulate energy, metabolism, and growth. However, some physiological responses produced are peculiar to certain species. In reptiles, thyroxine is associated with shedding of skin, and in amphibians it must be present for a tadpole to be able to change into a frog: tadpoles that have had the thyroid gland removed do not change.

The hormone called intermedin, or melanocyte-stimulating hormone, promotes different color

*Peptide hormones act as "first messengers," by binding to receptors on the membrane of the target cell, the resulting formation causing a "second messenger" to relay the hormonal message.*

changing results in different species. In humans intermedin does not play an important role in the normal behavior of melanocytes (cells that contain the dark pigment melanin). The effect is quite different, however, in many fish, amphibians, and reptiles, in which the melanocytes respond to dramatic color changes very quickly.

### Invertebrate hormones

Although invertebrate hormones have not been studied as extensively as have vertebrate hormones, there is evidence that hormones are important in the regulation of many invertebrate body functions.

Metamorphosis in insects is controlled by hormones. When insects grow, they periodically shed their hard exoskeletons. This phenomenon is called molting (see MOLTING). Cells in the insect brain produce a hormone that stimulates a pair of glands in the thorax to secrete ecdysone, which promotes molting and metamorphosis. Just behind the insect brain are a pair of glands, the corpus allata, which secrete juvenile hormone. This hormone delays maturity in the larval stage, by preventing ecdysone from promoting metamorphosis but not inhibiting molting. Secretion of juvenile hormone decreases as the larva grows. When the concentration of juvenile hormone becomes too low to inhibit the effect of ecdysone, the larva pupates (see LARVAE AND PUPAE). Then, when there is no juvenile hormone present, the pupa develops into the adult.

Squid and octopuses (cephalopods) produce stress hormones that control pigment cells by contracting muscles. Octopuses can turn pale and look larger and more threatening when danger looms. When food comes in sight, the color darkens. Some species can change into very bright colors. Squid can turn blue, purple, red, or yellow to blend into their environment when threatened.

## PLANT HORMONES

Like animal hormones, plant hormones are chemical messengers. Unlike animal hormones, they are not produced in particular glands and do not exert their effects only on specialized target cells. Plant hormones are produced in various parts of a plant in nonspecialized structures and can affect cells throughout the plant producing them; in the case of the hormone ethylene, even neighboring plants can be affected. Plant hormones control responses to environmental conditions such as gravity, light level, ambient temperature, availability of water, and seasonal changes. They also influence growth rate. There are three major groups of plant hormones: auxins, cytokinins, and gibberellins. There are also two other plant hormones that do not fall into these main groups: abscisic acid and ethylene.

### Auxins

The principal growth-stimulating hormone in plants and the first plant hormone isolated is the chemical

*Chameleons change color to blend in with their surroundings. The color change is caused by changes in the distribution of pigments in the skin cells. The distribution of these pigments is controlled by hormones.*

compound indoleacetic acid (IAA). It is often called simply auxin. Other auxins have been identified in plants, and there are also some important synthetic auxins: 1-napthaleneacetic acid stimulates root formation when applied to cut stems; 2,4-dichlorophenoxyacetic acid, better known as 2,4-D, stimulates the growth of broadleaf plants.

Scientists do not understand exactly how auxin moves through plants, although they know that in young plants it is transported from the tip of the shoot to the roots, where it stimulates growth. Auxin causes cells to lengthen rapidly by altering the permeability of the plasma membrane so that more water can enter the cell. It also promotes an increase in protein synthesis and new cell wall material. Fruit growers use auxin to stimulate fruit development in nonpollinated flowers.

## Cytokinins

Hormones that promote cell division were anticipated before they were isolated. In 1954, when tobacco pith was being grown experimentally in tissue culture, scientists found that a chemical called kinin stimulated cell division. Later, researchers showed that many other plant extracts and some bacteria contained similar chemicals, which became known as cytokinins.

Cytokinins are thought to be produced in the tips of roots. They travel upward through the plant and act to promote the development of branching, which auxin inhibits. As the plant grows and the auxin is produced farther from the lower lateral buds, less auxin reaches them. The rising cytokinins overcome the effect of auxin, and lateral buds grow.

## Gibberellins

Gibberellins were first isolated in a search for the cause of "foolish seedling" disease in rice plants in Japan. Some rice seedlings grew rapidly but were spindly, fell over, and seldom produced useful grain. A fungus, *Gibberella fujikuroi*, was found to produce the chemical that caused the rapid elongation of cells in infected rice plants. The isolated hormone was named gibberellin. Scientists have since identified more than 50 gibberellins, all similar growth-stimulating hormones.

Gibberellins are produced in young leaves near the growing shoots. These hormones stimulate rapid growth of cells and cellular differentiation in growing plants. Gibberellins are also thought to be produced by embryos and developing seedlings, where they stimulate enzymes that process reserves in the seed to nourish the embryo. They seem to be the main stimulants of root growth.

## Abscisic acid

Abscisic acid inhibits growth hormones. It turns off plant development when conditions for growth are unfavorable. When water is scarce, light is limited, or the temperature is too low for healthy growth, abscisic acid is produced in regions where there is a high concentration of the growth-stimulating hormone auxin.

## Ethylene

The gas ethylene plays an important role in senescence (aging) and the ripening of fruits (see AGING). It is produced when the level of auxin reaches a high concentration. Incomplete burning of kerosene also produces ethylene, and this substance can ripen plants as effectively as the ethylene produced naturally in the plants. Ethylene is used to bring fruits to market in prime condition. Unripe fruits can be picked and shipped safely and then ripened by treatment with ethylene just before sale.

Ethylene is an unusual hormone because it is released into the atmosphere. It acts not only on the producer but also on its neighboring plants and fruits. Apples continue to produce ethylene after picking, for example, and any wound on the surface of an apple promotes extra ethylene production. Therefore, if one apple in a barrel is damaged, it will age itself and its neighbors.

M. NAGEL

*The ripening of fruits such as these tomatoes is caused by the plant hormone ethylene.*

**See also:** ADOLESCENCE; AGING; AMINO ACIDS; ATP PRODUCTION; BIORHYTHMS; BLOOD; CHILD DEVELOPMENT; CIRCULATORY SYSTEMS; DIABETES; ENDOCRINE SYSTEMS; ENERGY; EPINEPHRINE AND NOREPINEPHRINE; FERTILIZATION; GROWTH DISORDERS; HOMEOSTASIS; INSULIN; KIDNEYS; LARVAE AND PUPAE; MENSTRUAL CYCLE; METABOLISM; MOLTING; PANCREAS; PREGNANCY AND BIRTH.

### Further reading:
Schulkin, J. 1999. *Neuroendocrine Regulation of Behavior*. Cambridge, U.K.: Cambridge University Press.

# HORNS

**Horns, made from bone and keratin, are used in defense, in sexual combat, and to show dominance in a herd**

*Male bighorn sheep (Ovis canadensis) have large, circular horns.*

## CONNECTIONS

● Keratin, an important component that surrounds the bony core of true horns, is also present in the claws of cats and in human **HAIR** and fingernails.

● In some animals, **HORMONES** trigger the growth of horns.

True horns, made of a bony core enclosed in an outer keratin (fibrous protein) sheath, are present in ungulate mammals belonging to the family Bovidae, which includes antelopes, cattle, sheep, goats, bison, and buffalo. The horns are unbranched and grow directly out of and are permanently attached to the animal's skull, unlike antlers, which branch and are shed and regrown each year (see the box on page 911). The pronghorn antelope (*Antilocapra*) is unique because it has horns but the keratin sheaths are shed annually much as antlers are. Giraffes and okapis are the only true ruminants whose young are born with horns. However, they are not true horns but ossicones. Covered with skin, ossicones are cartilaginous at birth, ossifying (becoming bony) and fusing with the skull as the animal grows. Ossicones get slowly larger throughout the animal's life.

## What is a horn?

The horn's core is made from bone, and every year it grows in diameter, as more bone is added (see BONE). It is possible to see annual rings by looking closely at the outer covering. The horn's outer covering is made from a fibrous protein called keratin. Horns grow on both males and females, although sometimes the females of some species do not develop them. This fact led to the belief that horns exist to provide males with weapons to fight rival males for access to females. Originally, scientists thought horn development was triggered by male hormones (such as testosterone), but they now think that epinephrine (also called adrenaline), a hormone possessed by all animals, is the trigger.

Horns come in various shapes and sizes. For example, bighorn sheep have backward-sweeping, forward-curving horns; kudus have curly, spiral horns; bison have upward-curving crescents that emerge from the sides of the skull; and mountain goats have small, ebony colored horns that taper backward from their foreheads.

---

### CORE FACTS

■ Horns grow out of and are permanently attached to an animal's skull.

■ True horns are made of bone with a covering of keratin.

■ Horns are present on both male and female animals.

■ The functions of horns include defense, courtship, and the indication of dominance.

## How did horns evolve?

The fossils of horned antelopes date back 25 million years, which is relatively recent in geological time. The original ancestors of horned animals are unknown, although scientists speculate that ancient giraffelike animals were their forebears.

The earliest horned animals developed extravagant, stabbing headgear, possibly as a means of defense. However, on the open grasslands, where these animals lived, the best defensive strategy was herding. Danger is more likely to be detected by many pairs of eyes, and long legs provide speed for flight. So, over time, their horns modified to more modest sizes and shapes. In contrast, musk oxen form a ring around young animals when danger threatens, with horned adults facing outward.

## The functions of horns

● **Dominance:** The size of an animal's horns may indicate its dominance within a social group. For example, when two male bighorn sheep meet, each tilts his head a bit toward the other to get a good view of the other's horns. When the horns are more or less the same size and equally impressive, fighting may ensue. If one male's horns are noticeably larger, the sheep with the smaller horns will back off, conceding the dominance of the better-endowed male. By displaying their horns, males often avoid physical contact, which can lead to injury. Usually the sheep in retreat is a juvenile, whose horns are smaller.

● **Sexual combat:** Although it is not their main function, horns sometimes play an important role in the males' fight for females. Females are attracted to males who have large horns because they indicate the bearer is strong and healthy, can defend a territory, and will pass on these desirable characteristics to their offspring. Male bighorn sheep, for example, engage in all-out combat for the sexual attentions of females. However, the horns are present more for protection than for injuring an adversary: beneath the horns lies a network of air-filled spaces, which absorb the shocks of collision and protect the animal's brain.

● **Defending resources:** Both male and female horned animals of some species defend their territory by head-butting intruders with their horns. Females are especially prone to this behavior when they are pregnant or have offspring to defend and feed.

N. GOLDSTEIN

**See also:** BONE; COMPETITION; DEFENSE MECHANISMS; MATING.

## Further reading:

Geist, V., and M. H. Francis. 2001. *Antelope Country: Pronghorns—The Last Americans.* Iola, Wis.: Krause Publications.
Vrba, E. S., and G. B. Schaller, eds. 2000. *Antelopes, Deer and Relatives: Fossil Record, Behavioral Ecology, Systematics, and Conservation.* New Haven, Conn.: Yale University Press.

## WHAT ARE ANTLERS?

Although male moose and deer, such as elks and white-tailed deer, carry impressive headgear during the mating season, these are antlers, not horns. True horns are permanently attached to an animal's skull and are never shed. Antlers, on the other hand, are shed each year and then regrow. They grow from small projections on the front part of the skull called pedicels, which are usually concealed by the skin covering the head. Several months before the mating season, beds of new, soft, flexible bone begin to form on the pedicels. As they grow, the immature antlers are covered with a downy fuzz, called velvet, which is filled with blood vessels to nourish the rapidly growing bone antlers. Once the antlers are fully formed, the bone hardens and becomes rigid. Finally the velvet peels off or is rubbed off by the animal. Antlers reach their maximum size when a stag is about nine years old and may decline thereafter.

Because antlers grow in time for the mating season and are shed shortly afterward, biologists believe they function as weapons during competition for females. Carrying a full rack of antlers requires great strength and health—characteristics that attract females to large-antlered males.

*Giraffes are born with skin-covered cartilaginous "knobs" that ossify and grow slowly throughout the animal's life. These knobs are called ossicones and are not true horns.*

## HORNS AND THE ROAD TO EXTINCTION

Horns are not always an animal's best friends. In the case of the rhinoceros, the loss of its habitat, its slow reproductive rate, and the insatiable demand for its horn (which is not a true horn but one made entirely of keratin that grows from the skin) has brought the animal to the brink of extinction. Not too long ago, there were tens of thousands of rhinoceroses in Africa and Asia. That number has dwindled alarmingly: in one African national park, a herd of 3,000 rhinos in the early 1900s had decreased to 15 by the 1980s.

In some parts of Asia, rhinoceros horn is ground up and used as a medicine. In other parts of Asia, men believe that rhinoceros horn will endow them with extraordinary sexual powers, and in the Middle East, men covet knives with rhinoceros horn handles. Many countries are now initiating educational programs to teach people about rhinoceroses and why they are in great danger.

AT RISK

# HUMAN EVOLUTION

*The skull of a Neanderthal man displays the jutting brow ridges and sloping forehead of an ape.*

## CONNECTIONS

● Humans have evolved the most sophisticated **BRAIN** of all **MAMMALS** and **VERTEBRATES**.

● Darwin proposed that all species evolved by a process called **NATURAL SELECTION**.

## Human evolution describes the process of development and formation of modern humans

Are humans related to snakes? How about a duck-billed platypus or the family dog? Although this sounds improbable, it is now generally believed that humans are related in some distant way to every living organism on Earth. Basic similarities in cell structure, gene mechanism, and metabolism suggest that every living thing evolved from the same simple, single-celled organism.

Biologists trace the roots of this family tree back over 3.5 billion years, soon after Earth's crust cooled and primordial seas formed. At this time single-celled organisms were beginning to form in the water, and from these organisms developed algae and bacteria and then sponges, fungi, and other increasingly complex organisms. Organisms adapted to their environments and in doing so developed fins, feathers, fur, and many other modifications to help them survive. Far out on one branch of this complex family tree are mammals—the class of warm-blooded vertebrates to which humans belong.

In this evolutionary scheme, apes are humans' closest relatives. When people speak of the evolution of humans, they usually mean the point at which human evolution diverged from that of the apes. Scientists have believed since the mid-1800s that apes are humans' nearest ancestors, yet many people reject this theory (see EVOLUTION).

### The roots of evolutionary theory

The first scientist to classify humans and apes together was a Swedish biologist named Carl von Linné (better known as Linnaeus; 1707–1778) His idea was resisted by his peers. Then, in 1797, English anthropologist John Frere (1740–1802) found evidence of humans' ancient roots in some flint tools discovered in Suffolk, England. (Frere was the great-great-great-grandfather of the 20th-century paleontologist Mary Leakey.) Frere speculated that the tools were made by an ancient people who did not have the use of metal. His discovery was ignored.

Some time between 1784 and 1802, Erasmus Darwin, grandfather of Charles Darwin, first suggested that all life sprang from a single source. In 1809 the French naturalist Jean Baptiste de Lamarck (1744–1829) formulated the first comprehensive theory of evolution. He noted that animals' organs grew larger or shrank, depending on how much they were used in an animal's lifetime. He assumed that these changes were passed on to later generations. His theory, called orthogenesis, influenced many scientists, although it was later proved to be wrong.

The most significant development for evolutionary theory came in 1859, with the publication of Charles Darwin's book *On The Origin of Species by Means of Natural Selection*. In it Darwin proposed that all species had evolved from a common ancestor, gradually over millions of years: as species developed adaptations to their environment, hereditary changes that aided survival would tend to persist and be passed on to succeeding generations. Organisms that failed to adapt adequately or whose environment changed abruptly would die off. Darwin called this process natural selection. Over time, the makeup of the species would change and a new species would

---

### CORE FACTS

■ Many scientists believe that all animals originated from the same simple, single-celled organism.

■ It is widely accepted among scientists that apes and humans evolved from the same ancestor. The closest living relatives to humans are therefore gorillas, chimpanzees, and orangutans.

■ The distinguishing features in human evolution are the development of a comparatively large brain, toolmaking skills, language, and bipedalism (walking on two feet).

evolve. Darwin did not explain how his theory applied to humans until 1871, when his book *Descent of Man* was published.

During the early 20th century, scientists refined Darwin's theory of evolution by natural selection. They learned that the code governing an animal's individual characteristics is carried in its genes (see GENETICS). Occasionally a gene mutates (see MUTATION) and thus changes that characteristic. If the mutation helps the animal survive in its environment, that mutation is passed on to future generations.

In spite of the scientific evidence, many religious leaders were opposed to the theory of evolution. In the 1920s several states passed laws banning the teaching of evolution in public schools. The issue came to a head in 1925, when a Tennessee high school teacher named John T. Scopes was convicted of violating a state law by teaching human evolution. The U.S. Supreme Court ruled in 1968 that such laws were unconstitutional.

This ruling has not stopped conservative religious groups from pressuring schools to teach the biblical story of creation. In 1981 Arkansas became the first state to pass a law requiring that creationism be taught along with evolution (see EVOLU-TION). A federal court, however, ruled that the law violated the First Amendment's guarantee of the separation of church and state.

## Not-so-distant cousins of humans

Most modern scientists have little doubt that humans evolved from the same ancestor as apes, but they cannot come close to agreeing on when, where, or how. To understand how humans separated from apes, one must first consider how much they still have in common. Both humans and apes belong to the order Primates, which includes 280 species of lemurs, lorises, tarsiers, monkeys, and apes. Primates are characterized by their forward-facing eyes, hands with opposable thumbs, flat fingernails and toenails, and relatively large brain.

The closest relatives of humans are gorillas, chimpanzees, and orangutans, known collectively as apes. Most people think humans' skin is a far cry from an ape's fur; in fact humans have as much body hair as apes—it is just shorter and finer. Even at the molecular level, humans and apes have much in common. Myoglobin, a protein in muscle tissue, is made of 153 amino acids strung together. The myoglobin of humans, gorillas, and chimpanzees differs by only one

## THE AQUATIC APE

In 1960 British zoologist Alister Hardy (right) raised the world's eyebrows when he claimed the long-sought missing link between apes and modern humans lay buried beneath the sea. According to Hardy, humans evolved from an ape that lived and swam among the fish. He had no fossils to support his theory, only some anecdotes that made great headlines for the tabloid press.

Hardy speculated that human's earliest ancestors did live on land but that competition for food pushed some of these apes to the shore. They began their aquatic shift by searching for shellfish and other food in shallow water. Gradually they learned to swim and even to dive down and catch fish with their hands.

To support his theory, Hardy compared several human traits with those of marine mammals. He pointed out that few other terrestrial mammals can swim and dive as well as humans. Lack of human body hair is another marine adaptation according to Hardy. He believed the aquatic ape shed its fur for streamlining when swimming. This ape-human retained luxuriant hair on its head because that was the only part of its body poking out of the water while swimming. Hardy said this hair offered protection from the sun.

Even a human's rotund physique is an inheritance from the aquatic ape according to Hardy. He explained that terrestrial apes are muscular and have little body fat. Humans, on the other hand, have a layer of fat much like the blubber that insulates whales and other marine mammals from the ocean's cold. Finally, Hardy speculated that human bipedalism evolved when these aquatic apes stood up on rocks to hold their heads out of the water and rest.

The controversial zoologist admitted he could not explain what became of the aquatic ape. Perhaps it was crushed and eaten by larger marine mammals, he said. Therefore, although following the principles of Darwinism, evolution of species by natural selection and adaptation, Hardy's theory has no evidence to support it.

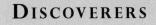

**DISCOVERERS**

## WALK LIKE A HUMAN

When paleontologists discovered a 4.4-million-year-old skull in Ethiopia in 1994, which they named *Ardipithecus ramidus*, they knew immediately that this ancient human ancestor had walked on two legs. The clue lies in the position of the foramen magnum, the opening through which the spinal cord enters the skull. In apes the opening faces toward the rear of the skull. In humans it is at the base of the skull. The shift in the location of the foramen magnum is among several adaptations that have enabled humans to walk upright while their simian (ape) cousins remain essentially on all fours.

Another adaptation for upright walking is the human spine and pelvis. In quadrupeds (animals that walk on four legs) the spine is straight and horizontal and supports organs suspended below. This positioning places the center of gravity well in front of the hind limbs. To move forward, the quadrupedal animal tightens the hind limbs and then stretches them out, and the body is propelled forward powerfully. If humans did the same thing, they would end up standing on tiptoes because the human center of gravity lies almost directly over the feet because of the vertical backbone, which supports weight above and in front. Thus, to move forward, humans momentarily shift their center of gravity ahead of one leg while pushing off with the back leg. They then bring the other leg forward to avoid falling.

The remains of the 3.2-million-year-old hominid named Lucy, discovered in 1974, show that she was better adapted for bipedal locomotion than her ancestors. Her ilia (broad blades on each side of the pelvis) flared out more than modern woman's and thus her hips had greater stability. Another unusual feature of Lucy's pelvis is its oval shape, which gave her a birth canal that was broad but short from front to back. The shape of the hips worked for Lucy because any offspring would have had heads no larger than those of a baby chimpanzee. As human ancestors' brains grew larger, the female pelvic cavity had to become rounder. It expanded from front to back but narrowed from side to side. Accommodating both bipedal walking and a birth canal large enough for a human infant's brain remains a problem for modern-day woman. Human births are among the most difficult in the animal kingdom.

Another adaptation in humans is a knee that can withstand greater stress during extension than the knees of other primates. Also, humans' ankles are modified to support the entire body weight; the foot's arch works as a shock absorber; and the toes are shorter than those of the apes because their function is propulsion and not grabbing or clinging to branches. Moving out of the trees also meant that humans' ancestors did not need such long fingers and arms.

### A CLOSER LOOK

amino acid. The molecules of blood and other body tissues are also very similar among apes and humans. The difference between a human's genetic code and that of a chimpanzee is 0.7 percent.

What separates humans from apes more than any physical characteristic is human intellectual superiority. No other species has adapted to life in virtually every habitat and changed their environment as humans have. No species has matched a human's ability to make tools (although there are many examples of animals using tools), solve complex problems, or make fire. Apes have relatively sophisticated communication skills but nothing remotely approaching the complexity of human language.

Another significant difference is bipedalism, that is, the ability to walk on two feet. Apes can mimic the human walk for short periods of time but are better suited for walking on four limbs (knuckle walking).

### Branching off from the family tree

For two centuries, scientists have sorted through countless fragments of bone, teeth, and stone in search of the human family tree's roots. With each new find, the roots seemed to shift, often reaching back farther than anthropologists had imagined.

Scientists generally agree that the most recent common ancestor of humans and apes was a primate about the size of a modern chimpanzee. This primate, called both *Proconsul* (Africa) and *Dryopithecus* (Europe), has been identified in fossils that date back 22 million years to the early Miocene epoch. Proconsul's skeleton suggests it was a generalized ape, lacking specific adaptations for swinging from branches, leaping among trees, or walking on the ground. It probably moved slowly through the trees and walked on all four limbs.

The era of *Proconsul* and similar Miocene apes descended from it is followed by a gap of some seven million years. To date, no well-documented remains

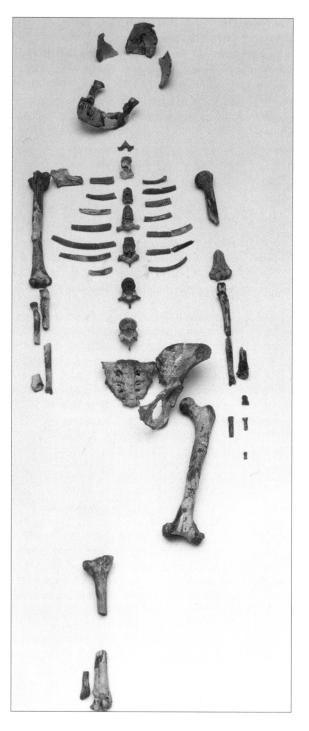

*The photograph to the right shows the fossil hominid skeleton,* Australopithecus afarensis, *known as Lucy, discovered by U.S. paleoanthropologist Donald Johanson (b. 1943) in 1974.*

of apes or hominids (humanlike animals) have been found from this period, which is called the late Miocene gap. Paleontologists continue to search for remains from this period, looking for the missing link.

In 1974 the fossil record began to be filled in, with the discovery of the famous 3.2-million-year-old Lucy skeleton. This small female hominid was human's oldest known direct ancestor.

In 1994 a team of paleontologists Tim White, Gen Suwa, and Berhane Asfaw narrowed the gap when they unearthed fossils of a previously unknown 4.4 million-year-old species (see the box on page 914). This species looked more like a chimpanzee than Lucy did, yet the shape of its head and backbone, canine teeth, and elbows indicated clearly that it had already split from the apes. This discovery was named *Ardipithecus ramidus*, *ramidus* suggesting humanity's root species. No one is certain, however, that it was indeed the first hominid. Genetic studies indicate that the first hominids probably evolved no more than six million years ago, leaving open the possibility of an earlier species than *A. ramidus*.

White, Suwa, and Asfaw unearthed the ramidus remains about 140 miles (225 km) northeast of Addis Ababa, in Ethiopia, a region rich in ancient fossils. Some 45 miles (72 km) to the north, in Hadar, the partial skeleton named Lucy had been discovered in 1974. Lucy surprised the scientific community with the small size of her brain, coupled with a pair of legs suggesting bipedal, upright locomotion. Anthropologists had previously thought that upright walking came only after the brain's expansion. Although Lucy was in her late teens or early 20s when she died, she stood only about 45 inches (114 cm) tall—the height of an average 6 year old—and weighed about 60 pounds (27 kg). Her species was named *Australopithecus afarensis*, *afarensis* meaning "southern ape from afar."

Scientists have found Lucy's australopithecine relatives throughout southeast Africa. The first fossils were discovered in South Africa by anatomy professor Raymond Dart in 1925. Dart named the species *Australopithecus africanus*. The skull had a relatively flat face and humanlike teeth. The foramen magnum, the hole where the spinal cord enters the skull, indicated that *A. africanus* was able to walk upright, although its brain was still much smaller than a modern human's. *A. africanus* lived between two and three million years ago and reached a height of about 50 inches (127 cm) and a weight of about 75 pounds (34 kg), the size of an average 10 year old.

Some paleontologists now argue that *A. africanus* and *A. afarensis* belong to the same species. The larger fossils, they believe, belonged to males. Such consistent differences between males and females of the same species are called sexual dimorphisms (see DIMORPHISM AND POLYMORPHISM). There does, however, seem to be greater dimorphism in *A. afarensis* compared with *A. africanus*.

The outer branches on the *Australopithecus* limb of the evolutionary tree are occupied by two bigger and heavier species, called *Australopithecus robustus* and

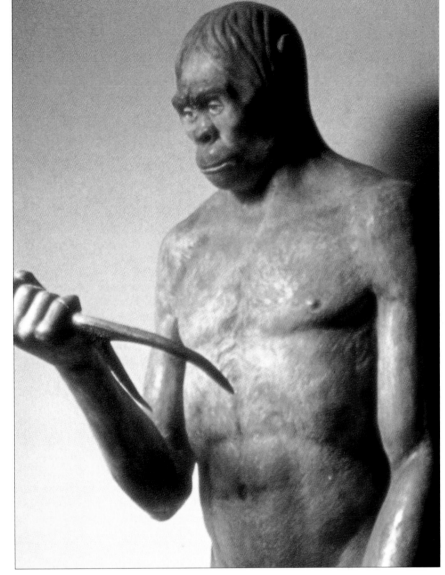

*A. boisei*. These species weighed between 88 and 176 pounds (40 and 80 kg), although they were approximately the same height as the earlier slender australopithecines. The first remains of this hefty species were discovered by English paleontologist Mary Leakey in 1959, in Tanzania's Olduvai Gorge.

Scientists still speculate about the relationship between the different types of *Australopithecus* and early humans. Three views now predominate. The first puts *A. afarensis* as the common ancestor of the two lineages, the first that divided through *A. afarensis* to *A. robustus* and *A. boisei* and the second to *Homo erectus*. The second view puts *A. afarensis* as an ancestor to *A. africanus* but *A. africanus* as the common ancestor of the *Homo erectus* and *A. robustus/boisei* lineages. The third scheme supports the theory that *Australopithecus* and *Homo erectus* share a common older ancestor that is as yet undiscovered in the fossil record.

## The first humans

In 1964 the English paleontologist Louis Leakey (1903–1972) and his colleagues proclaimed the discovery of the oldest remains that could be considered human. The fossils they found in Olduvai Gorge,

*A reconstruction of Java man, renamed* Homo erectus, *who lived in Africa, Asia, and Europe from 1.6 million to less than 300,000 years ago.*

## *RAMAPITHECUS'S* BRANCH ON THE FAMILY TREE

For a decade, beginning in the 1960s, a small, 12-million-year-old apelike creature named *Ramapithecus* occupied an important branch on the human family tree. Then came the 1970s, and *Ramapithecus*'s fall to an obscure branch, illustrating how quickly theories about human evolution can change.

The first *Ramapithecus* fossils were discovered in 1932, in India's Kashmir province. They were dated at 12 million years old. *Ramapithecus* displayed several humanlike features, including a somewhat flat face, small canine teeth, and a rounded lower jaw. (Ape jaws are more angular.) Fossils dating back at least 14 million years were found later at Fort Ternan in Kenya. These finds bolstered the convictions of those who viewed *Ramapithecus* as a direct human ancestor. In his 1977 book, *Origins*, paleontologist Richard Leakey devoted several pages to theories on how and why *Ramapithecus* stood up on two feet, used tools, and fostered the evolution of *Homo sapiens*.

By the late 1970s, *Ramapithecus*'s status had become dubious. Studies of protein structure in chimpanzees and humans suggested a more recent ancestor for human and ape, dating the split to no more than 7 to 10 million years ago. Moreover, fossils of *Ramapithecus* found in Turkey, Pakistan, and China showed an angular jaw and other features that made it less human than previously thought. The morphology of the *Ramapithecus* skull is quite different from that of other African apes, although these characteristic structures are also seen in modern orangutans. Scientists now believe *Ramapithecus* is an ancestor of the modern orangutan and not closely linked to the evolution of humans.

*The diagram below shows the skeletal structure of a monkey, an ape, and a human, from left to right, respectively. The ability to walk on two legs is determined by the angle of rotation and the shape of the pelvis (as shown in red).*

Tanzania, dated back 1.7 million years. They were found alongside the remains of stone tools and dubbed *Homo habilis*, meaning "handy man."

From the start, scientists could not agree on whether the species was an apelike human or a humanlike ape. *H. habilis* clearly showed human traits not found in *Australopithecus*. For one, it had a type of opposable thumb that could be rotated to form a human's unique precision grip. Most important, *H. habilis* had a large brain, which had been lacking in all *Australopithecus* fossils.

Since Leakey's discovery, remains of some 20 *H. habilis* individuals have been found at Olduvai

Gorge. They show a species that stood about 50 inches (127 cm) tall and weighed about 90 pounds (41 kg). It had a flatter face than *Australopithecus* yet rounder than a modern human's. There is still some controversy as to whether there were two different species of early *Homo* around at the same time or whether *Homo habilis* merely displayed a huge variation in size and morphology (body structure).

In 1891, decades before the rush to discover human traces in Africa began, a Dutch physician named Eugene Dubois had discovered fossils of a primitive man on the Indonesian island of Java. Originally dubbed Java Man the species in the 1950s was renamed *Homo erectus*, and is now considered humanity's immediate ancestor.

*H. erectus* lived in Africa, Asia, and Europe from 1.6 million to less than 300,000 years ago. The richest site for discoveries is in Zoukoudien, China, where the remains of more than 40 individuals have been found. The area has many caves, where anthropologists believe *H. erectus* lived between 460,000 and 230,000 years ago.

*H. erectus* stood about 5 feet (1.5 m) tall, walked like modern humans, and looked much like them, except for the shape of the head. With a low, sloping forehead and prominent brow ridges, *H. erectus* still resembled the ancestral apes. Compared with *H. habilis*, the face, teeth, and jaw were proportionately smaller, and the brain larger.

In 1921 workers in northern Zambia (formerly Rhodesia) uncovered a skull that had the large upper jaw and jutting brows of *Homo erectus* and the prominent chin, large brain, and domed cranium of modern humans. Paleontologists dated the skull between 130,000 and 150,000 years old. Since then several similar fossils have been found in Europe, Africa, and China, and the species has been recognized as an ancient form of the human species, *Homo sapiens*. Modern human's subspecies is named *Homo sapiens sapiens*. No one knows just when *H. sapiens* replaced *H. erectus*. Anthropologists point to a gradual shift between 400,000 and 100,000 years ago.

One of the most interesting fossil finds was in the Neanderthal, near Düsseldorf, Germany, in 1856, three years before the publication of Darwin's *Origin of Species*. Skulls uncovered at a lime quarry there displayed the jutting brow ridges and sloping forehead of *Homo erectus*. The last thing people then wanted to admit was that these fossils could be human. Those who did acknowledge a link said that the bones had belonged to a brutish cretin.

The bones were those of a species now called Neanderthal man. Neanderthals were shorter and stockier than *Homo sapiens* and had a brain that was as large if not larger than their modern cousins. Remains are dated from 70,000 to 35,000 years ago and have been found scattered throughout Europe and the Middle East. The robust torso of the Neanderthals suggests that they were adapted for life in a cold climate. Anthropologists for a long time regarded Neanderthal man as a subspecies of *Homo sapiens*, but DNA evidence has

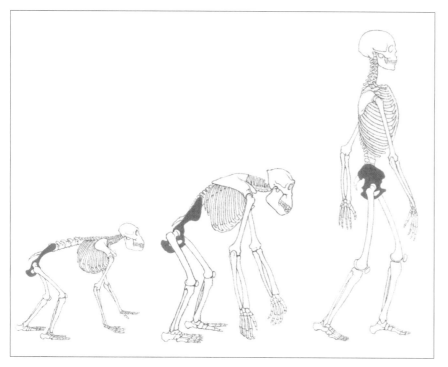

confirmed that Neanderthal man is different enough from humans to warrant its own species. It is now called *Homo neanderthalensis*.

Scientists are not sure what led to the Neanderthals' disappearance some 30,000 years ago. Some speculate that they evolved into Cro-Magnon man. Cro-Magnons are *Homo sapiens sapiens*, who look much like modern Europeans, with slightly broader faces. Fossils disprove that theory, however, because there was an overlap between the Neanderthal and Cro-Magnon eras. Another theory is that Cro-Magnons who settled in Europe from other places brought with them diseases that killed the Neanderthals. Some scientists believe the hardier Cro-Magnons won out over Neanderthals in the competition for food and shelter, while others suspect the Cro-Magnons killed off their competitors.

## Where humanity was born

Since the first hominid fossils were discovered, humans have puzzled over the site of their family tree's roots. In the late 1980s, genetic research appeared to provide the answer. Genetic studies centered on the DNA present in mitochondria, cellular organelles that provide energy in the form of ATP (see CELL BIOLOGY; ENERGY). Mutations occur in DNA at a predictable rate; therefore, these mutations can be used as a type of molecular clock. By seeing how much variation there is in the genetic material of the mitochondria from different people living in a particular region, geneticists can estimate the length of time that those people have inhabited the area.

Mitochondrial DNA studies showed the greatest diversity among people in Africa. This finding suggests humans have lived there the longest, and thus, their DNA had more time to change. According to this theory, all *Homo sapiens sapiens* emerged from a small population of humans who lived in sub-Saharan Africa 150,000 to 200,000 years ago.

However, fossils suggest a much earlier migration. The focal point of the opposing theory is Java, where Eugene Dubois found his first human remains in 1891. Scientists had estimated the age of the Java man fossil at one million years and classified it with fossils found in China as *Homo erectus*. Most were convinced that, until then, Africa had been the only part of the world inhabited by humans.

High-tech dating techniques in the mid-1990s, however, indicated that remains of Java man were 1.6 million years old. The oldest *H. erectus* fossils in Africa are dated between 1.8 and 1.7 million years. If the Out of Africa theory is true, then *H. erectus* must have migrated from Africa shortly after evolving from *Homo habilis*—a possibility because Indonesia then was connected to Africa by lower sea levels.

Multiregionalists, on the other hand, have long believed that humans evolved simultaneously from *H. erectus* in several parts of the world. Their strongest evidence comes from Australia's aborigines, who first migrated to Australia from Indonesia some 50,000 years ago. These aborigines have several traits reminiscent of the *H. erectus* remains found in Java, traits that precede those of the African *Homo sapiens*, believed to be the root of modern civilization. Many scientists are skeptical of this theory, however, and contend that such a long period of isolation for the aborigines is unlikely. Their view is supported by recent DNA analysis.

## The advent of culture

As human ancestors developed a larger brain, they began using it in ways unimaginable for any other species. They made tools for hunting and cultivating crops. They sculpted and painted their visions on the walls of their caves. They also developed language and music. Anthropologists generally date the dawn of the age of culture back some 40,000 years, when the crude stone tools of the Neanderthals gave way to smooth, polished axes, spearheads, and arrowheads. The earliest known sculptures date back around 30,000 years. They were carved from stone, bone, antlers, and horns and often depicted animals. Language appears to be a more recent accomplishment. Some linguists trace an Indo-European protolanguage back 6,000 to 7,000 years.

C. WASHAM

**See also:** CELL BIOLOGY; DIMORPHISM AND POLYMORPHISM; ENERGY; EVOLUTION; FOSSILS; GENETICS; MUTATION; PRIMATES.

## Further reading:
Bromage, T. G. and F. Schrenk, eds. 1997. *African Biogeography, Climate Change, and Early Hominid Evolution*. New York: Oxford University Press.
Leakey, R. E. 1996. *The Origins of Humankind*. Science Masters Series. New York: Basic Books.
Lewin, R. 1999. *Human Evolution*. Malden, Mass.: Blackwell Science.
Tattersall, I. 1995. *The Last Neanderthal*. New York: Macmillan.

## PILTDOWN MAN

In 1912 an amateur archaeologist named Charles Dawson, digging in a gravel bed on Piltdown Common in Sussex, England, appeared to have stumbled on the missing link between humans and apes. The nine pieces of cranium, the jawbone, and the molars he found fitted together to form a skull that was certainly human, though more primitive than *Homo sapiens*. It had the protruding jaw and receding chin of an ape, yet its other features were more like those of humans, something scientists would expect of the missing link. The fossil was dated at about 200,000 years old and dubbed *Eoanthropus dawsoni*, "dawn man of Dawson."

Over the next 30 years, paleontologists found many hominid fossils in Africa, but none resembling Piltdown man. In 1948 scientists used the then-new fluorine dating technique on the skull. Because bones absorb fluorine from the ground water surrounding them, scientists can estimate the bones' age by measuring the amount of fluorine they contain. The test shocked scientists when it revealed that the skull was no missing link; it was a hoax.

The jaw belonged to a medieval orangutan. The pieces of skull were only slightly older, and the very young canine tooth had been filed down to look old. Investigators searched for the perpetrator of the hoax but never found definite proof, and it remains an unsolved mystery in the history of science.

# HUMAN GENOME PROJECT

**The Human Genome Project is an effort to map and sequence the genetic information on human chromosomes**

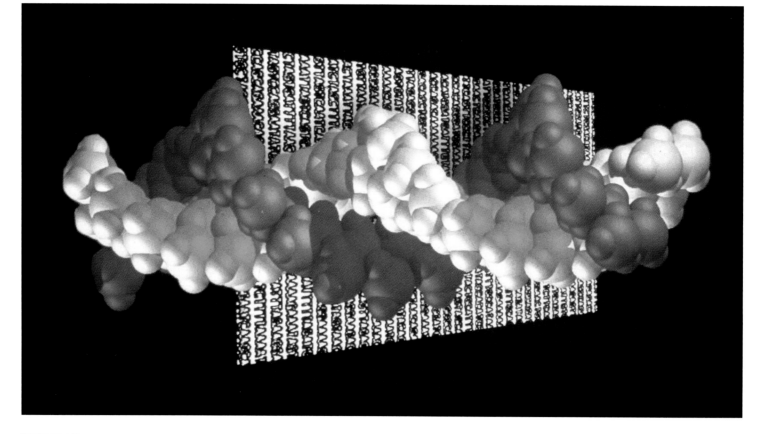

*An artist's impression of a DNA molecule, showing its characteristic helical arrangement.*

## CONNECTIONS

● Application of the findings from the Human Genome Project is likely to rapidly accelerate advances in **GENE THERAPY** and thus increase the potential for treating a wide range of **GENETIC DISEASES**.

● Advances in the knowledge of **GENETICS**, made possible by the Human Genome Project, have raised concerns in the area of medical **BIOETHICS**. Some people fear such knowledge could lead to the **SELECTIVE BREEDING** of humans for "desirable" traits.

In February 1953, British scientist Francis Crick (b. 1916) walked into the Eagle public house in Cambridge, England, and announced that he and U.S. researcher James Watson (b. 1928) had found the secret of life—the structure of DNA (deoxyribonucleic acid; see DNA). DNA is the chemical that carries the natural code for the construction and maintenance of living organisms. The chemical is packaged within chromosomes in the nucleus of cells. Along the length of a chromosome are numerous genes—units of inheritance that determine particular functions within a cell and that determine the features of the organism as a whole.

The human genome is the full set of genetic information carried within the genes and chromosomes of a human cell (see CELL BIOLOGY; CHROMOSOMES). Each cell in the body—except the reproductive cells (eggs and sperm) and some of the cells that give rise to them—carry two sets of 23 chromosomes; one set inherited from the female parent and the other from the male. Human body (somatic) cells therefore have 46 chromosomes. The 46 chromosomes form 23 pairs of homologous chromosomes (so called because the members of a homologous pair are structurally similar). One pair of the 23 are sex chromosomes, which determine the sex of the individual. This sex chromosomal pair are homologous in females and are designated XX because of their shape. In males, the pair are nonhomologous (XY). The X chromosome is the same as the one present in females, but the Y chromosome is smaller. For this reason, in mapping the human genome and establishing its DNA sequence, scientists need to study 24 chromosomes, not 23.

Each gene consists of a long string of nucleotides, the building blocks of DNA (see GENETICS). Each nucleotide is made up of a deoxyribose sugar, a phosphate group, and a nitrogen-containing base. There are four types of nucleotides, and the difference between them lies in the nature of the base. The four possible bases in DNA are: adenine (designated A), thymine (T), guanine (G), and cytosine

## CORE FACTS

■ The Human Genome Project (HGP) aims to construct a complete "blueprint" of human genetic information.

■ A draft sequence of the human genome was completed in June 2000, and the detailed sequence was finished in April 2003.

■ More than 100 laboratories in at least 19 countries are involved in various aspects of the Human Genome Project.

■ The project's applications include finding the genes that cause up to 4,000 inherited diseases and tailoring medication to the genetic background of the individual.

(C). When the nucleotides are joined together, the sequence of bases forms a code, which is read off (translated) within the cell. The code is read off in groups of three nonoverlapping bases, called triplets, so that the sequence CCTCTA, for example, would be read as CCT, CTA.

Each triplet codes for an amino acid, a building block of a protein, or acts as signal to start or stop translation of the code (see AMINO ACIDS; PROTEINS).

Another molecule, called messenger RNA (mRNA), acts an intermediate stage between the DNA itself and production of a protein (or part of a protein) coded for by a gene. Messenger RNA carries the coded message from a DNA strand to a ribosome in the cytoplasm of the cell where the appropriate protein (or protein component) is assembled. The protein functions as an enzyme (biological catalyst) or as a structural part of cells, giving functional expression to the gene. The protein therefore determines the characteristic that is coded for by the gene.

DNA is double stranded (has two complementary strands), the bases on one strand pairing with bases on the other. When researchers talk of the length of DNA, they are usually talking about double-stranded DNA—in other words, a sequence of base pairs. The human genome is about three billion base pairs long. Once the base pair sequence is known, it would take a person more than nine years to read out the entire base sequence at the rate of 10 bases per second, without rest.

Ever since Watson and Crick's discovery of the structure of DNA, it was clear than an ultimate goal for human genetics would be to map all the chromosomes and genes in the human genome and to determine the sequence of bases (nucleotides) in the DNA. By the late 1970s, techniques were available to do both, although the technology of the time was extremely laborious.

By the late 1980s, several foremost molecular biologists were campaigning for the establishment of a project to map and sequence the entire human genome. The payoffs in doing so would be enormous. It would enable researchers to pinpoint genes associated with specific diseases and find new ways to treat these diseases. It would also enable researchers to begin to truly appreciate how genes interact to control the development and function of cells in the human body.

Walter Gilbert, a Harvard University professor and cofounder of the biotechnology company Biogen, called finding the human genome sequence "the grail of human genetics." Francis Collins, Director of the National Human Genome Research Institute, saw this achievement for molecular biology and medicine as comparable to the foremost achievements in other sciences and technologies, such as putting a man on the Moon or splitting the atom.

The Human Genome Project (HGP), formally launched in October 1990 and nationally coordinated by the Department of Energy and the National Institutes of Health, was planned to run for 15 years. So successful has been the international cooperation on the project and the implementation of technological advances that, despite the emerging complexities in unravelling the human genome, the detailed sequence was completed in spring 2003.

The aims of the HGP are to map the positions of all the genes on human chromosomes and to determine the sequence of bases for the entire human genome. In addition, the human genome is being compared with the genomes of model organisms, including a mouse (*Mus* spp.), a roundworm (*Caenorhabditis elegans*), yeast (*Saccharomyces cerevisiae*), and a fruit fly (*Drosophila melanogaster*).

The HGP is international, with at least 18 governments operating their own national programs. They contribute to the international initiative that is coordinated by the Human Genome Organization (HUGO) and other scientific bodies.

## Mapping the genome

There are various ways of mapping the human genome. Maps fall into two categories: a physical map measures the distance between two genes in terms of bases (or nucleotides), and a genetic linkage map measures the distance between two genes according to the likelihood that both genes will be inherited by an individual offspring (see the diagram on page 921). During the formation of egg and sperm cells, genes on a chromosome may become separated in a process called crossing over (see CELL BIOLOGY). Genes that tend to stay linked during crossing over are put close together on genetic

*How proteins are derived from the genome. DNA in the human genome consists of 24 separate pairs of chromosomes. Each chromosome contains many genes, which are the basic physical and functional units of heredity. Genes are precise sequences of bases (A, T, C, G) that encode instructions on how to make proteins.*

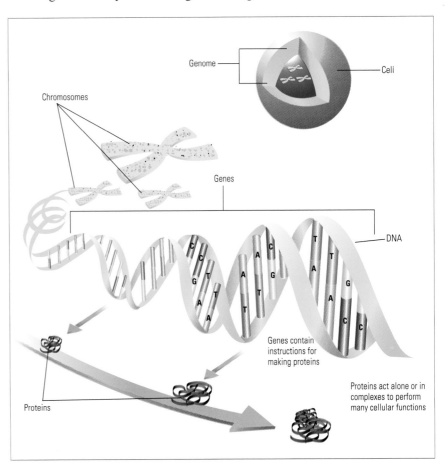

Genome

Cell

Chromosomes

Genes

DNA

Genes contain instructions for making proteins

Proteins

Proteins act alone or in complexes to perform many cellular functions

**Frederick Sanger, seen here examining a DNA molecule, developed a sensitive and rapid method of mapping the exact sequence of DNA using gel electrophoresis.**

## HOW MANY GENES?

When scientists first embarked on the Human Genome Project, they estimated that there were probably 100,000 genes in the human genome. By 2001 the estimate had dropped to less than 40,000, only about three times the number of genes in a fruit fly or twice that of a roundworm.

Deciding what is a functional human gene can be quite a problem. For example, a human gene is rarely a single discrete section of DNA. It is usually dispersed as several lengths of DNA called exons separated by long noncoding regions called introns. The products of exons are spliced together during transcription (when messenger RNA is assembled alongside the DNA template). A single mRNA strand is compiled from several exons.

To identify functional genes, researchers draw on several lines of evidence. One approach compares known human messenger RNA (mRNA) with complementary DNA (cDNA) held in databases of human DNA sequences. Another approach compares the DNA sequences for mouse genes with those in the human genome (most mouse genes correspond to human genes). When clues such as these are not available, researchers resort to gene-predicting computer programs. These programs are mathematical algorithms (rules that specify a sequence of actions) that compare DNA sequences with the properties of genes previously identified.

Assuming the estimate of 40,000 human genes is more-or-less correct, then some genes are undoubtedly responsible for determining more than one human trait. The products of exons can be spliced together in more than one way, the result being several gene products from a single gene. Furthermore, a single human protein can have more than one function—performing, for example, one role in the human immune (defense) system, another role in the nervous system, and yet a third in blood clotting. This type of complexity means that simple comparisons between the human genome and that of a fly or worm are not valid. Humans are much more complex than the number of human genes suggest.

**A CLOSER LOOK**

linkage maps. Genes that frequently tend to separate are put farther apart. Physical maps range from those at the lowest resolution—regions of the chromosome that are visible with a light microscope and vary in their tendency to attract stain—and, at the other extreme, the DNA sequence itself, which is beyond direct visualization but can be determined by chemical means. The DNA sequence is represented on paper as a sequence of nucleotides, denoted by the four bases: A, T, G, and C.

The first physical maps of chromosomal DNA were produced in the 1960s and were based on staining guanine-rich regions of the chromosome. The first maps for entire human chromosomes were published in 1971. They depicted banding patterns on chromosomes, based on guanine density. More detailed landmarks on the chromosome are called markers and are identified using chemical probes, short lengths of DNA that bind to the complementary base sequences on marker sites.

The earliest markers were restriction fragment length polymorphisms (RFLPs; pronounced *riflips*). They denote places where a particular type of restriction enzyme (so-called biochemical scissors) can cut. Markers of the second generation were called microsatellite repeat sequences (MRSs; repeating sequences of two, three, or four bases). Researchers look for RFLPs and MRSs when seeking to identify the location of a particular gene in which they have an interest.

Bearing in mind that a single chromosome may contain 100 million nucleotides and more than 1,000 genes, searching for a particular gene is like searching for a needle in a haystack. When tracking down a particular defective gene, researchers may seek out large, extended families in which an inherited disease is known. Comparing blood samples from affected and unaffected family members, they look for RFLPs that are closely linked with the culprit gene (RFLPs that are common to those with the disease but are absent in those without). The close association of the RFLP and the disease suggests the two are linked genetically (the RFLP and the disease-causing gene are physically close together on the same chromosome or are at the same location). This approach has led to the discovery of many genes, including those for cystic fibrosis, which causes breathing difficulties, and Huntington's disease, which results in mental deterioration (see BRAIN; GENETIC DISEASES).

Another gene-hunting strategy involves the study of people who are missing part of a chromosome. Such deletions typically cause recognizable mental retardation and physical problems. By studying the DNA of people possessing chromosomal deletions, researchers can begin to figure out the genes responsible for certain characteristics and their location. For example, the study of the DNA of one boy who was missing part of his X chromosome led to the discovery of the gene for the muscular disorder Duchenne muscular dystrophy (see MUSCULAR SYSTEMS).

## DNA sequencing

DNA sequencing is the greatest technical challenge for the HGP. The most popular sequencing method was first developed by British biochemist Frederick Sanger (b. 1918) in 1977 (for which he won his second Nobel Prize). Like other DNA sequencing methods, it employs the technique of gel electrophoresis (see ANALYTICAL TECHNIQUES). Charged molecules (in this case, lengths of DNA) can be separated by size using an electric current. The chemical mixture being tested is applied to a suitable support and transport medium, usually a gel block or gel-filled capillary tube of agarose or acrylamide. When an electric voltage is applied across the block or tube, smaller DNA fragments travel farther than larger ones. This method distinguishes fragments differing in length by as little as one nucleotide.

Sanger's method employs nucleotides that are nearly identical to those in DNA, but these nucleotides are dideoxynucleotides. They differ from deoxynucleotides in that the deoxyribose sugar lacks one of its oxygen atoms. When a dideoxynucleotide attaches to a growing DNA strand, it halts the growth of the strand. It is a chain terminator. Sanger's approach is called the dideoxy, or chain termination, method.

To sequence DNA using modifications of Sanger's approach adopted by the HGP, human chromosomes are first broken into fragments of about 150,000 bases. The fragments are cloned to produce multiple copies by inserting them into bacterial artificial chromosomes (BAC). The researchers use DNA probes to identify major markers on each BAC insert. Investigators already know the position of these mark-

ers on the human chromosome. Their presence on BAC inserts allows researchers to map the position of BAC inserts in the human chromosome.

Before DNA sequencing, each of the BAC inserts is "shotgunned," that is, broken into pieces 500 to 1,500 base pairs long. Each is then sequenced. The shotgunning produces fragments of different lengths that overlap. Computers analyze the sequences of fragments and, by joining them where they overlap, determine the whole sequence of the original BAC insert.

To sequence a DNA fragment, it is used as a template to generate a set of identical complementary sequences but which differ in length by a single base. The complementary-sequence fragments are separated by gel electrophoresis, and the different end-termination bases (A, T, G, or C) are identified by a different fluorescent dye. A laser scans the colored

## WHOSE DNA?

The human genome project (HGP) aims to produce a reference sequence that is a composite of more than one person's genome. It is based on DNA samples taken from the blood (in the case of females) or sperm (for males) from a limited number of donors selected at random from a much larger sample. Neither donors nor researchers know precisely whose DNA is being sequenced.

Private human genome projects are complementing the HGP. The human genome sequence being generated by the U.S. company Celera Genomics is based on DNA samples taken from five donors—between them representing African-American, Asian, Caucasian, and Hispanic ancestry.

### A CLOSER LOOK

*Chromosome maps and gene sequences. The diagram below shows the relationship between linkage maps and physical maps and the different levels of resolution. The first human chromosomal maps produced in the 1960s, used a stain that bound to tha DNA base guanine (G). The resolution of the maps has increased as scientists have found more and more markers.*

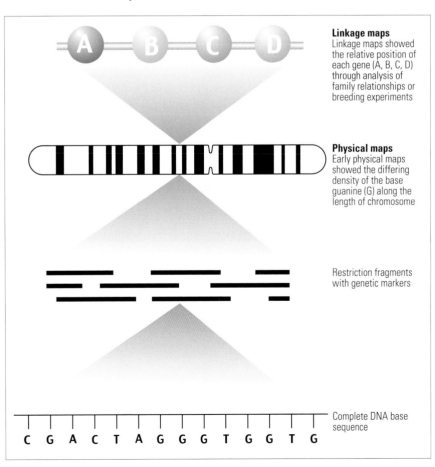

**Linkage maps**
Linkage maps showed the relative position of each gene (A, B, C, D) through analysis of family relationships or breeding experiments

**Physical maps**
Early physical maps showed the differing density of the base guanine (G) along the length of chromosome

Restriction fragments with genetic markers

Complete DNA base sequence

C G A C T A G G G T G G T G

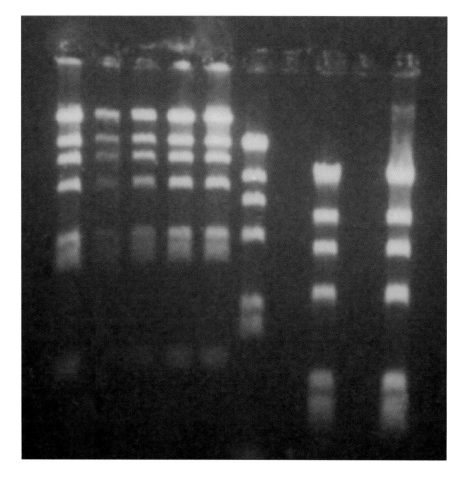

*This electrophoresis gel shows DNA fragments separated from at least eight samples by an electric current. DNA samples are applied at specific locations at the top of the gel. When an electric current is used on the samples, the smallest DNA fragments travel the farthest distance (toward the bottom).*

bands produced on the gel. The order of colors gives the base sequence of the original DNA fragment.

A modern automated DNA sequencer can read a sequence of 500 bases (nucleotides) or more with each run. Computers then assemble these sequences into long continuous stretches by combining overlapping data with that from other runs. After being quality checked, the finished sequence for that part of a chromosome is submitted to major public databases. The data is made freely available on the Internet to whoever wishes to have access.

A modern sequencing machine can read 150,000 bases a day. Done manually, a person would take one year to identify 50,000 bases. When the HGP was first launched, the sequencing cost per base was about $10 U.S. dollars. By 2001 it had dropped to 10 to 20 cents.

### Draft and finished sequences

In producing a draft DNA sequence, researchers determine the order of bases in each chromosomal region at least four or five times. Most draft sequence data is in the form of 10,000-base fragments for which the approximate location on a chromosome is known. The completion of a working draft for the human genome was announced in June 2000 and published in February 2001.

To generate a high-quality, or finished, sequence, a chromosomal region is sequenced 8 to 10 times and any ambiguities resolved. The agreed-on standard for a final HGP sequence is an error rate of one base or less in every 10,000. It is this high-resolution sequence that researchers anticipate will be completed by spring 2003 for all 24 human

chromosomes. Even so, this sequence will not represent all the DNA in the chromosomes. It will cover exons (polynucleotide sequences in the nucleic acid that code information for protein synthesis) and introns (sequences that do not code such information) but not the chromosome tips (telomeres), centers (centromeres), or regions packed with certain types of sequence repeats. However, researchers anticipate that the sequenced regions will cover all the gene-rich areas that are translated into mRNA during gene expression.

### Single nucleotide polymorphisms

Although more than 99 percent of DNA is the same in all people, somewhere between 0.1 percent and 0.3 percent varies from person to person. Many of these differences affect a single nucleotide. The existence of more than one nucleotide at a particular site on the DNA strand is called a single nucleotide polymorphism (SNP, pronounced *snip*). SNPs occur every 100 to 300 bases in the human genome, and there are estimated to be about 3 million SNPs in all. They occur in both introns and extrons.

There is some in-built redundancy in the genetic code, so an alternative nucleotide may still code for the same amino acid. Alternatively, the nucleotide change may code for a different amino acid, but this change may have no effect on the function of the gene's protein product. Medical specialists are particularly interested in SNPs that do change protein function. Such changes could make a difference to a person's susceptibility to a particular disease or his or her ability to respond to drug treatment.

In many cases, a single SNP may make a marginal contribution to a person's susceptibility to a particular disease, but several SNPs at different gene loci may interact and markedly affect the likelihood of developing cancer, diabetes, circulatory disorders, or even some forms of mental disorders (see CANCER; DIABETES; CIRCULATORY SYSTEMS). By mapping SNPs, researchers expect to find patterns of gene combinations associated with particular diseases.

Several groups are working on SNP maps, especially the U.S. Human Genome Project and the SNP consortium, which is a coalition of 10 large pharmaceutical companies in association with the U.K. Welcome Trust. The SNP consortium's aim is to map 300,000 common SNPs.

### Gene oases, gene deserts

One feature of the human genome is its varied landscape. On a given chromosome, regions that are densely packed with genes are interspersed by gene-poor regions that are millions of base pairs long. What function to these gene deserts serve?

More than half the human genome consists of "junk DNA"—repeat sequences that have no known function. Most are derived from so-called transposable elements, or transposons—stretches of DNA that replicate and insert copies elsewhere in the genome. In the human genome, these transposons seem to have slowed or stopped their tendency to roam about the genome. However, about 50 genes have been identified that are based on transposon elements. It seems that transposons have played some useful role in the human genome's evolution.

Even in gene-rich regions, there are segments of considerable duplication, and sometimes DNA sequences on one chromosome are repeated on another. During evolution, it seems that the genome "experimented" with duplicates of DNA sequences, while keeping the original functional genes intact.

In all, genes make up only about 2 percent of the human genome. The noncoding regions may contribute to the structural integrity of the chromosome. They may also contain regulatory regions that control the expression of genes.

## New opportunities, new dangers

The Human Genome Project has spurred an explosion in genetic knowledge. Scientists have pinpointed more than 30 disease-associated genes, including those related to Huntington's disease and several inherited forms of cancer. Such findings allow researchers to begin a targeted search for a cure. The HGP also opens the door to testing people for disease-associated genes. Yet these advances create new ethical, legal, and social concerns (see BIOETHICS). Should expectant couples use genetic tests to determine whether their unborn child has inherited a disease? If the child does have a disease, what action should the couple take?

The signs and symptoms of some genetic diseases, such as Huntington's disease, do not appear until middle age. Would people carrying the faulty gene want to know in advance whether they will develop a crippling disease for which no cure exists? Would people want to know whether they are likely to develop an inherited form of cancer? Would they want their employers or health insurers to know that they carry such disease genes?

Some ethicists fear that the new genetic knowledge will lead to selective breeding, that is, attempts to create "superior" humans. To prevent the misuse of genetic information and encourage debate on these issues, the U.S. Genome Project has devoted up to 5 percent of its budget to the study of the project's ethical, legal, and social implications (a program called ELSI). Similar programs are running in several European countries.

## Beyond the HGP

The mapping of human chromosomes and sequencing of human DNA are the beginning rather than the end of the HGP's accomplishment. Numerous projects will follow the HGP. Applications include using HGP knowledge to study how environmental changes, such as the presence of specific microorganisms, influence the expression of human genes and could trigger disease. Comparing base sequences of humans with those of other organisms will also shed further light on the evolutionary origins of humans. One thing is sure: the HGP will massively alter humans' understanding of who they are.

T. DAY

## PATENTING GENES?

The Human Genome Project (HGP) was set up from the outset to enable its findings to be readily available to the commercial world. Private companies, such as Celera Genomics headed by Craig Venter (below left, with Francis Collins of the National Human Genome Research Institute, which is leading the project), have been carrying out their own DNA sequencing and filling in gaps using HGP data. Private companies, many of which are operating as nonprofit organizations, are filing patent applications for human genes and DNA fragments. Although, in general, it is not possible to patent raw products of nature, it is possible to patent DNA products that have been "isolated, purified, or modified" to produce a form not found naturally. By 2001 over three million patent applications had been made worldwide for genome-related products and processes.

*Craig Ventor (left) and Francis Collins announce the human genome sequence, 2001.*

## SCIENCE AND SOCIETY

**See also:** AMINO ACIDS; ANALYTICAL TECHNIQUES; BIOETHICS; BRAIN; CANCER; CELL BIOLOGY; CHROMOSOMES; CIRCULATORY SYSTEMS; DIABETES; DNA; GENETIC DISEASES; GENETICS; MUSCULAR SYSTEMS; PROTEINS.

**Further reading:**
Baker, C. 1999. *Your Genes, Your Choices.* Washington, D.C.: American Association for the Advancement of Science.
Cantor, C. R., and C. Smith. 1999. *The Genomics: The Science and Technology behind the Human Genome Project.* New York: John Wiley.
Chervas, J., and J. Gribbin, eds. 2002. *The Human Genome.* New York: Dorling Kindersley.
Davies, K. 2001. *Cracking the Genome Future: Inside the Race to Unlock Human DNA.* New York: Free Press.

# HYDROPONICS

**Hydroponics is a method of growing plants with their roots in solutions of nutrients instead of in the soil**

Research
Nutrient
Requirements
of Peppers

*Using water and land more efficiently than traditional agriculture, hydroponics is useful in dry climates.*

## History

People have known for centuries that it is possible to grow plants without soil. In the late 1600s, John Woodward in England compared plants grown in polluted river water with those grown in rainwater and concluded that dissolved solids assisted in the plant's growth. In 1860 the German scientist Julius von Sachs grew plants without sand or gravel, using only water and nutrients, and published the first soilless growing formula. In the 1920s scientists experimented with other nutrient solutions. Gericke was able to grow tomato plants to a height of 25 feet (8 m)—so high that he had to climb a ladder to harvest them. With news of his success, many people developed soilless culture as a hobby, and some commercial ventures began.

The first large-scale use of hydroponics came during World War II (1939–1945), when the technique was used to provide fresh vegetables for the troops on Pacific island bases. The late 1960s also brought renewed interest because some people felt the land would not supply them with enough food.

## How the system works

Hydroponic plants must have the same essentials as those grown in fertile soil: a balanced nutrient solution for their root systems and a support to keep them in a position so that the green part of the plant can receive sufficient light. Correct temperature and humidity are also important.

So that plants can make food using photosynthesis, adequate supplies of carbon dioxide, light, heat, and nutrients are necessary. A total of 16 chemical elements is required. Carbon, hydrogen, and oxygen come from air and water. (Carbon dioxide is a combination of carbon and oxygen; water, of course, is a combination of hydrogen and oxygen.) Nitrogen, phosphorus, potassium, calcium, magnesium, and sulfur are called macronutrients, as they are needed in large quantities.

Seven other elements, called micronutrients, are also required. Although only a few parts per million are needed by the plant, a deficiency in one of the

Hydroponics is a way of growing plants with their roots in a special solution of essential nutrients in water instead of in soil. The word "hydroponics" comes from two Greek words: *hydor* meaning "water," and *ponos* meaning "work." This name was given to the process in 1929 by Dr. William F. Gericke of the University of California, Berkeley, who first developed today's hydroponic methods. Gericke said that hydroponics literally meant "water working."

micronutrients will result in weaker plants, which are more susceptible to disease and less likely to survive. The micronutrients are boron, chlorine, copper, iron, manganese, molybdenum, and zinc. All these elements enter the plant through the roots, either dissolved in soil, in water, or as part of the hydroponic growing formula.

## TYPES OF CULTURE

There are two types of hydroponics: water culture and aggregate culture. The only difference between the two methods is the way in which the plants are supported.

### Water culture

In water culture, plants are simply suspended on a frame that submerges the roots in water containing nutrient salts. The roots absorb water and nutrients, but do not anchor the plants. As the roots need to take up oxygen, air must be regularly pumped or mixed into the solution.

Gericke developed the method of filling shallow tanks with nutrients and then covering them with wire mesh. Plant roots were permitted to grow through the open spaces in the mesh to feed on the solution below. The wire surrounding the roots held the plants upright.

### Aggregate culture

In aggregate culture, sand, perlite (a heat-expanded volcanic glass), small gravel, glass marbles, or stone chips are used to support the plant roots, and since these substances are inert (inactive), they do not interfere with the growing process.

The nutrient solution flows around the inert growing medium and feeds the roots. The solution itself may be applied from above and left to drain through the growing medium, or it may be pumped from a tank beneath the container and then allowed to drain for reuse—the method that is favored by most commercial growers.

The main advantage of the aggregate technique over water culture is that less care is needed in sprouting and planting the seeds. The medium supports the plants and holds them erect. Forcing air into the nutrient solution is also unnecessary when using the aggregate method.

### Success of hydroponics

In Glendale, Arizona, a 10-acre (25 ha) complex with concrete seedbeds, pipes, pumps, and rows of fiberglass greenhouses has been built on a covered landfill. This showplace, called the Magic Gardens, is one of many hydroponic farms.

In the United States and Canada hydroponic farms have become big business. Thousands of these operations provide food for many millions of people. Hydroponic growing is particularly popular in Hawaii, where land is so expensive that growers must achieve the greatest efficiency from their crops. In addition, many private gardeners also use hydroponics to produce their own food.

## ADVANTAGES AND DISADVANTAGES OF HYDROPONICS

### Advantages
- Uses land more efficiently because plants can be grown closer together. Tomatoes grown in soil yield 5 to 10 tons per acre (11 to 22 tonnes per ha); with hydroponics the yield rises to 60 to 300 tons per acre (134 to 672 tonnes per ha).
- Less water is required, and the water used can be recycled.
- Crop rotation is unnecessary. Nutrient levels can be maintained throughout the growing cycle, so the same type of crop can be grown in endless succession.
- Automation and low energy costs mean that the process is economical.
- By changing the nutrient solution, different crops can be grown to order.
- There is no weeding to do.
- There is no growing season, and crops can be produced 12 months a year.
- Like factory or office workers, hydroponics workers have a job for the whole year, instead of the few months of seasonal labor possible with soil culture.

### Disadvantages
- Initial setting up costs are high, and concrete beds, pipes, and pumps must be constructed and installed before a single plant is grown.
- The hydroponic grower must learn more about plant physiology and nutrients than the soil gardener and needs a technical support team of scientists and analysts.
- Plant disease may be a problem, especially if the disease is present in the circulation medium.
- In subfreezing areas, plant beds must be placed in greenhouses, which are expensive to maintain.

Nations throughout the world have recognized the value of hydroponics for growing food crops. In the Middle East, countries including Lebanon, Kuwait, and Israel have successful hydroponic operations. The soil in these desert countries is too dry to cultivate, and there is not enough water for irrigation.

European countries, including Holland and Belgium, have applied hydroponics to growing flowers as well as to growing food. In the United States, the San Diego and Bronx Zoos use giant hydroponic trays to raise food for animals.

### The future

Hydroponics is a logical way of growing a wide range of agricultural products. Scientists foresee huge hydroponic towers within major cities, where vegetables can be grown all year round.

Research into hydroponics takes place in many universities and experimental stations. One day soilless beds on space flights may provide the technology to feed colonies on the moon and beyond. The future of hydroponics is extremely bright.

E. KELLY

See also: AGRICULTURE.

**Further reading:**
Duren, L. 2001. *Home Garden Hydroponics.* Bloomington, Indiana: 1st Books Library.
Resh, H. M. 2001. *Hydroponic Food Production: A Definitive Guidebook of Soilless Food-Growing Methods.* 6th ed. Beaverton, Oreg.: Woodbridge Press.

# HYPNOSIS

**Hypnosis is an artificially induced trance state, characterized by heightened susceptibility to suggestion**

*Hypnosis is carried out by trained hypnotists, who use a special procedure to transport the subject into a trancelike state of mind.*

## CONNECTIONS

● Under hypnosis, the subject is in a state between waking and sleeping, according to the **BRAIN**-wave patterns he or she exhibits.

● The use of hypnosis to help treat cases of **ADDICTION**, smoking, for example, has had some success.

The idea of hypnosis may bring to mind a familiar scene: a person walking and talking in a trance-like way, while obeying the instructions of a hypnotist. The word *hypnosis* comes from the Greek word *hypnos*, meaning "sleep." At first glance, people under hypnosis might seem to be sleeping or sleepwalking, but the brain waves of a hypnotized individual are more similar to the brain waves of an awake person than a sleeping person.

## Responsiveness to hypnosis

The hallmark of hypnosis is the subject's responsiveness to suggestions. These are instructions from the hypnotist regarding what the subject should see, hear, taste, feel, or do. The sensations produced by suggestions can be wholly imaginary or can recall past experiences in the subject's life. A suggestion can even be untrue, such as that the subject see the sky as green in color. Some suggestions continue to influence the individual even after he or she has woken from the hypnotic state; these types of suggestions, known as posthypnotic suggestions, are used in some medical applications, such as helping patients control pain, or deal with obsessive or addictive behavior.

Some people are more likely to follow suggestions and therefore are more easily hypnotized. Conversely, other people cannot be hypnotized at all, either because they are inherently less hypnotizable or because they deliberately resist hypnosis. The hypnotist is not all controlling: a hypnotized subject can resist or disobey suggestions if they run contrary to strongly held beliefs. What seems clear, however, is that there must be certain characteristics for different degrees of suggestibility in people. It is quite untrue, for example, that a hypnotist can

order a subject to do something in public that the person would never normally do. Nevertheless, hypnosis can implant false memories. This situation is particularly dangerous with the increasing use of hypnosis to uncover repressed memories of past sexual abuse or other trauma. An unethical hypnotist could implant such memories where none previously existed and thus lead the subject to believe, for example, that he or she had been abused—when in fact there had been no such abuse.

## The early history of hypnotism

Hypnotism has its roots in the work of the Austrian Franz Anton Mesmer (1734-1815), who maintained that the human body contained "animal magnetism." Mesmer believed that he could influence this magnetism by passing his hands downward across a patient's body and thus redirect magnetic fluids that had become disrupted and had produced illness in the patient. A later practitioner, Englishman James Braid (1795–1860), coined the term *neurohypnosis* in 1843. The modern term *hypnosis* is a shortened form of Braid's term.

## Uses of hypnotism

Hypnosis has found wide application in both medicine and psychology, although carefully constructed scientific studies of its effects are relatively rare. Clinical studies suggest that it can reduce discomfort and speed the recovery of surgery patients. Similarly, it may be an aid to patients undergoing chemotherapy for cancer.

In the area of behavioral science, hypnosis has been used to help smokers, alcoholics, and compulsive eaters change their habits, although researchers disagree on how well the effects of hypnosis have been documented. Hypnosis can also help subjects recover past memories through hypnotic regression (returning to an earlier state). Such information can be used as a guide for future therapy or as a basis for criminal prosecution, although legal acceptance of recovered memories has varied greatly.

However, despite its apparent usefulness, hypnotism has suffered from a poor reputation, attributable to its use in theater acts and other nonscientific settings. Some scientists remain doubtful that hypnosis is an altered state of conciousness at all, believing that it merely represents an extreme on the normal scale of suggestibility.

V. KIERNAN

**See also:** MEDICINE, HISTORY OF; PSYCHOLOGY.

**Further reading:**
Temes, Roberta, and Marc Strauss, eds. 1999. *Medical Hypnosis: An Introduction and Clinial Guide.* New York: Churchill Livingstone.

# IMMUNE SYSTEMS

**The immune system is a collection of cells and proteins that defends the body against harmful foreign invaders**

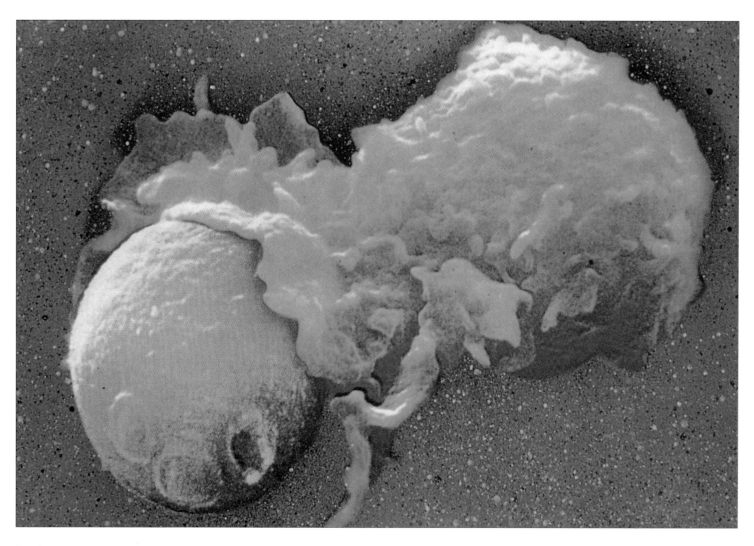

*A lymphocyte (white blood cell)—the main defense of the immune system—engulfs a foreign particle.*

The body has its own protection against disease-causing invaders, such as viruses and bacteria. The cells and proteins that make up these defenses are called the immune system. The basic role of an immune system is to distinguish the organism's own cells, or "self," from foreign substances or cells (nonself) entering the body and remove these intruders. Almost all animals, from sponges to humans, and some plants have mechanisms that allow for protection against invading organisms (see the boxes on pages 931 and 932). The immune system is also involved in protecting the body against cancer and in rejecting tissue after transplant surgery. Sometimes the immune system mounts reaction against harmless substances, such as pollen, causing allergies, or even attacks the body's own tissues to cause autoimmune diseases (see AUTOIMMUNE DISORDERS).

The immune system has two main types of defenses: natural (innate) immunity, which is nonspecific and includes external barriers, such as the skin, and fast-acting processes, such as phagocytosis and inflammation; and acquired (adaptive) immunity, in which specific attacks are mounted against foreign invaders. The later type of defense depends on certain types of white blood cells with a "memory" of invaders that have been encountered previously. Acquired immunity is most effective on subsequent exposure to foreign invaders.

## Natural immunity

In animals the first line of defense against invading organisms is physical barriers, such as healthy, unbroken skin (see IMMUNOLOGY). In addition, sweat,

### CORE FACTS

- The immune system protects an organism against foreign invaders.
- Animals and plants have immune systems.
- The immune system works by distinguishing self from nonself and destroying nonself.
- There are two types of immunity: natural immunity, which is nonspecific, and acquired immunity, which is specific and has memory.

## CONNECTIONS

- Some diseases, such as **ARTHRITIS** and **MULTIPLE SCLEROSIS**, are **AUTOIMMUNE DISEASES**, in which the immune system attacks its own tissues.

- The study of immune systems is called **IMMUNOLOGY**.

- Active immunity (exposure to an antigen) and passive immunity (injection of ready-made **ANTIBODIES**) are common forms of **IMMUNIZATION**.

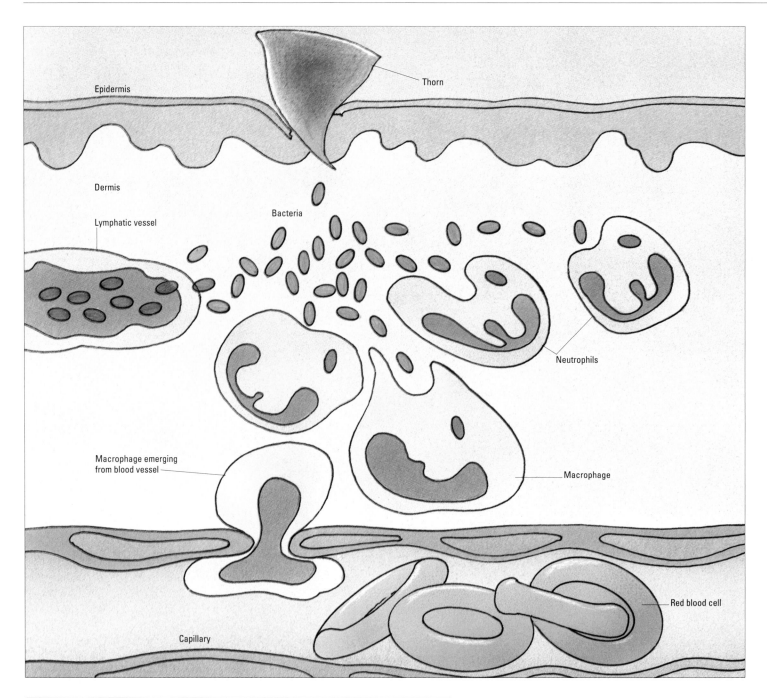

Epidermis

Thorn

Dermis

Lymphatic vessel

Bacteria

Neutrophils

Macrophage emerging
from blood vessel

Macrophage

Red blood cell

Capillary

## EVOLUTION OF THE IMMUNE SYSTEM

The simplest invertebrate animals, such as sponges and starfish, evolved almost 600 million years ago. All invertebrates have amoeboid phagocytic cells that recognize and engulf any foreign invaders that do not have "self" labels—proteins that occur on the surface of their own cells. Invertebrates also have proteins called lectins, which appear to tag foreign invaders for phagocytosis and may be the evolutionary precursors of antibodies. Some invertebrates, such as earthworms, have lymphocyte-like cells; others, such as crabs, evolved a nonspecific complement-like defense. Invertebrates do not seem to have an immunity with a memory (acquired immunity), unlike vertebrates. The earliest vertebrates, such as lampreys (jawless fish), appeared about 500 million years ago. They have an immune system based on lymphocytes but do not have distinct B- and T-cells. The modern vertebrate immune system, with B- and T-cells, first arose in sharks 450 million years ago. The shark's immune system is very similar to that of other fish, amphibians, reptiles, birds, and mammals.

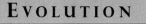

**EVOLUTION**

*In natural immunity, neutrophils and macrophages ingest and destroy foreign invaders such as bacteria.*

tears, and saliva contain an enzyme called lysozyme that can destroy bacteria by cleaving a component of the bacterial cell wall. Microorganisms may also gain entry through mucous membranes, moist surfaces that line the mouth, nose, eyes, intestines, and genital and urinary tracts. Hairs in the nose prevent entry of microorganisms; sneezing and coughing also helps to expel them. Mucus produced by the mucous membranes of the respiratory tract traps microorganisms. The mucus is swept away by cilia (tiny hairs lining the respiratory tract) and swallowed or expelled from the body through the mouth or nose. Any swallowed microorganisms are usually destroyed by acid in the stomach. Microorganisms that do reach the intestine often die because they cannot compete with normal intestinal flora (harmless and beneficial microorganisms that live in the intestine). Vomiting and diarrhea are also the body's attempt to remove patho-genic agents in the digestive tract. If microorganisms enter the body through a tear in the skin or a mucous membrane, nonspecific cellular and chemical responses attack to prevent them from multiplying and causing harm. This second line of natural defense includes the white blood cells called neutrophils and macrophages. These cells kill through phagocytosis, a process in which the foreign invader is engulfed within a sac inside the cell. This sac then fuses with a lysosome. Lysosomes contain a variety of antibi-otic enzyme activities, some of which work in a man-ner similar to bleach by oxidizing the proteins of the engulfed bacteria. Another type of white blood cell, the natural killer (NK) lymphocyte, destroys cells that have been infected by viruses (see IMMUNOLOGY)

Proteins important in nonspecific defense are complement and interferons. The complement sys-tem consists of about 20 different proteins that are components of blood plasma. The presence of bacte-rial or fungal cell wall proteins in the body triggers a cascade of complement cleavage reactions that pro-

## EVADING THE IMMUNE SYSTEM

The immune system destroys microorganisms that enter the body by recognizing specific antigens on their cell surfaces. However, some microorganisms manage to evade the immune system by a process called antigen shifting, or variation. To fool the host, the microorganisms mutate (genetically change) their surface antigens to avoid recognition. Disease-causing microorganisms that use antigen shifting include the flu and cold viruses and trypanosomes (protozoans that cause African sleeping sickness). Because microorganisms reproduce quickly, they evolve rapidly and can produce variations in their surface antigens relatively quickly, often before the body has had a chance to wipe out the infection with specific antibodies directed against the microorganism's old surface. Many scientists believe that humans may never be able to create vaccines against some disease-causing germs, such as flu or cold viruses, because they can change their identity regularly. The African trypanosmome parasite has several thousand different versions of the genes for its surface antigen; it keeps one step ahead of its host's immune system by repeatedly changing its surface antigen. As the immune system overcomes the latest surface antigen, so a new variant is generated. People with this disease rarely overcome the infection. Other ways of evading the immune response adopted by microorganisms include shedding all surface antigens or acquiring a coat of host proteins to appear as "self" to the immune system.

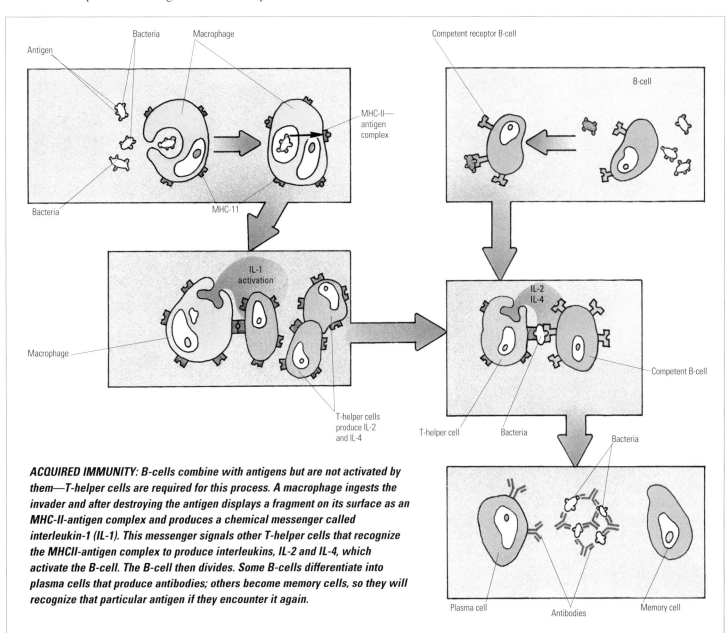

***ACQUIRED IMMUNITY: B-cells combine with antigens but are not activated by them—T-helper cells are required for this process. A macrophage ingests the invader and after destroying the antigen displays a fragment on its surface as an MHC-II-antigen complex and produces a chemical messenger called interleukin-1 (IL-1). This messenger signals other T-helper cells that recognize the MHCII-antigen complex to produce interleukins, IL-2 and IL-4, which activate the B-cell. The B-cell then divides. Some B-cells differentiate into plasma cells that produce antibodies; others become memory cells, so they will recognize that particular antigen if they encounter it again.***

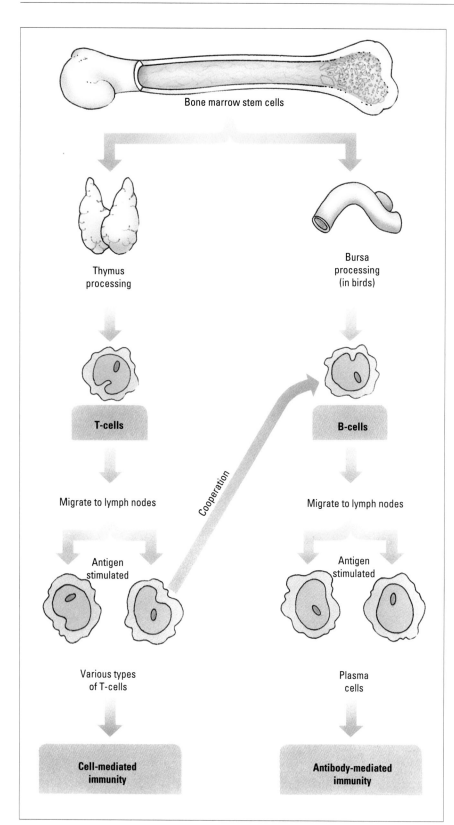

Bone marrow stem cells

Thymus processing

Bursa processing (in birds)

**T-cells**

**B-cells**

Migrate to lymph nodes

Cooperation

Migrate to lymph nodes

Antigen stimulated

Antigen stimulated

Various types of T-cells

Plasma cells

**Cell-mediated immunity**

**Antibody-mediated immunity**

*T-cells develop in the thymus gland. In most vertebrates, B-cells are thought to mature in bone marrow. In birds, however, they develop in a lymphatic organ called the bursa of Fabricus.*

beta, and gamma. Healthy cells take up interferon and make antiviral proteins to protect themselves against further infection. Interferons inhibit viral replication but there is a great deal of interest in their value as anticancer agents. However, high concentrations are needed, which produce unwanted side effects.

Another nonspecific response is the inflammatory response. Infected or injured cells release chemicals such as histamine and prostaglandins, which dilate surrounding blood vessels and cause fluid to leak from the vessels into the surrounding tissue. The increase in blood flow brings phagocytic cells to the area of infection (see IMMUNOLOGY).

## Acquired immunity

If an invader manages to get past the natural immune system defenses, it faces the second line of defense called acquired, or adaptive, immunity. Acquired immunity allows the body to remember past specific infections and respond rapidly if the same infectious agent is encountered (in other words, immunity has been acquired against that particular infectious agent). Acquired immunity, which is complex and not fully understood, occurs only in vertebrates. Therefore, many diseases, such as measles and chicken pox, rarely affect the same individual twice.

The cells responsible fot the acquired immune response, called B-lymphocytes (B-cells) and T-lymphocytes (T-cells), must first recognize invading antigen nonself proteins that are different from the body. Once recognized, two pathways establish the counterattack through humoral (humor refers to body fluid) or cell-mediated responses. In the humoral response, B-cells produce proteins called antibodies (immunoglobulins), which neutralize the invading antigen and stimulate its removal. Cell-mediated responses are directed by cytotoxic T-cells, which lyse any cell recognized as nonself as well as viral- or parasite-infected cells.

## Humoral immunity

This type of acquired immunity is especially important in defending the body against bacteria, viruses, and toxins. After a complex process involving the recognition of foreign antigens, B-cells produce antibodies. Antibodies are soluble proteins consisting of two identical short polypeptides, called light chains, and two identical long polypeptides, called heavy chains. The chains are held together by disulfide bonds to form the characteristic Y-shaped structure of the antibody. The "arms" of the antibody are variable regions that fit specific antigens. Each B-cell produces an antibody with a different variable region, and every human can synthesize more than 100 billion different variable regions. These regions are highly specific and are able to distinguish between two protein antigens that differ by only one animo acid.

There are five classes of antibodies in mammals (see the box on page 931). The antibodies act as receptors for antigens, attached to the membrane of B-cells. When an antibody encounters an antigen that it recognizes or fits, the B-cell secretes more of the anti-

duce active enzymes. One type is a membrane attack complex that punches holes in the invader cell, much as the perforins produced by NK cells do. The cells then swell and burst. The complement system also attracts phagocytes to the site of infection and coats invaders so the phagocytic cells can ingest them easily.

When an organism is infected with viruses, lymphocytes and other cell types secrete interferons, proteins that act as signaling molecules to trigger a wide variety of cellular responses that fight the infection. There are three main types of interferons: alpha, bodies to combat that particular antigen. The B-cell is then activated by a T-cell to divide into new cells, called plasma cells. These cells manufacture vast numbers of exactly the same type of antibody. Once the antigens of a foreign invader are coated in antibodies, it is marked for destruction by phagocytic cells, such as macrophages, and also by the complement system, which causes the invading cell to swell and burst.

## Cell-mediated immunity

This type of acquired immunity is involved in defense against viruses, against cancer cells, and in rejecting tissue transplants. Two types of T-cells are the key players in cell-mediated immunity: helper T-cells and cytotoxic, or killer, T-cells.

Macrophages engulf antigen-bearing particles, such as viruses. These cells then process the viruses, breaking them up and combining viral antigens with cell surface proteins called class II major histocompatibility complex (MHC) molecules on the macrophage cell surface (see the box on page 932). The macrophages then release a substance called interleukin-1, which signals to helper T-cells that have specific receptors on their surface that bind to the viral/MHC molecules. When a particular helper T-cell recognizes the viral/MHC II complex, it releases interleukin-2. This substance stimulates cytotoxic T-cells to multiply and destroy body cells infected with that antigen. (Interleukin-2 also stimulates B-cells to become plasma cells.)

Cytotoxic T-cells are also stimulated when they recognize antigens complexed with MHC I molecules on cell surfaces. The cytotoxic cell multiplies and destroys any cell infected with that particular antigen. Scientists also think that cytotoxic cells recognize cancer cells and cells from transplanted tissue as nonself and destroy them in a similar way.

Other types of T-cells include inducer T-cells, which are in charge of T-cell development in the thymus gland, and suppressor T-cells, which terminate a cell-mediated response when the foreign

---

## WHEN THE IMMUNE SYSTEM GOES WRONG

Sometimes the immune system does not work effectively or causes damage. Problems with the immune system include immunodeficiencies, autoimmune disorders, and allergies. When the immune system cannot work effectively and is unable to combat infections, this condition is called immunodeficiency. Immunodeficiency, which may be due to a genetic disorder and may be present at birth (congenital immunodeficiency), leads to recurrent infections and failure to grow normally. Immunodeficiency that develops after birth (acquired immunodeficiency) has various causes, including the HIV virus, which causes AIDS by attacking and destroying helper T-cells, and some drugs.

In autoimmune diseases, the immune system behaves abnormally and starts forming antibodies or white blood cells that attack the body's own tissues, making them inflamed and damaged. The causes of these diseases are poorly understood, but genetic factors, infections with certain viruses, or some drugs and hormones may be triggers. Examples of autoimmune disorders include rheumatoid arthritis, in which connective tissue in the joints are attacked, and multiple sclerosis, in which the myelin sheath that surrounds nerves in the brain and spinal cord is damaged, thus affecting the transmission of nerve impulses.

In allergies, the body mounts an abnormal immune response to a foreign substance (called an allergen) in susceptible people. In most people, the trigger substance is harmless and does not produce symptoms. There are two main forms of allergy: immediate hypersensitivity, in which B-cells produce antibodies to an allergen immediately, and thus, symptoms appear seconds or minutes later; and delayed hypersensitivity, in which T-cells launch an abnormal immune response with symptoms appearing within 48 hours after exposure to the allergen.

In immediate hypersensitivity, the first contact with the allergen leads to the production of IgE antibodies, which bind to cells called mast cells and basophils. A second exposure leads to the allergen binding to the IgE on these cells, which are then stimulated to release various chemicals, including histamine, that cause symptoms of anaphylaxis. Pollen (responsible for hay fever); certain drugs, such as penicillin; and some foods, such as peanuts, are substances that commonly cause immediate hypersensitivity. Often the symptoms are mild, such as watery eyes or a runny nose, but in some people widespread histamine release, which causes blood vessels to dilate, can block the airway and so affect breathing or lead to anaphylactic shock, a life-threatening drop in blood pressure. In delayed hypersensitivity, the immune response is triggered by T-cells releasing compounds called lymphokines. An example of this type of allergy is the rash caused by contact with certain plants, such as poison ivy.

### AT RISK

---

## IgA, IgD, IgE, IgG, AND IgM: WHAT IS IN THE ALPHABET SOUP?

The five classes of antibodies, or immunoglobulins (Ig), are receptors for antigens and are manufactured by B-cells. Some are bound to the surface of the B-cells that produce them; others are free floating.

● **IgM** (about 10 percent of total antibody) is the first to be secreted in a primary immune response and acts as a receptor on the B-cell surface. IgM also makes antigen-bearing particles or microorganisms stick together (agglutinate); thus, they are easier to destroy.

● **IgG** is the most common class of antibody in the blood plasma (80 percent of total antibody). It is secreted in a secondary response by B-cells. Therefore, it is the first antibody to respond after reinfection with the same microorganism or after a booster vaccination. IgG lives for about 25 days, which is up to four times as long as the lifespan of the other classes of antibodies. In addition, it is the only antibody (immunoglobulin) that can cross the placenta from mother to fetus.

● **IgD** is present in trace amounts in the serum and on the surface of B-cells in combination with IgM. It probably is part of the mechanism to signal antibody production.

● **IgA** is the main class of antibody in external secretions, such as saliva, mucus, and tears, and is often a first-line defense against invaders. It is also secreted in breast milk to provide newborn babies some protection while their immune system is developing. About two-thirds of all antibodies in humans are IgA.

● **IgE** is the least common antigen in most people and is secreted by B-cells in the skin and tonsils and in the respiratory and digestive systems. IgE stimulates the inflammatory response and mediates the anaphylactic response. However, in some people it can also react to harmless substances, such as pollen, and produce the symptoms of allergy.

### A CLOSER LOOK

## THE MAJOR HISTOCOMPATIBILITY COMPLEX

The major histocompatibility complex (MHC) is a set of genes that code for glycoproteins on the surface of vertebrate cells. These surface glycoproteins are called MHC proteins (in humans they are called HLA, or human leukocyte antigens, and are encoded by genes on chromosome 6). They help T-cells to distinguish between tissue that is "self" and "nonself." It is rare for two individuals to have the same MHC glycoproteins because the genes of the MHC have many forms—some genes in humans have up to 170 variants, or alleles. There are two classes of MHC proteins: MHC-I, which are present on every cell with a nucleus in the body, and MHC-II, which are present only on macrophages, B-cells, and a subtype of T-cells. When foreign particles or cells enter the body, certain cells called antigen-presenting cells digest these invaders and complex the invaders antigens with MHC proteins on the cell surface. T-cells recognize only the antigens in association with the MHC proteins and then launch an immune response.

The MHC was first discovered when scientists found that organ transplants between two humans, or two animals, were nearly always rejected by the recipient. For this reason, surgeons now try to match the MHC profile of the organ donor with that of the recipient. Transplants between identical twins are the most successful. However, because it is difficult to find MHC profiles that match exactly, organ recipients are given drugs that suppress the immune system to prevent rejection.

**A CLOSER LOOK**

invader has been cleared. Human immunodeficiency virus, which is responsible for causing AIDS (acquired immune deficiency syndrome; see AIDS), devastates the immune system because it infects and destroys helper T-cells, which then cannot activate cytotoxic cells to kill infected cells.

### Immune memory

Some of the activated B- and T-cells remain circulating in the bloodstream or reside in lymphatic organs as memory cells. On re-encountering the antigen to which they specifically bind, these cells rapidly deal with the invader. An infectious microorganism can be eliminated in two or three days, compared with five or seven days the first time it invaded that individual. As people grow older, they acquire more and more memory cells; therefore children are more susceptible to infectious diseases than are adults.

### Development and organization of the immune system

The white blood cells of the immune system, including T- and B-cells, develop from self-renewing stem cells in the bone marrow (see STEM CELLS). B-cells are released from the bone marrow and circulate in the blood and lymphatic systems (see box on page 929 ) until they encounter specific antigens. T-cells migrate from the bone marrow to the thymus (hence the *T* in their name: the *B* in B-cell comes from the word *bursa*, a region in birds where these cells are processed). The thymus is a gland present in the upper part of the chest behind the breastbone. Here the T-cells develop receptors enabling them to recognize antigens. Depending on which class of MHC molecule a T-cell recognizes, it then matures into one of several types of T-cells, including helper T-cells and cytotoxic T-cells.

Mature B- and T-cells increase their chance of finding foreign antigens by circulating between the blood and lymphatic systems, which are connected. The lymphatic system is a collection of vessels, nodes, and tissues, such as the thymus gland, tonsils, and spleen, that drains colorless tissue fluid (lymph) back into the bloodstream and fights infection. Drained tissue fluid often contains particles such as bacteria. This fluid passes through nodes, which are tightly packed with lymphocytes and other white blood cells. The nodes filter the lymph, trapping foreign particles, which are then destroyed by the immune cells.

J. GODDARD

**See also:** AIDS; AUTOIMMUNE DISORDERS; BLOOD; CIRCULATORY SYSTEMS; LYMPHATIC SYSTEMS; STEM CELLS.

## IMMUNE SYSTEMS OF PLANTS

Plants defend themselves from disease-causing microorganisms with an immune system similar to that of animals. As animals have skin, plants have a protective epidermis to block the entry of potentially harmful microorganisms. However, plants also have defenses at the cellular level to prevent disease.

Plants appear to have genes that produce proteins that recognize and trigger a reaction called the hypersensitive response (HR) if infected by a disease-causing microorganism. This response effectively seals off the area of infection by causing the plant cells around this site to rapidly die. In this way, the plant prevents the infection from spreading. The chemicals hydrogen peroxide and nitric acid are involved in HR. An alternative strategy to HR involves the cell walls of cells near a localized infection thickening to help prevent the spread of a plant disease.

In addition to localized responses, plants also have a general response to invasion. This response, called systemic acquired resistance (SAR), allows the plants to respond quickly if reinfected. However, it is short-term, lasting for only a few days, and nonspecific, unlike the acquired immunity of vertebrates. Plants are also known to produce antimicrobial agents: substances such as phytoalexins.

**A CLOSER LOOK**

### Further reading:
Edelson, E. 1999. *The Immune System*. New York: Chelsea House Publications.
Roitt, I. M., J. Brostoff, and D. K. Male. 2001. *Immunology*. St. Louis: Mosby.

# IMMUNIZATION

**Immunization stimulates the body's defenses or supplements them to fight off foreign cells or molecules**

Immunization against specific microorganisms or viruses makes it possible for the body's immune system to eliminate these organisms before they have a chance to cause disease. Immunization is usually carried out by injecting an antigen (a foreign substance, such as part of a disease-causing organism) into the bloodstream. The immune system responds by producing specialized cells that manufacture proteins called antibodies (see ANTIBODIES; IMMUNE SYSTEMS; IMMUNOLOGY) to destroy and eliminate the antigens. The immune system retains a memory of the initial exposure to the antigen and is prepared to fight any future infection.

## The history of immunization

In ancient China and India, people knew that children who were given a powder made from the scabs of people recovering from smallpox seldom developed full-blown smallpox themselves. The powder had to be inhaled or applied to a scratch on the skin. This practice was risky because 2 percent of those receiving the treatment died, but the death rate for people who developed natural smallpox was 20 to 30 percent. This treatment spread to the West and was practiced until the early 19th century.

In the 18th century, people noticed that dairymaids who milked cows with cowpox (caused by a virus related to the smallpox virus) often had a mild pox infection themselves. However, they soon recovered and then seemed to be protected from the deadly smallpox. English doctor Edward Jenner (1749–1823) noticed the connection between exposure to cowpox and resistance to smallpox (see JENNER, EDWARD). In 1796 he injected an eight-year-old boy with pus from cowpox pustules. Several months later, he injected the same boy with pus from smallpox pustules. Luckily for the boy, Jenner's experiment worked: he did not develop smallpox. News of Jenner's success soon spread, and by 1802 this new process became commonplace.

The Indian and Chinese children who received powder from smallpox scabs did not receive disease-causing smallpox viruses but viruses made harmless by the donor's immune response. The dairymaids and Jenner's boy received cowpox virus, a virus

*A small boy being vaccinated against measles in northern India.*

## CONNECTIONS

● Some U.S. children receive vaccinations for **TUBERCULOSIS** (TB). The vaccine induces the production of **ANTIBODIES** against *Mycobacterium tuberculosis*, which causes TB. Thus, critical tests for TB exposure are useless because everyone vaccinated tests positive.

● The term *vaccine* comes from *Vaccinia*, the name of the virus that **JENNER** used to make the first vaccine.

### CORE FACTS

■ Immunization is a method of acquiring or inducing resistance to infection.
■ Active immunization, or vaccination, introduces antigens into the body, where antibodies are synthesized against the disease-producing organism.

## How does immunization work?

There are two types of immunization: active and passive.

• Active immunization: Jenner's method remains the basis of active immunization, or vaccination. Bacteria or viruses that have been killed or modified so they can no longer cause disease are injected or ingested. The oral polio vaccine, for example, is made from a modified polio virus that can no longer cause disease. To the immune system, the vaccine looks just like the real thing because antigenic proteins are still present on the viral coat. Two types of white blood cells (lymphocytes) are primarily responsible for the immune response to the viral antigen. One type, B-lymphocytes, manufactures antibodies in response to contact with antigens foreign to the body. The second type, T-lymphocytes, act in partnership with B-lymphocytes to determine the strength of the antibody defense (see ANTIBODIES). When activated by antigen, a class of T-lymphocytes called T-helper cells secrete stimulatory factors called cytokines that activate the B-cells and increase the level of antibody they produce.

Critically, once T- and B-cells have encountered polio virus antigens, a small number of them become so-called memory cells, which lie in wait for another infection by the same organism. In many cases, these memory cells live for decades after immunization. Following each encounter with the antigen, the immune system responds better and faster than the time before; thus, people are often given several doses of the same vaccine, months or years apart.

• Passive immunization: Doctors can inject a person directly with antibodies specific for a particular organism. These antibodies live for about a month before they are broken down. The person is protected against the disease only for that time because antibodies alone cannot induce specific memory in lymphocytes. Passive immunization happens naturally when a mother passes antibodies to her baby through the placenta and after birth through breast milk. These antibodies play an important role in protecting the baby against infections while its own immature system develops enough to fight disease.

Passive immunization is useful if a quick response is required and the body does not have time to develop antibodies. For example, in response to the bite of a poisonous snake, a physician may inject antibodies specific for the toxins in the snake venom. If injected quickly enough after the bite, the antibodies can bind to the toxins and neutralize them.

that looks like smallpox virus to the immune system but does not cause severe illness in humans. The immune systems of these people made antibodies to the viruses with which they had been injected, and these antibodies were also active against the smallpox virus (see IMMUNE SYSTEMS; IMMUNOLOGY).

Mass immunization has been a great success story. In 1980 the World Health Organization declared that smallpox was the first disease to be eradicated worldwide through vaccination. (The last case of smallpox resulting from natural infection was in Somalia in 1977.) Polio, measles, mumps, rubella, and whooping cough may be eliminated in the early part of the 21st century.

*Babies that breastfeed naturally take in antibodies with their mother's milk. These antibodies protect against infections common in the outside environment.*

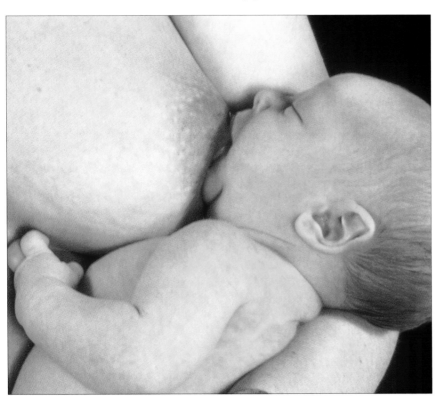

## Vaccines and vaccine production

Following Jenner's development of the smallpox vaccine, the second giant step toward controlling public health through immunization came from French scientist Louis Pasteur (1822–1895; see PASTEUR, LOUIS). Pasteur was trying to determine the cause of cholera in chickens by growing a microorganism isolated from the sick birds on a culture plate. One day, he accidentally let his cultures incubate too long before injecting them into chickens. Instead of developing cholera, as chickens injected with fresh cultures did, the chickens remained well. When Pasteur injected the same chickens with disease-causing microorganisms a few weeks later, the chickens still did not become infected. The genes of the old bacterial cultures had changed (mutated) in a way that allowed them to grow and induce an immune response without causing disease. Such bacteria are said to be weakened, or attenuated.

## Attenuated organisms

Many modern viral vaccines, including those for polio (the form given by mouth), yellow fever, measles, mumps, and rubella, are made from live, attenuated viruses. There are also attentuated vaccines against bacterial disease. For example, a strain of bovine tuberculosis bacteria called BCG (Bacille Calmette-Guerin) is used to make a vaccine against tuberculosis (TB) in humans. BCG does not cause TB in humans but produces an immune response to *Mycobacterium tuberculosis*, the causative agent of human TB.

Some organisms are still attenuated using methods similar to those used by Pasteur over 100 years ago. Some organisms, such as Jenner's cowpox virus, are considered attenuated because they cause disease in cows but not in humans. Other disease organisms are grown successively in less susceptible animals. This method has the effect of reducing their ability to produce disease. Yet other disease organisms are mutated deliberately to render them harmless.

Attenuated viruses can grow and reproduce inside the body, and so they generate a very strong immune response resulting in lifelong immunity. Attenuated bacterial vaccines are less effective.

## Inactivated organisms

Some viruses and bacteria are inactivated (killed) for the development of effective vaccines. Inactivated vaccines cannot infect cells or cause disease, but they still induce a specific immune response. Polio (given intravenously), influenza, and rabies vaccines are made from inactivated viruses. The vaccines protecting against pertussis (whooping cough), cholera, and bubonic plague are made from inactivated bacteria.

These vaccines must contain larger amounts of the organism compared with attenuated preparations because inactivated bacteria and viruses cannot multiply inside the body. Inactivated vaccines often induce a weaker immune response than attenuated vaccines, so several doses are required.

## Subunit, toxoid, and genetic vaccines

Antibodies bind to only one or a few surface antigens on viruses or bacteria. In some cases, scientists can identify and purify large amounts of specific antigenic proteins to make so-called subunit vaccines. The surface antigens of hepatitis B and influenza A viruses and the outside capsule of some bacteria, including those causing pneumococcal pneumonia and bacterial meningitis, are effective vaccines. Advances in genetic engineering have also enabled scientists to build subunit vaccines for the herpes simplex virus.

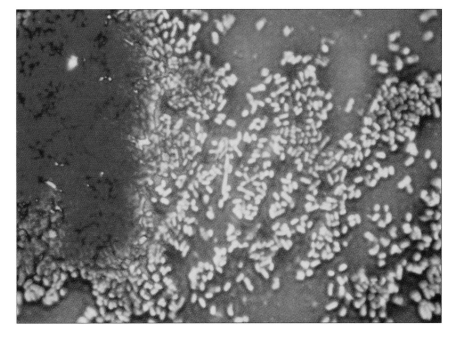

Some bacteria are dangerous because they make powerful toxins. At the beginning of the 20th century, English scientist Alexander Glenny discovered that diphtheria toxin treated with formalin was no longer toxic but still induced an immune response. The altered toxin was called a toxoid. Formalin is still used to prepare diphtheria and tetanus toxoids. Scientists can also insert genes coding for microbial antigens into harmless viruses and infect animals with them to make vaccines. Antigens from the hepatitis B, herpes simplex, and influenza viruses have been inserted into viruses in this way.

*Vibrio cholerae, **the bacterium that cause the disease cholera. When these bacteria are inactivated, they can be used to vaccinate against the disease.***

## Vaccination schedules

The vaccines commonly given to infants and children are measles, mumps, and rubella (MMR, a combination

---

## ADVERSE REACTIONS TO VACCINES

As with any medicine, some people develop side effects to some vaccines; very rarely, these are severe. Depending on the vaccine, the side effects might be slight stiffness or swelling in the joints, a rash, slight fever, or soreness, redness, and swelling where the shot was given. These problems are mild and usually last only a day or two. However, vaccines may cause more serious problems. The pertussis part of the DTP vaccine, for example, occasionally causes long bouts of crying, high fever, or a shocklike collapse. These reactions do not have long-term effects. The pertussis vaccine causes long-lasting severe brain damage in about one out of 300,000 cases. Before the pertussis vaccine was developed, 2 million Americans developed whooping cough each year; 7,000 died.
In Britain, after a few severe reactions to the vaccine became widely known, vaccination levels dropped to 30 percent. Some years later, more than 120,000 people developed whooping cough, and 28 died. Clearly, the benefits of the pertussis vaccine are very much greater than the attendant risks.

Occasionally, attenuated virus vaccines change back into disease-causing strains, and the vaccine causes the disease it is meant to prevent. One of the three attenuated polio virus strains used to make the oral polio vaccine, for example, will sometimes revert to its old, disease-causing form. It will cause polio in about 2.5 out of 1 million vaccinations.

## AT RISK

*A contemporary illustration of Edward Jenner vaccinating a child. The process was called* vaccination *because Jenner was injecting infants with the* Vaccinia *virus, which is the cause of cowpox.*

antibiotics should not receive live, attenuated vaccines. Some viral vaccines are first grown in chicken embryos; people who have serious allergies to eggs should not receive these vaccines. Doctors do not recommend vaccination of pregnant women, because the vaccine may harm the fetus.

## The global war against disease

Vaccines are among the safest, cheapest, and most powerful tools for preventing disease. Vaccination programs have had a dramatic effect on the health and well-being of the U.S. population. U.S. federal law requires that all children be immunized before they can enter school. As a result, 87 percent of all U.S. school-age children have been fully immunized, and most life-threatening childhood illnesses are effectively held in check.

Despite this success, there remains some debate over mandatory vaccination programs. Successful vaccination programs must provide an effective vaccine and appropriate educational materials for health care workers and the general public. A major concern is that parents in developed countries will become complacent about the need for immunizations, and the rates of childhood disease will rise.

Despite the obvious benefit of vaccination programs, much of the world's population is not immunized. In 1974 the World Health Organization began the Expanded Program on Immunization (EPI), with the goal of immunizing all children against diphtheria, pertussis, tetanus, measles, polio, and tuberculosis by 1990. Although the EPI did not reach the goal (in 1990, the worldwide vaccination rate was 80 percent), they made great progress. In 1974 when the program started, fewer than 5 percent of the world's children were fully immunized.

Experts estimate that between six and eight million children die each year from diseases that could be prevented by effective vaccines. Children in developing countries are most at risk. Although vaccines are generally inexpensive, especially when compared with the high cost of treating disease, they are sometimes luxuries in areas where there is not enough money to buy food. Scientists are therefore seeking ways to make immunization easier in developing countries. They want to develop a safe, effective vaccine that would protect against a number of diseases. Ideally, the vaccine would need to be given only once, would not require costly refrigeration, and would be inexpensive. A good immunization program, backed up by better sanitation, education, and nutrition, is the key to controlling serious diseases in the world.

S. LATTA

vaccine), diphtheria, pertussis and tetanus (DPT, another combination vaccine), polio, hepatitis B, and *Haemophilus influenzae* type b (Hib, the cause of bacterial meningitis). Doctors suggest booster shots of tetanus toxoid every 10 years. They also strongly recommend that some people, especially those over the age of 65, have a vaccination against the influenza virus every year. This virus rapidly mutates to new strains, and so scientists must predict which strain will appear each year and develop a new vaccine.

For most people, the benefits of vaccination are much greater than the risks. There are a few people who should not be immunized or who should delay their immunizations. People who have a hard time fighting infection (because they have cancer, AIDS, or are taking drugs that suppress the immune system) or people who have serious allergies to certain

**See also:** ANTIBODIES; BACTERIA; IMMUNE SYSTEMS; IMMUNOLOGY; PASTEUR, LOUIS; VIRUSES.

## Further reading:

Paoletti, Lawrence C., and Pamela M. McInnes, eds. 1999. *Vaccines: From Concept to Clinic. A Guide to the Development and Clinical Testing of Vaccines for Human Use.* Boca Raton, Fla.: CRC Press.

# IMMUNOLOGY

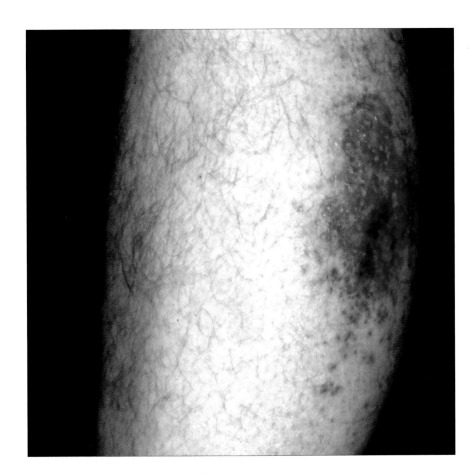

*The abrasion on this leg makes it susceptible to potentially dangerous infection. The human immune system helps safeguard against infection.*

## CONNECTIONS

● **ALLERGY** is an exaggerated immune response to certain antigens.

● Immunology is the study of the **IMMUNE SYSTEM**.

● **CHEMOTHERAPY** and radiotherapy, which are used to treat cancer, harm the performance of the immune system.

The study of immune systems is called immunology. The immune system protects vertebrates from foreign material that may damage cells. Potentially dangerous pathogens (disease-causing agents; see INFECTIOUS DISEASES), including viruses, bacteria, fungi, protozoa, and worms, constantly bombard the body, and the immune system defends against these unwelcome intruders. Vertebrate bodies must also deal with the appearance of abnormally developing cells that periodically appear and, if not eliminated, could develop into life-threatening cancerous tumors.

The first protective barrier to infection is the skin and the mucus lining of the lungs and stomach. These external barriers cannot normally be penetrated, but minute cuts and abrasions may allow the passage of unwanted objects. When these barriers are breached, the body's internal defense mechanisms must fight the invaders. The immune system responds in two ways: providing natural (innate) and acquired (adaptive) immunities.

## INNATE IMMUNITY
Innate defenses (sometimes called natural defenses) come into play very soon after the appearance of a pathogen in the body. Innate defenses are nonspecific and therefore target any invader. The skin is considered to be one level of innate protection, as are the cilia (hairlike structures), which sweep out airborne pathogens from the lungs. Bacteria-destroying enzymes (such as lysozyme) in tears, nasal secretions, and saliva are also innate, nonspecific defenses.

### The inflammatory response
The inflammatory response occurs when a body is injured or invaded by microorganisms. As the small blood vessels near the injury or infection dilate, the blood supply increases, and the result is the characteristic redness and heat. The blood vessels also become more permeable, and fluids move from the blood into the tissue and thus cause swelling.

The inflammatory response is initiated by chemical signals. One of these chemicals is called histamine. Histamine is contained in certain cells in the blood and connective tissue and is released when these cells are damaged. Other chemicals that promote blood flow to the site are also released. Blood leaking from the wound clots (forms a scab). Clotting is the first stage in repairing the damage to the body. The scab also blocks any pathogens from getting through the skin. Pus that accumulates at the site of an infection consists of dead cells and the fluid leaked from the capillaries during the inflammatory response.

### Phagocytes
When pathogens do penetrate the external barriers, white blood cells called phagocytes (meaning "cell eaters") are the first to wage war on the intruders. These specialized cells are the rapid deployment force; they migrate toward infected areas, attracted by chemical signals. When they arrive at the infected site, phagocytes engulf the foreign invaders. Phagocytes also act as a holding force that keeps the infection at bay until the adaptive immune system has time to muster its forces. They also clean up dead cells and generally keep the body's fluids clean.

There are a number of phagocytic cells involved in innate immunity. However, the most important cells are neutrophils and macrophages. Neutrophils make up 60 to 70 percent of all white blood cells, while macrophages make up only 5 percent.

---

### CORE FACTS
■ There are two phases to the immunological response: innate immunity, which attacks all foreign bodies, and adaptive immunity, which targets specific invaders.
■ The body's first line of defense is the skin. When the skin is broken, the blood clots to fill the gap and thus stops anything from getting inside.
■ The main defenders of the body are white blood cells. These cells patrol the blood and lymph, destroying invaders. Some cells remember if the body has been attacked by a particular pathogen before and by doing so speed up their protective response.

Neutrophils live for only a few days and self-destruct when destroying pathogens. Macrophages (meaning "big eaters") are the largest phagocytic cells and, despite their relatively small numbers, provide effective defenses. These amoeba-like cells extend pseudopodia (false feet) that grab the pathogens and drag them inside the cell. Once enveloped by the macrophage, digestive enzymes destroy the pathogens.

However, many pathogens have evolved methods to counter the attacks of macrophages. Certain bacteria have capsules around them to which macrophages cannot attach, while others have evolved resistance to the digestive enzymes; some pathogens can even reproduce within the macrophage.

### The complement system

At least twenty proteins in the blood serum also play a role in the nonspecific immune response. These proteins make up the complement system and are named for their ability to complement or assist the activity of antibodies and augment the nonspecific attack against invading bacteria. Complement proteins have several functions: they play a regulatory role in the inflammation response, attract phagocytic cells, and cause lysis of cells that are coated with antibodies. One complement system pathway is activated in the presence of bacterial cell wall components. The result is production of a complement protein-derived membrane attack complex, which by punching holes in the invading bacteria's membranes, allows entry of enzymes that kill the bacteria. Several complement system proteins also activate phagocytes, and some of these cells produce additional complement components at the site of infection. Bacteria coated with complement proteins are more easily recognized by phagocytes, which carry specific receptors on their surfaces for complement proteins.

### Natural killer cells

A further type of white blood cell, the natural killer cell, also provides innate, nonspecific immunity. These cells do not attack microorganisms but the body's own infected cells, especially those harboring viruses. They also destroy abnormal body cells that could develop into tumors. Natural killer cells do not attack body cells by phagocytosis. Instead, they kill on contact. The killer binds to its target and then delivers a lethal burst of chemicals that produce holes in the target cell's surface membrane. Fluids seep in and leak out, causing the cell to burst. In several immunodeficiency diseases, including AIDS (acquired immune deficiency syndrome), natural killer cells do not work properly (see AIDS).

In the presence of certain microorganisms, macrophages produce endogenous pyrogen (Interleukin-1), which stimulates the anterior hypothalamus to produce prostaglandins. Prostaglandins are chemicals that raise the body temperature and produce fever. Some white blood cells of the immune system are more active at higher temperatures. Fever also speeds up phagacytosis and may speed up the repair of tissue.

## ADAPTIVE IMMUNITY

While pathogens are being assaulted by nonspecific defense mechanisms, other cells launch a specific immune response. While the innate system attacks pathogens in a general way, the body also targets specific pathogens, such as certain species of bacteria. This response is called the adaptive immune response.

Small white blood cells called lymphocytes are responsible for carrying out the activities of the adaptive immune system. There are approximately one trillion lymphocytes circulating in the human body. Almost all of these lymphocytes are produced by the bone marrow. Initially all lymphocytes are alike, but later they differentiate into two main types: B-cells and T-cells. B-cells further their development in the bone marrow, while T-cells mature in the thymus.

Mature B-cells and T-cells are most concentrated in lymphatic organs, such as the lymph nodes and the spleen. Both B-cells and T-cells are equipped with receptors on their plasma membranes, which recognize specific antigens. Any foreign substance that causes an immune response is called an antigen. Components of pathogenic microorganisms are antigenic and stimulate strong immune responses. Pollen, venom, transplanted organs, abnormal cells, and a variety of other substances are also antigens.

The specificity and diversity of the immune system relies on the lymphocyte receptors. When antigens bind to the receptors on the surface of the lymphocytes, the lymphocytes are activated to divide and differentiate, giving rise to a population of effector cells (or clones). Effector cells defend the body in the immune response. The effector cells of B-cells are called plasma cells, and they secrete antibodies. Effector cells of T-cells can be one of two types: cytotoxic T-cells, which kill infected cells and cancer cells, or T-helper cells, which secrete chemicals that regulate the actions of B- and T-cells. T-helper cells play a vital role in controlling adaptive immunity.

Just as there are two types of cells that provide different defensive functions, adaptive immunity can be divided into two types: humoral immunity and

*Scanning electron micrograph of lung cilia. These fine hairlike projections sweep out much unwanted airborne material. Along with the lung's mucosal lining, cilia help to protect the lungs from damage and infection.*

cellular immunity. Humoral immunity employs B-cells to secrete soluble proteins called antibodies into the body's fluids, or humors. These antibodies interact with circulating antigens, such as bacteria and toxic molecules but are unable to penetrate living cells. Humoral immunity relies on the indirect action of B-cells via the antibodies they produce. These antibodies bind to foreign antigens and neutralize their toxic effects or target the invading antigen for destruction. In contrast, cellular immunity uses T-cells to eliminate foreign material by attacking body cells that have been hijacked by viruses or changed into cancerous cells. Cellular immunity depends on the direct action of T-cells.

## Immunological memory

The immune system can remember antigens it has encountered before; it is extremely quick to attack bacteria or viruses that have previously infected the person. This characteristic is called acquired immunity. When an antigen invades for the first time, lymphocytes multiply to form effector cells. This response is called the primary immune response. The time between the initial exposure to the antigen and the maximum production of effector cells is 5 to 10 days. If at a later date the body is exposed to the same antigen, the response is faster (1 to 2 days), and the quantity of antibody is much greater owing to larger effector cell numbers. This response is the secondary immune response. The antibodies produced at this stage are also more efficient at binding to the antigen than those produced by the primary response.

The immune system's ability to remember a previously encountered antigen, called immunological memory, is due to memory cells, which are produced on initial antigen exposure along with effector cells. These memory cells are long-lived and remain inactive until they are again exposed to the antigen. On second exposure to the same antigen, the memory cells proliferate rapidly, giving rise to new memory cells and new effector cells. This mechanism prevents people from catching the same disease twice. A childhood infection of chicken pox, therefore, leads to lifetime immunity. With the common cold, on the other hand, there are over 200 different viral strains. Although a person is unlikely to be infected by the same strain again, there are plenty of other cold viruses around for him or her to catch.

## Active and passive immunity

The immunity created from recovering from a bout of chicken pox is called active immunity because it relies on the response of the body's' own immune systems. Active immunity can also be acquired artificially by vaccination. Vaccines are usually inactivated bacterial toxins, dead microorganisms, or living but weakened (attenuated) microorganisms. They no longer cause disease but retain the antigen and stimulate an immune response. Therefore, if a pathogen invades at a later date, the immune

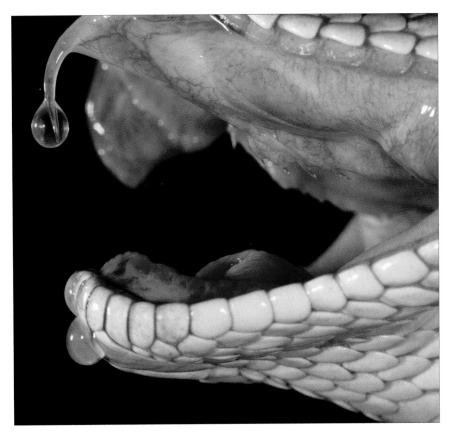

*Snake venom is a powerful and potentially lethal antigen. Such antigens provoke an adaptive immune response from the lymphatic system.*

system will recognize the invader and launch a fast secondary immune response against it.

Passive immunity occurs when antibodies are transferred from one individual to another, as occurs naturally between a mother and her baby in the womb. Antibodies produced in the mother's body are passed across the placenta, and the fetus gains temporary immunity to whatever diseases the mother is immune to. Passive immunity is also transferred through the mother's milk. This immunity persists for only a few months and then fades, as the child's own immune system starts to develop.

Passive immunity can also be transferred artificially, as in the case of the rabies vaccine. Rabies infections are treated with an injection of antibodies taken from a person who has already been vaccinated against the disease. This approach gives temporary immunity. The onset of rabies is extremely rapid, and without the vaccine the infected person's immune system would not have time to cope with the disease. The person would die before his or her body could produce its own antibodies.

## Self-nonself recognition

The immune system also has the ability to distinguish between the molecules of the body and foreign molecules. This ability is extremely important because the body would not be able to defend against invaders if it could not tell them apart from its own cells. Failure of self and nonself recognition can lead to autoimmune diseases, where the immune system starts attacking healthy body cells.

The lymphocytes called B-cells and T-cells are responsible for destroying foreign invaders, but how do these cells distinguish foreign antigens?

*Transplanted organs, such as this heart, trigger an immune response in the patient, as the tissue is foreign to its new body. It is most often for this reason, rather than for surgical ones, that many organ transplants are unsuccessful. The immune system can reject the new organ and prevent it from functioning properly.*

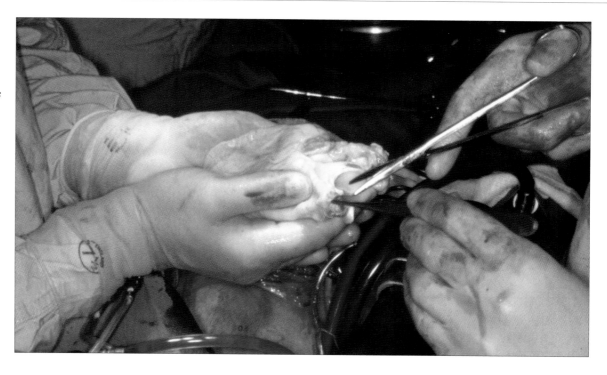

Discovering the antigen and therefore detecting non-self objects is carried out by antigen receptors on the lymphocytes' surfaces. Normally there are no lymphocytes that act against the body's own molecules. This self-tolerance develops as the B- and T-lymphocytes are maturing. Any lymphocytes that are produced with antigen receptors for the body's own cells are destroyed, leaving only lymphocytes that attack nonself cells.

Body cells also have self-marker molecules (self antigens) on their surface. These molecules are encoded by a family of genes called the major histocompatibility complex (MHC). MHC was discovered during the course of tissue transplantation experiments. As MHC genes and the molecules they encode vary widely from one individual to another, transplanted organs are very likely to be identified as foreign and rejected by the immune system. Only in the case of a transplant between identical twins would the MHC genes be the same and the tissue or organ not be rejected by the immune system.

## Transplants

Despite differences in the MHC, it is possible to transfer a variety of tissues and organs, including kidneys, hearts, and lungs, from a healthy donor to an ailing recipient. However, organ transplantation is difficult. Foreign MHC molecules are antigenic and cause the T-cells to mount a cellular immune response against the transplanted organ. The immune defense overrules the fact that the organ is needed for the body's continued survival. Successful

## AIDS

Acquired immune deficiency syndrome (AIDS) is perhaps one of the most devastating immune diseases of recent years. It was first recognized in the United States in 1981, following a sharp rise in cases of cancer and pneumonia, normally only contracted by patients who are severely immunosuppressed. By 1983 the agent that caused this immune deficiency was identified as a virus that made infected individuals vulnerable to illnesses that the healthy immune system would normally overcome with ease. The main targets of the virus are T-helper cells. The virus enters these cells and replicates inside them. The newly formed viruses then leave the host cell and infect other T-helper cells. As T-helper cells play a vital role in regulating cellular and humoral immunity, their disruption essentially paralyzes the adaptive immune system. The virus also impedes some B-cells, macrophages, and natural killer cells.

HIV escapes the attack of the immune system because it affects the white blood cells involved in immune defense and also because it remains virtually invisible for years after the initial infection by inserting a DNA copy of the viral genome into the genome (genetic material) of the host cell, forming a provirus. Another important factor is that HIV is continually changing its genetic sequence and constantly altering viral-encoded antigens so that immunological memory of the invader is useless. The virus has an extremely high mutation rate, so when it replicates, it accumulates nucleotide changes. The immune system is therefore constantly battling with what it sees as different viruses. Eventually, the immune system is overwhelmed by an accumulation of new and different antigens, the number of T-helper cells drops drastically, and the cellular immunity collapses, allowing opportunistic diseases or cancer to take hold.

AIDS is the name given to the late stages of HIV infection. The virus may have an extremely long incubation period, from 10 to 40 years, but death is the eventual result unless the later stages of the disease are held off with continued medication to halt virus reproduction. HIV is contracted primarily through sexual contact and requires the transfer of bodily fluids such as blood or semen. Unprotected sex and drug users sharing needles account for most of the AIDS cases reported in the United States and Europe.

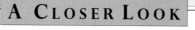

A CLOSER LOOK

transplantation depends on the similarities between the recipient's and the donor's MHC. To minimize rejection, attempts are made to closely match the MHC of the donor and recipient. Drugs are also used to suppress the recipient's immune response; the disadvantage of this suppression is that the recipient is then more vulnerable to infection.

## Privileged immunity

A fetus developing in the mother's womb carrying foreign antigens (inherited from the father) is not rejected by the mother's immune system. Why do the foreign antigens not trigger rejection? The answer is that the mother's uterus is an "immunologically privileged" site, where immune responses are subdued. Scientists do not fully understand how the rejection response is restrained, but there are a number of theories. One theory is that the developing child produces a protective substance against the mother's antibodies. The uterus may further produce a substance to help disguise fetal antigens. It has also been suggested that the embryo may be shielded from the mother's immune system by not expressing its antigens. Whatever the reason, the separation of mother and child is not perfect. Mothers can produce antibodies against their fetus. This situation is common when the baby carries a surface antigen on its red blood cells, called Rh factor (inherited from the father), that is not found on the mother's red cells. The production of maternal antibodies against the fetus does not usually cause problems in the first pregnancy, but the memory cells produce a much stronger reaction for a second pregnancy, and the increased production of antibody could put the fetus in danger. This problem can be prevented by tying up the maternal antibody before it reacts with the child, by injecting anti-Rh factor antibodies into the mother's bloodstream during and after the pregnancy.

## IMMUNOLOGICAL DISEASES

The immune system's job is to regulate the body's internal environment, by helping to remove foreign agents and abnormal or worn out cells. It protects the body, promotes good health, and prolongs survival. However, under certain circumstances the immune system may bring more harm than it does good, as in organ transplant rejection. What happens, therefore, when the immune system starts to go wrong and makes inappropriate immune responses that are excessive, insufficient, or misdirected?

## Hypersensitivity

The most common immune disorder is an unusually strong immune response (hypersensitivity) to antigens that should be harmless. Antigens that most commonly cause hypersensitivity reactions are dust, pollen, and animal fur. While some people are hypersensitive to insect stings, others are hypersensitive to medications and certain foods and food additives. There are four classifications of hypersensitivity based on the immunological events that occur

### KEY FEATURES OF THE IMMUNE SYSTEM

The immune system can recognize and eliminate microorganisms and other foreign material. It produces antibodies and activates lymphocytes to launch an attack on intruding antigens. The antigens that trigger the immune response are chemical substances (proteins, polysaccharides, and other macromolecules) on the invaders that are recognized as foreign. Each antigen has a very specific molecular shape, which stimulates the production of an exact type of antibody that can bind to that antigen. Thus, the immune response is extremely specific and highly efficient. The immune system also has the ability to recognize millions of different types of invaders. This diverse response is possible because of the huge number of lymphocytes present, each with receptors for a particular antigen.

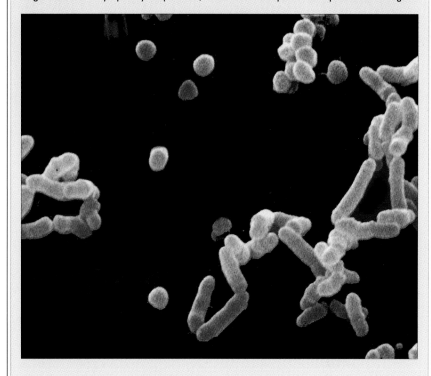

*Rod-shaped bacteria are attacked by lymphcytes. Lymphocytes with receptors specific to the particular bacteria bind to and kill the bacteria (cluster, top right).*

## A CLOSER LOOK

for each type. One kind of type 1 hypersensitivity is commonly referred to as allergy. Allergic reactions usually take place after the second exposure to a particular antigen, known as the allergen. The symptoms of allergy are related to the point of entry of the allergen and vary from merely annoying symptoms, such as itchy eyes and a runny nose, to life-threatening anaphylactic shock responses that may result in death from circulatory collapse or respiratory failure.

Most of these symptoms are caused by a particular kind of immune system cell found in connective tissue, called a mast cell. Mast cells contain granules of histamine and other chemicals that regulate the inflammatory response. During an allergic response, the chemicals released by mast cells cause anaphylaxis, a family of responses that includes smooth muscle contraction, dilation of blood vessels, coughing, sneezing, congestion, itching, and watery eyes. Severe anaphylaxis can be life threatening. Simple skin tests are performed to determine

# THE LYMPHATIC SYSTEM

The body's defensive cells need an efficient transport system if they are to effectively tackle disease. Two transport systems are involved: the circulatory (blood) system and the lymphatic system. The lymphatic system is the main defensive highway and is patrolled by phagocyte and lymphocyte defenders. This network of vessels is spread throughout the body; it is similar to the circulatory system and almost as extensive. However, the flow of lymphatic fluid is slower than blood because its movement relies on external pressure from muscle contraction and respiratory movements rather than a heart pumping it along.

The lymphatic system keeps the environment around the body's cells constant. All cells are bathed in interstitial fluid, which is transported in the lymphatic vessels and delivered back into the bloodstream. Once the interstitial fluid enters the lymphatic vessels, it is called lymph, a milky fluid similar to blood in content, but without any red blood cells. However, lymph does contain lots of waste material, bacteria, and dead cells collected from between the body's living cells.

As lymph flows through the lymphatic vessels, it passes through a variety of defensive filters called lymph nodes, which sieve out and destroy the bacteria, toxins, and dead cells. The lymph nodes house a high concentration of phagocytes and lymphocytes that attack the pathogens present in the lymph. There are more than 100 tiny oval lymph nodes scattered along the lymph vessels, although they tend to be clustered at points where the lymphatic vessels converge, in the neck, groin, and armpits. They

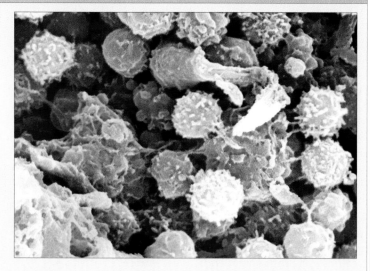

*Microscopic lymphocytes—a type of white blood cells—among a network of connective tissue in one of the body's lymph nodes.*

are generally pea sized but swell up when fighting infection. In addition to the lymphatic vessels and nodes, there are a variety of organs that are important in the body's defense system, including the thymus, adenoids, tonsils, appendix, and the largest lymphoid tissue, the spleen.

## A CLOSER LOOK

which allergens should be avoided by an allergic individual. Autoimmunity is a misdirected immune response. The immune system malfunctions, producing abnormal antibodies or white blood cells that attack and destroy the body's own tissues. There are a variety of autoimmune diseases, including rheumatoid arthritis, a crippling autoimmune disorder in which the immune system slowly destroys the cartilage and bone in joints. Multiple sclerosis, anemia, and certain types of diabetes are also autoimmune disorders.

### Immune deficiency
In contrast to overactive or misdirected immune responses, an underactive immune system can also be harmful. In someone who is immunodeficient, the mechanisms that combat disease are in a weakened state and thus allow pathogens to cause damage to the body. Immune deficiency can be congenital (present at birth) or acquired (appearing later in life). Congenital deficiencies involve the failure of the immune system to develop properly, while acquired deficiencies are the consequence of damage to the immune system later in life. For example, certain cancers, such as Hodgkin's disease, damage the lymphatic system and make the person more susceptible to infections. The viral disease AIDS causes severe depression of the immune system. Immunosuppressant drugs that are used in organ transplants may also cause immune deficiency, while

chemotherapy and radiotherapy, used to treat cancer, also impair the immune system's performance.

There is growing evidence that physical and emotional stress have suppressing effects on immunity. Hormones that are secreted during stress have also been shown to affect the numbers of white blood cells and may suppress the immune system in other ways. Networks of nerve fibers that penetrate deep into the lymphoid tissue, including the thymus, physically link the nervous system and the lymphatic system. Receptors for chemical signals secreted by nerve cells have been discovered on the surface of lymphocytes. It is even possible that chemicals secreted by nerve cells when a person is happy could have beneficial effects on immunity.

T. JACKSON

**See also:** AIDS; BACTERIA; BLOOD; CELL BIOLOGY; IMMUNE SYSTEMS; IMMUNIZATION; INFECTIOUS DISEASES; LYMPHATIC SYSTEMS; VIRUSES.

**Further reading:**
Berger, W. E. 2000. *Allergies and Asthma for Dummies.* New York : John Wiley and Sons.
Clancy, John, Jr., ed. 1998. *Basic Concepts in Immunology: A Student's Survival Guide.* New York : McGraw-Hill, Health Professions Division.
Peakman, Mark, and Diego Vergani. 1997. *Basic and Clinical Immunology.* New York : Churchill Livingstone.

# INDIAN MEDICINE

**Indian medicine cares for the body and the mind, using massage, exercise, food, and herbs to treat disease**

An American visiting a practitioner of Indian medicine for the first time might wonder about the purpose of the practitioner's questions. Do you like your showers hot or cold? Do you prefer hot soup or cold yogurt? Are you a light eater or a hearty one? The physician is trying to determine whether the patient's type is earth (kapha), air (vata), or fire (pitta), so he or she will know which foods, herbal medicines, massages, and exercises to prescribe.

While this concept is new to many Americans, the principles of Indian medicine date back to the 2nd millennium BCE, and thus, it is one of the world's oldest systems of medicine.

For centuries, Indian medicine was virtually unknown outside southern Asia. Then, during the 1980s, it was taken up by practitioners in Western nations, as many people, frustrated with the impersonal nature of conventional (allopathic) medicine, began seeking alternative therapies. Indian medicine's appeal lies in its emphasis on disease prevention through the nurturing of the body and the mind.

## Rooted in religious beliefs

Indian medicine comprises three principal disciplines —ayurveda, siddha, and unani. The most widespread is ayurveda (pronounced *eye-yuhr-VAY'-dah*), which means "science of long life" (from *ayur*, meaning "life," and *veda*, meaning "knowledge"). It is the only Hindu tradition that has taken root outside southern Asia. In the United States, best-selling books have been written by the ayurveda specialist Deepak Chopra, and thousands of people have

*A traditional village doctor uses diagnostic methods similar to mainstream Western medicine but prescribes herbal preparations as remedies.*

## CONNECTIONS

● Other alternative therapies, such as **HOMEOPATHY** and **HERBAL MEDICINE,** also use plants in their treatments.

● Many ayurvedic practitioners also rely on conventional **MEDICINE.**

## CORE FACTS

- Indian medicine began in the 2nd millenium BCE, and is one of the oldest systems of medicine in the world.
- The main concept behind Indian medicine is the care of the mind and the entire body.
- Indian medicine can be divided into three main disciplines: ayurveda, unani, and siddha, of which ayurveda is the most widespread.
- Indian medicine is now practiced alongside conventional medicine in southern Asia but remains unrecognized in the United States.

## AYURVEDA IN THE UNITED STATES

Deepak Chopra, a U.S. physician born in New Delhi, is often credited with introducing ayurveda to the United States. He has proclaimed the virtues of the Hindu science in several popular books, including his 1993 bestseller, *Ageless Body, Timeless Mind*. Chopra also directs the Maharishi Ayurveda Health Center for Stress Management and Behavioral Medicine in Lancaster, Massachusetts, and holds frequent seminars on ayurvedic medicine.

Chopra's regimen of diet, massage, herbs, meditation, and exercise is designed to relieve the stress that plagues many Americans. His diagnoses are based in part on patients' answers to questions about their lifestyle. Those who are creative, worrisome, easily fatigued, and averse to the cold are said to be vata types. Pitta personalities are more ambitious and outgoing and tend toward early graying or baldness. Kaphas are generally loving, calm, tolerant, and prone to obesity.

After a long struggle for acceptance in the medical community, Chopra managed to have an article promoting ayurvedic medicine published in 1991 in the highly respected *Journal of the American Medical Association*. However, Chopra and his unorthodox practices were later condemned by the journal. The editors pointed out that the herbs, massage oils, and meditation classes that Chopra prescribed generated profits for organizations with which he was involved.

In spite of the journal's opposition, interest in ayurveda in the United States continued to rise. Enrolment in the country's first school of Indian medicine, the Ayurvedic Institute in New Mexico, has increased substantially from its opening in 1984, and approximately 200 students graduated from the year-long program during its first 10 years. Although the United States does not license ayurvedic practitioners, many graduates earn accepted medical credentials and incorporate ayurveda medicine in their practices.

### A CLOSER LOOK

attended his seminars and clinic in Massachusetts. The Ayurvedic Institute in Albuquerque, New Mexico, enables Americans to study Indian traditions, although the U.S. government does not yet recognize ayurvedic medicine as being efficacious.

Ayurveda evolved during Indian medicine's Vedic period, which began in the 2nd millennium BCE and ended around 800 BCE. Vedic medicine was based on the belief that diseases were caused by demons punishing people for their sins. Treatments were based on rituals to expel demons, and a doctor (shaman) would recite chants, give the patient medicinal herbs and vegetables, and perform a ceremonial bath designed to wash the demons from the body. Patients who believed the demons were being banished may indeed have recovered.

The concepts of early Indian medicine were found in sacred writings called Vedas. Indians believed the principles were given to Brahmans (wise men). From its earliest days, Indian medicine was concerned about more than physical health. Its main mission was to help foster spiritual enlightenment, as Hindus believed that humans could achieve their full potential only by having healthy bodies.

Ayurveda is based on the belief that all substances in the body arise from three *dosas*—vata, kapha, and pitta—which are akin to the Greek humors. Practitioners believe that perfect health can be attained only when all three dosas are balanced through a modest, unselfish lifestyle and a healthy diet.

Another important Indian medical tradition is siddha, which evolved from ayurveda in southern India and remains the major traditional system of medicine in this region. Like ayurveda, siddha holds that body and mind work together in sickness and health and that illness stems from an imbalance of the three dosas. A unique characteristic of siddha is that it uses the pulse in diagnosis. Siddha practitioners detect dosa imbalances by taking the pulse in each wrist, with three separate fingers. They claim that there are 600 different pulse readings, indicating a range of medical and psychological conditions.

Unani, the third Indian medical system, is an Islamic system based on Greek traditions. It is the major system in Pakistan and is also popular in northern India and Bangladesh. Muslim scientists adopted Greek practices when Islam conquered the Byzantine Empire in the 6th century CE. They began adapting their own practices, drawing from the traditions not only of the Greeks but also of the Chinese, Persians, and Egyptians.

Like the other Indian medical traditions, unani also emphasizes holistic diagnosis and treatment (the care of the entire patient in all aspects) and attributes disease to an imbalance in the body's substances. Unani, sometimes spelled yunani, flourished between the 8th and 13th centuries. The achievements of this era included the successful treatment of mental illness and the introduction of the licensing of women, who were probably the world's first female doctors. The fall of Baghdad in 1285 and the Western Caliphate in 1492 brought an end to unani's golden era. By the 19th century, it had become limited largely to the Indian subcontinent.

### Current medical practices in southern Asia

Allopathic biomedical practitioners now work alongside traditional Indian doctors throughout southern Asia. Specialists in ayurveda and unani train in medical colleges like their counterparts in the West. They have adopted many biomedical practices, particularly the use of synthetic drugs.

Physicians trained in modern biomedicine practice in major southern Asian cities. People who can afford biomedical treatment seek it when they believe their illness can be cured with surgery or drugs. Yet even wealthy people prefer traditional medicine for chronic, less specific complaints, such as rheumatism. Rural residents rarely have any choice but the local traditional healers.

C. WASHAM

**See also:** ALTERNATIVE MEDICINE.

### Further reading:
Chopra, D. 2001. *Perfect Health: The Complete Mind-Body Guide.* New York: Crown Publishing.
Ninivaggi, F. J. 2001. *An Elementary Textbook of Ayurveda: Medicine With a Six-Thousand-Year-Old Tradition.* Madison, Conn.: International Universities Press.

# INFECTIOUS DISEASES

Infectious diseases are illnesses caused by microorganisms such as viruses, bacteria, protists, and fungi

Microorganisms that invade the body cause infectious diseases, which are transmitted in various ways. In developed countries, most infectious diseases are spread by airborne transmission, direct skin contact, bloodborne transmission, or sexual contact. In developing countries, where infectious diseases are a major cause of death, insectborne, waterborne, and foodborne infection are common modes of transmission. In addition, some infections can cross the placenta from an infected mother to her unborn baby.

In developed countries, the number of cases of infectious diseases has decreased significantly over the last century owing to improved hygiene, pest control, sanitation, and water purification; effective drugs, such as antibiotics and other antimicrobials that can destroy disease-causing organisms; immunization, which provides immunity against many infections; and improvement in standards of nutrition, which has strengthened people's immune system.

In addition to microorganisms, larger organisms such as flukes and roundworms can also cause disease in humans. Together with external parasites, such as lice and scabies, these colonizations are called infestations rather than infections (see PARASITES).

## Insect- and arachnid-borne infections
Insects and arachnids (a group of eight-legged arthropods that includes spiders, ticks, and mites) carry diseases but do not usually cause them. A mosquito, for example, can carry the protozoa (single-celled protists) that cause malaria and inject them into the victim's blood through its bite. Such carriers are called vectors. When the pathogen (disease-causing microorganism) grows or reproduces in the insect or arachnid, the carrier is called a biological vector. When the carrier simply spreads pathogens by picking them up on its feet and body, it is called a mechanical vector. Many types of flies are mechanical vectors; by picking up microorganisms from feces and then landing on food, they spread disease-causing organisms. This mode of transmission commonly spreads intestinal infections.

*A health worker demonstrates how a latrine works to village sanitation workers in Tamil Nadu, India.*

## CONNECTIONS

● **PESTICIDES** are used to eradicate **INSECTS** and **ARACHNIDS**.

● **VIRUSES, BACTERIA, PROTISTS,** and **FUNGI** can cause disease in humans.

● **ANTIBIOTICS AND ANTIMICROBIALS** are used to treat many infectious diseases.

## CORE FACTS
■ Vectors are animals that transmit infectious diseases.
■ Diseases can be caused by viruses, bacteria, protists, and fungi.
■ In developing countries, most infectious diseases are transmitted by insects and contaminated water and food.
■ In developed countries, most infectious diseases are transmitted by airborne droplets from or skin contact with an infected person.

*An engorged deer tick feeds on its host. Its biting mouthparts, embedded in the animal, can easily spread infectious diseases from one host to another.*

Serious infectious illnesses spread by insects acting as biological vectors include malaria and filariasis, which are both transmitted by mosquitoes; sleeping sickness, which is transmitted by tsetse flies; leishmaniasis, which is transmitted by sand flies; epidemic typhus, which is transmitted by lice; and plague, which is spread by rat fleas (see the box on page 950). In addition, various arthropods, including mosquitoes, sand flies, and ticks, transmit arboviruses, which cause diseases such as yellow fever, dengue, and some types of viral encephalitis.

About 30 species of anopheles mosquitoes can carry plasmodia, the single-celled protozoa that cause malaria. Worldwide, this disease affects more than 200 million people annually and kills about 2 million, mostly children. Four species of plasmodia affect humans.

The protozoa reproduce inside the mosquito, and stages in the life-cycle called sporozoites migrate to the insect's salivary gland, exiting the insect when it bites. Once in the host's bloodstream, the sporozoites travel to the liver, invade the cells, and reproduce. The swollen liver cells burst, spilling the malarial parasites into the host's blood. These parasites then infect red blood cells and multiply again. The red blood cells rupture, releasing the parasites into the bloodstream to infect more red blood cells. Symptoms coincide with the rupture of the blood cells and include chills, fever, and sweating.

Culex mosquitoes transmit filariasis, a group of tropical diseases caused by various nematodes (parasitic worms) and their larvae. Symptoms of certain types of filariasis include massive disfiguring swellings—called elephantiasis—in the limbs or scrotum.

Tsetse flies are bloodsuckers that carry African trypanosomiasis, also called sleeping sickness. This disease is caused by the protozoan parasite *Trypanosoma brucei*. The parasites multiply in a victim's blood and lymph vessels. The infection is characterized by a feverish illness, followed by progressive damage to the nervous system, coma, and death.

The bites of infected sand flies can transmit leishmania protozoa, which cause leishmaniasis. The most serious form of the disease, which occurs in some parts of Asia, Africa, South America, and the Mediterranean, causes an enlarged spleen and anemia and is fatal if not treated.

Reduviid (assassin) bugs transmit the disease American trypanosomiasis, or Chagas' disease. These insects, also called kissing bugs because they bite people on the lips, become infected by sucking blood from people or animals carrying *Trypanosoma cruzi*, a parasitic protozoan. The parasite multiplies in the bug's gut and is deposited on human skin when the bugs come to feed on blood. The parasite enters the body through tears that the bug makes in the skin or mucous membranes. Over time, *T. cruzi* damages the host's heart and intestines.

The body louse *Pediculus humanus corporis* acts as a vector for diseases such as relapsing fever (which is caused by the bacterium *Borrelia recurrentis*), epidemic typhus (caused by the rickettsia *Rickettsia prowazekii*), and trench fever (caused by the rickettsia *Rochalimaea quintana*; (see the box on page 950). Rickettsia are parasitic bacteria that live inside cells and invade small blood vessels, where they multiply. In severe cases, blood vessels collapse and the blood pools in spaces between the vessels.

Ticks are blood-feeding arachnids. They are about 0.1 inch (3 mm) in length but become much bigger once they have fed and are bloated with blood. They can spread infectious microorganisms from animals to humans by their bites and are responsible for transmitting the following rickettsial infections: ehrlichosis (due to *Ehrlichia* strains) , Q fever (due to *Coxiella burnetti*), tick typhus (due to *Rickettsia conori* ), and Rocky Mountain spotted fever (due to *Rickettsia rickettsii*). Ticks also spread other bacterial infections, most notably Lyme disease (due to *Borrelia burgdorferi*) and tularemia (due to *Francisella* strains), and the protozoal infection babesiosis (due to *Babesia* species). Most tick-borne infections produce flulike symptoms, including fever, chills, nausea and vomiting, headache, muscle pains, and often, a characteristic rash.

Viral infections spread by arthropods are called arboviral diseases. They include many tropical diseases such as yellow fever, dengue fever, and West Nile virus, which has recently started to make some impact in the United States (see the box below). Arboviral diseases often cause encephalitis (swelling of the brain). The virus responsible for yellow fever is transmitted to humans by certain mosquitoes, such as *Aedies aegypti*. Yellow fever causes severe jaundice, in which the skin turns bright yellow, and can be fatal in up to 50 percent of cases. In dengue fever, also called breakbone fever, which is again spread by the bites of infected *Aedes aegypti* mosquitoes, the symptoms include fever, headache, back pain, muscle ache, and joint pain.

In addition to arthropods, other animals can transmit disease. For example, a person can develop rabies if bitten by a mammal such as a dog carrying the rabies virus.

## WEST NILE VIRUS

West Nile virus is an arboviral infection (a viral disease transmitted by insects and other arthropods) that is emerging in the Western Hemisphere. First identified in Uganda in 1937, the infection is most common in Africa, Eastern Europe, West Asia, and the Middle East, and since the early summer of 1999, the United States. By mid-2002, there had been almost 200 confirmed cases of West Nile virus infection in people in the United States, many of these cases in the New York area. Eighteen of the cases resulted in death.

West Nile virus is transmitted from infected animals, including birds, to humans by mosquito bites (the virus is located in the insect's salivary glands), such as from Culex mosquitoes. The incubation time for symptoms to appear is between 3 and 15 days after being bitten. In most cases, the infection causes no symptoms or a mild flulike illness. However, in rare cases, life-threatening inflammation of the brain, called viral encephalitis, develops, usually in elderly people or those with a weakened immunity. Symptoms may then include headache, high fever, disorientation, tremors, convulsions, paralysis, and coma. Animals known to become infected with and killed by West Nile virus include horses, cats, bats, rabbits, squirrels, and wild game.

There is no specific treatment for the West Nile virus in humans. Serious cases of the disease usually involve intensive care in the hospital. At present, several biotechnical companies are working toward developing a vaccine to prevent the disease.

## AT RISK

*Natural disasters, such as flooding (pictured above), often lead to large-scale waterborne disease epidemics because drinking water supplies become contaminated and sanitary conditions decline.*

## Airborne infections

Many diseases can be spread by the inhalation of airborne droplets containing infectious organisms that have been exhaled, coughed, sneezed, or even discharged through speaking. Infection may even be picked up from contaminated dust. Common viral infections transmitted by inhaling airborne droplets include chicken pox, which is caused by the varicella-zoster virus; the common cold, which is caused by many rhinoviruses and coronaviruses (see COLD, COMMON); and influenza, commonly called flu.

Chicken pox produces an itchy rash and can be serious in adults. The virus lies dormant in the nerves and can resurface in later life as a painful rash called herpes zoster, or shingles. Other viral illnesses that can be spread by droplets include measles, mumps, rubella, which is also called German measles, and poliomyelitis; all these infections can be prevented by immunization (see IMMUNIZATION). In addition, the disease of animals, foot-and-mouth disease, is transmitted by air (see the box opposite, top right).

## ANATOMY OF A WATERBORNE DISEASE OUTBREAK

In 1993 residents of the area in and around Milwaukee, Wisconsin, were the victims of an outbreak of cryptosporidiosis, an infection caused by the protozoan Cryptosporidium. In March of that year, residents noticed that their water seemed cloudy and tasted off and had a noticeable odor. By early April, many residents had diarrhea, and pharmacies began selling out of antidiarrheal medicines. Examination of stool samples revealed the protozoal culprit, which is usually a common cause of diarrhea in calves. Health officials found high levels of the organism in one of the city's two water-treatment plants and issued an advisory note to boil all water.

Over 400,000 people became ill with the infection in the Milwaukee area, more than 4,000 were hospitalized, and 54 died. Officials suspect that runoff from dairy farms was responsible for the high levels of the protozoan in the water supply. The water-treatment plant had misused a new type of coagulant that should have gotten rid of most of the protozoa. It is thought that the protozoa, cysts, which are resistant to chlorine, slipped through the filtration system and contaminated the city's water supply.

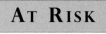

Bacterial infections spread by airborne droplets include pertussis, pneumonia, and tuberculosis. Pertussis, or whooping cough, is caused by the microorganism *Bordetella pertussis* and is now rare in developed countries owing to routine immunization. Pneumonia (inflammation of the lungs) can be caused by the bacterium *Streptococcus pneumoniae*; it can also be caused by other infectious agents, such as certain viruses. Tuberculosis (TB) is caused by *Mycobacterium tuberculosis*. Worldwide, TB is the most fatal bacterial infection in adults. In recent years, there has been a resurgence in TB because drug-resistant strains of *M. tuberculosis* have evolved, and also people with HIV infection and AIDS are more susceptible to TB because their immunity is lowered (see TUBERCULOSIS).

Certain fungal infections can result from inhaling airborne fungal spores. These infections include aspergillosis (due to *Aspergillus* species), histoplasmosis (due to *Histoplasmosis capsulatum*), coccidioidomycosis (due to *Coccidioides immitus*), and blastomycosis (due to *Blastomyces dermatitidis*). These diseases are most common in people with reduced immunity, such as those with HIV infection and AIDS.

## Waterborne infections

Waterborne diseases occur when drinking, washing, or swimming water is untreated, improperly treated, or accidentally contaminated by disease-causing microorganisms. Waterborne diseases are common in developing countries, where sanitation is poor. In developed countries, occasional local outbreaks of waterborne disease occur. They also commonly occur after a natural disaster, such as a flood or earthquake, when sewer lines break or back up into the water supply.

Waterborne viral diseases include viral gastroenteritis (symptoms of which are vomiting, diarrhea, headache, and fever) caused by Norwalk and Norwalk-like viruses; hepatitis A, which causes flulike symptoms and liver damage; and poliomyelitis, commonly called polio, which has symptoms of sore throat but in less than one percent of cases affects the nervous system and causes paralysis. Polio has been eradicated in many areas of the world since the World Health Organization began widespread vaccination programs.

Waterborne bacterial diseases include cholera (caused by *Vibrio cholera*) and typhoid fever (caused by *Salmonella typhi*). Epidemics of these diseases are usually caused by drinking water contaminated with the feces of infected people. Cholera kills over 100,000 people each year in Africa and Asia. The infection leads to profuse diarrhea and dehydration. In typhoid fever, symptoms include diarrhea, a rash, headache, and fever. With treatment, the vast majority of people survive these infections.

Other disease-causing bacteria that are spread by contaminated water include *Legionella pneumophila* (which causes the serious pneumonia-like Legionnaire's disease) and various other bacteria such as *Campylobacter*, *Salmonella enteriditis*, *Shigella*, and

*Escherichia coli*, all of which cause what people often call "traveler's diarrhea."

Protozoan waterborne diseases include amebiasis (due to *Entamoeba histolytica*), giardiasis (due to *Giardia lamblia*), and cryptosporidiosis (due to *Cryptosporidium parvum*). These infections cause watery diarrhea. Amebiasis affects up to 500 million people worldwide and kills up to 100,000 yearly. Cryptosporidiosis is very serious in people with reduced immunity, such as those with HIV infection and AIDS. There are occasional outbreaks of these diseases in developed countries (see the box on page 948).

The prevention of waterborne disease requires good sanitation and a clean water supply that is adequately filtered and treated and regularly tested for the presence of disease-causing microorganisms.

## Foodborne infections
Foodborne infection may result from eating meat or milk from animals that harbored disease-causing microorganisms or from eating food that has picked up disease-causing microorganisms, usually as a result of flies acting as mechanical vectors and spreading microorganisms from feces. There are over six million cases a year of food poisoning in the United States. Most foodborne infections cause vomiting and diarrhea in those affected.

Many of the bacteria and viruses that can be transmitted in food, such as Norwalk viruses, *Salmonella*, *Campylobacter*, and *E. coli*, are also transmitted by water. Other bacteria include *Staphylococci*, *Clostridium botulinum*, which causes botulism, and *Listeria monocytogenes*, which causes listeriosis. The bacterium that causes listeriosis spreads to humans in contaminated soft cheeses, milk, patés, and salads; the disease is very serious in people with reduced immunity. Botulism is transmitted by eating contaminated preserved and canned food; a toxin produced by the bacteria damages the nervous system and causes paralysis.

Parasitic worms, such as tapeworms, can pass to humans who eat undercooked fish or meat that contains parasitic cysts (see PARASITES).

In addition, a very rare disorder called Creutzfeldt-Jakob disease (CJD), which is caused by an infectious protein called a prion, has been linked to eating beef from cattle with a disorder called bovine spongiform encephalopathy (BSE). CJD leads to progressive degeneration of the brain and is usually fatal within three years of diagnosis (see ANIMAL DISEASES; PRIONS). Most foodborne infections can be prevented by hygienic preparation and storage and correct cooking of food.

## Sexually transmitted infections
Certain infectious diseases, called sexually transmitted infections (STIs) are spread primarily by sexual intercourse. These diseases include the viral infections hepatitis B (caused by hepatitis B virus), genital warts (caused by papillomavirus), genital herpes (caused by herpes simplex virus), and HIV infection

and AIDS (caused by human immunodeficiency virus and also a bloodborne disease). Sexually transmitted bacterial infections include syphilis (caused by *Treponema pallidum*), gonorrhea (caused by *Neisseria gonorrhoeae*), and chlamydial infections (caused by various strains of *Chlamydia*).

## FOOT AND MOUTH DISEASE

Also called hoof-and-mouth disease, foot-and-mouth disease is a highly contagious viral disease of cloven-hoofed livestock, such as cattle, pigs, and sheep. The disease can be fatal, especially in young animals, but usually it leaves livestock debilitated and commercially unfit for meat and milk production. This disease very rarely affects humans, but they may act as carriers of the virus, which can remain in human nasal passages for up to 28 hours. The virus is also spread by movement of soil, for example, on tires, shoes, and animals' feet, and by air.

In February 2001 an epidemic of the disease began on a pig farm in the north of England. The strain responsible for the outbreak was identified as the Pan O Asian strain, which is believed to have originated in Asia. The disease spread rapidly around the United Kingdom and into some European countries. By the closing stages of the epidemic in September 2001, over six million animals had been slaughtered and burned in the United Kingdom.

An outbreak of hoof-and-mouth disease in the United States would cost the livestock industry billions of dollars. With the threat of the disease reaching the United States, the United States Department of Agriculture (USDA) banned the importation of livestock and meat products from Europe. Other measures, such as disinfecting the shoes of travelers coming into the country who had visited rural areas in Europe, were also carried out.

A vaccine does exist for hoof-and-mouth disease, but European countries do not use it for commercial reasons, although it is being considered: some countries free of the disease, such as the United States, do not import the meat of vaccinated animals because vaccinated animals may still be carriers of the virus.

### AT RISK

## LYME DISEASE

Ticks that normally live on deer transmit Lyme disease, which is caused by the bacterium *Borrelia burgdoferi* and was first recognized in patients in Old Lyme, Connecticut, in 1975. The disease exists in geographic ranges that contain ixodid ticks. *Ixodes dammini* is the principal vector in forests in the northeastern United States and in Wisconsin and Minnesota. The disease is also a problem in Europe, Russia, China, Japan, and Australia.

Transmission occurs when an infected tick becomes embedded in the skin and feeds for several hours. A red dot may appear at the site of the tick bite. This dot grows into a reddened area up to ¼ inch (5 mm) across. Symptoms may initially be flulike and include fever, headache, and muscle pain and may be followed by joint pain from inflammation, most commonly in the knees and other large joints. Left untreated, the disease can produce complications up to two years later, including meningitis (inflammation of the protective coverings of the brain and spinal cord) and arrhythmia (abnormal heartbeat). Arthritis may be a long-term effect of the infection.

The tick may also simultaneously transmit other pathogenic bacteria, such as strains of *Ehrlichia*, which can cause ehrlichiosis. This infection also produces flulike symptoms, joint pains, and sometimes a rash. Rarely complications occur, such as anemia or damage to the liver, lungs, kidneys, and nervous system.

Early treatment with antibiotics soon after the bite minimizes the risk of complications. Vaccines are now available against Lyme disease. People who work, camp, or walk in tick-infested wooded regions should keep their arms and legs well covered to reduce the risk of being bitten by ticks.

## TRENCH FEVER

Trench fever is now a rare disease. It used to be common among louse-infested soldiers fighting in World War I and World War II, especially those living in overcrowded and unhygienic conditions—such as in the trenches. The disease is caused by the rickettsia (a small type of bacterium) *Rochalimaea quintana*, which is carried by body lice (*Pediculus humanus corporis*). Body lice, which live in clothing worn close to the body, only come onto the body to feed on blood. When feeding, infected lice release *R. quintana* in their feces. Infection is transmitted when louse feces, which are left on the skin during feeding, are scratched or rubbed into the wound left by the bites of the lice. The symptoms of trench fever include pain behind the eyes, in the legs, and in the back. In some cases, it also produces a rash. The infection can be treated successfully with antibiotics.

infestation with the mite *Sarcoptes scabiei* burrowing under the skin to lay eggs; and ringworm, an infection caused by dermatophyte fungi that produce red, scaling areas of skin, often with a central healed area, hence the ring shape. Ringworm can also be caught from contact with affected animals.

### Across the placenta

Some infections can cross the placenta, including HIV infection, gonorrhea, and rubella. Fetuses affected by the rubella virus may be born with severe defects, such as deafness, heart disease, learning difficulties, cataracts (clouding of the lens of the eyes), and cerebral palsy (movement and posture problems caused by brain damage).

JOLYON GODDARD

Trichomoniasis is another STI, caused by the protozoan *Trichomonas vaginalis*. In addition, infestation with the insect pubic louse (*Phthirus pubis*) is also considered an STI. Many STIs can be prevented by practicing safe sex, including the use of condoms. Contact tracing, in which the sexual partners of people with STIs are traced and urged to be examined and treated, is an essential part in the management of STIs.

### Infections transmitted by skin contact

Some infections are transmitted by direct contact with skin. These infections include chicken pox and impetigo, in which bacteria—often staphylococci—enter cracks in the skin to form fluid-filled blisters; scabies, in which intense itching occurs due to

**See also:** ANIMAL DISEASES; ARTHROPODS; COLD, COMMON; IMMUNE SYSTEMS; IMMUNIZATION; PARASITES; PRIONS; TUBERCULOSIS.

### Further reading:

Farrel, J. 1998. *Invisible Enemies: Stories of Infectious Disease.* New York: Farrer, Straus, and Giroux.
Garret, L. 1995. *The Coming Plague: Newly Emerging Diseases in a World out of Balance.* New York: Penguin.
Holloway, M. 2001. Outbreak not contained. *Scientific American* (April): 20–22.
Honigsbaum, Mark. 2002. *The Fever Trail: In Search of the Cure for Malaria.* New York: Farrar, Straus, and Giroux.

## PLAGUE

Plague is a serious disease and its cause—the bacterium *Yersinia pestis*—was discovered in 1894 by Swiss scientist Alexandre Yersin. The disease predominantly affects rodents, such as rats, but can be passed on to humans by the bites of infected fleas that live on the rodents.

There are two principal types of plague: bubonic plague, in which the lymph nodes swell, become dark and painful (called buboes), and often bleed; and pneumonic plague. In pneumonic plague, the lungs are affected, and this type can spread between people by coughed-up airborne particles containing *Y. pestis*. Symptoms of pneumonic plague include severe coughing that produces a bloody, frothy sputum and breathing difficulties. Both types of plague produce fever and chills.

The Black Death,which killed over 25 million people (a third of the population) in the 14th century, and the epidemics that followed every 10 to 15 years for the next three centuries are thought to have been plague. However, some researchers have recently challenged the idea that *Y. pestis* was the cause of the Black Death. By studying old records, they believe it spread too fast for a rat and flea-borne disease. Researchers suggest that it may have been a viral disease with symptoms similar to those of bubonic plague that spread from person to person probably via airborne droplets. Reservoirs of bubonic plague still exist in Asia and North America; there are about 10 cases a year in the United States. Eliminating the fleas that carry the disease is difficult.

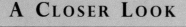

A CLOSER LOOK

# INFLUENZA

**Influenza is a common infectious respiratory disease caused by rapidly mutating viral strains**

Coughing, headaches, muscle pain, aching joints, fever—most people have suffered the symptoms of influenza at some time. There are between 10,000 and 40,000 deaths attributable to this highly contagious disease every year, and worldwide outbreaks (pandemics) can kill millions. Influenzas are caused by a group of viruses called the orthomyoxoviruses. Because these viruses mutate rapidly, their genetic material (RNA or DNA) changes and thus outmaneuvers the body's the immune system; as a result an individual can catch flu many times, each time from a different strain of the virus.

The illness starts with a short incubation period, in which the virus replicates in the trachea (windpipe), followed by the onset of headache, painful joints and muscles, and fever severe enough for most people to have to go to bed. Respiratory symptoms, such as bronchitis and coughing, may persist for weeks, especially in people with asthma.

Influenza can spread very rapidly, borne on mucus droplets coughed out by infected people. In poor communities with crowded living conditions, sickness and death rates can be extremely high. As the virus mutates, exceptionally virulent strains can arise and cause pandemics (outbreaks that affect many people over a wide area). In 1918 toward the end of World War I, there was an outbreak of Russian influenza (named for the country of its first recorded outbreak) in which 20 million people died worldwide, including 50,000 Americans. The 1918 pandemic was characterized by a high death rate from viral pneumonia caused by the flu virus. This condition was also a feature of an Asian flu pandemic in 1957, which caused 60,000 deaths.

Scientists have studied antibodies in the blood of people born from the 1850s onward (most earlier samples were taken from bodies in graves). They found that the flu epidemics of 1889–1890, 1918, 1946–1947, 1957, and 1968 were all variants of one virus, the A virus—the first to be discovered. (There are three main types of viruses, A, B, and C.)

Outbreaks of flu are usually seasonal, starting in the late fall and becoming more severe in January. In tropical climates, flu coincides with the rainy season. Unlike diseases such as hepatitis and typhoid, influenza does not have symptomless human carriers; the virus survives by passing rapidly from host to host. The virus also survives by jumping species—from humans to horses, swine, poultry, and seals.

## Prevention and treatment

Every year new vaccines are developed to target those strains of flu that doctors expect to be prevalent in the upcoming months. These vaccines are made from killed viruses and are between 80 and 90 percent effective. However, these vaccines have some drawbacks: it may take nine months or more to

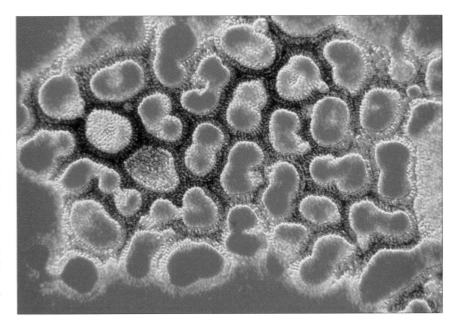

produce a vaccine in sufficient quantities; most vaccines can protect against only a few strains of flu, and they are usually not effective against the following year's crop of flu viruses. Also, some people should not get the flu shot (women who are pregnant or nursing), and still others may suffer mild to severe reactions. A few medicines, such as amantidine or rimantidine, can offer short term protection against type A, but not type B influenza.

E. SAREWITZ

**See also:** ENVIRONMENTAL DISEASES; IMMUNE SYSTEMS; IMMUNIZATION; VIRUSES.

### Further reading:

Davenport, Penny. 1995. *The Natural Way with Colds and Flu*. Rockport, Tx.: Element.
Nicholson, Karl G., and Robert G. Webster. 1998. *Textbook of Influenza*. Boston: Blackwell Science.

*The influenza viruses (shown as red in this electron micrograph) belong to the Orthomyxovirus class of RNA viruses.*

## CONNECTIONS

● The success of the flu virus is based predominantly on its rapid **MUTATION** rate. New strains of flu, against which the **IMMUNE SYSTEM** has no defenses, are always developing.

## A MOLECULAR JURASSIC PARK

In January 1977, hundreds of U.S. Army recruits returning to Fort Dix, New Jersey, after Christmas were struck down with the flu. The Centers for Disease Control identified the virus as a close relation of the 1930 strain, the swine flu virus, but the origin of this virus was, in fact, the killer strain of the 1918 pandemic, which had survived in pigs. This "living fossil" had reemerged and, contrary to all previous experience, had jumped from a less-evolved animal back to humans. The decision to vaccinate the nation against this flu was triggered by three factors: past experience of pandemics; the tendency of viruses to increase in virulence as they spread; and a large nonimmune population. By December that year, 43 million people had been vaccinated, but the virus had another surprise in store. Despite its fearsome past, it fizzled out. The lessons learned from this episode were that the influenza virus was utterly unpredictable and that with flu viruses, there always be a next time.

# INFORMATION SCIENCE

**Information science is the study of information and the systems that use it**

## CONNECTIONS

● **Feedback loops** help control the release of **HORMONES** in the body's **ENDOCRINE SYSTEM**.

● The **GAIA HYPOTHESIS** views Earth as a self-regulating system of feedback loops and **HOMEOSTASIS** mechanisms.

● **Feedback** mechanisms are vital parts of automated systems such as **ROBOTICS IN MEDICINE**.

The collection, storage, communication, and transmission of information is termed *information science*. This information includes words and numbers, electrical and electronic signals, the nerve signals of living organisms, and the chemical signals carried by hormones. Early studies of information handling dealt with documentation: examining how the information in reference books and scientific journals was arranged and how techniques such as indexing, cataloging, and creating abstracts helped people access it. In the 1940s the development of electronic computers spurred a mathematical approach to the study of information.

Two major advances in information science appeared then. One was the information theory model published in 1949 by U.S. mathematicians Claude Shannon (1916–2001) and Warren Weaver (1894–1978). Inform-ation theory is the application of mathematics to the study of information—defining and measuring the amount of information contained in messages and coding and decoding it. Shannon also pioneered the use of digital information coding using ones and zeros as "bits" of information—the basis of modern computers and digital electronics. Next came the theory of cybernetics, developed by U.S.

### CORE FACTS

■ Two of the most important aspects of information science are information theory and cybernetics.
■ Information theory is the mathematical study of information processing.
■ Cybernetics studies the information flow in control and communication systems.
■ The basis of cybernetics is the feedback loop.
■ Negative feedback limits the activity of a system, while positive feedback increases the activity.

mathematician Norbert Wiener (1894–1964). Wiener's theory, published in 1948, described how information is transmitted and processed by control and communication systems in machines. He coined the term *cybernetics* from the Greek word *kybernetikos*, meaning "helmsman," because control systems keep a machine running on course and prevent it from straying outside definite limits.

The addition of information theory and cybernetics to the study of documentation led to the creation of information science, the theories of which have been widely adopted by other branches of science, such as management science, computer science, and engineering. These theories, essential components of cybernetics, can also be applied to living organisms and ecosystems.

### Cybernetics and feedback loops

At the heart of cybernetics is the feedback loop, which compares the result of an action with the desired

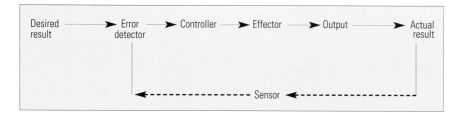

result. A simple system containing a feedback loop has four main components—an effector, a sensor, an error detector, and a controller. The effector carries out the action and produces a result, or output. The sensor measures the output and sends this information (feeds it back) to the error detector. The detector compares the result with the desired result. If there is a difference between the two, the detector signals the controller, which instructs the effector to increase or decrease its activity to eliminate the difference. A common example of a system containing a feedback loop is a furnace controlled by a thermostat.

## Positive and negative feedback

Feedback may be negative or positive. Negative feedback limits the activity of a system to prevent the output from rising too high. In the example of the furnace, negative feedback switches off the furnace when the room reaches the desired temperature.

Positive feedback causes the output of a system to keep on increasing. If a furnace was working on a positive feedback system, an increase in room temperature would make the furnace produce even more heat. Positive feedback systems must have an escape mechanism to break the cycle.

## Biological feedback systems

Feedback systems also control processes in living organisms. One biological example of negative feedback is the control of blood glucose, a sugar that provides the body with energy. The level of blood glucose is regulated mainly by the hormones glucagon and insulin (see HORMONES; INSULIN). If blood glucose levels fall too low, the pancreas secretes glucagon, which prompts the liver to release glucose. As the blood glucose level rises, the secretion of glucagon decreases. If the glucose level becomes too high, the pancreas secretes insulin, which makes muscle and liver cells take up more glucose. As the blood glucose level returns to normal, the secretion of insulin decreases. Thus, two feedback systems—one based on glucagon and the other on insulin—help keep the blood glucose level fairly constant. The balance of physiological processes made possible by feedback systems is called homeostasis (see HOMEOSTASIS).

## Feedback in childbirth

Most biological feedback systems use negative feedback, but an important positive feedback system is involved in childbirth (see right). When a woman gives birth, the hypothalamus in the brain sends signals to the pituitary gland (1), which releases oxytocin hormone. The hormone stimulates the uterus to contract rhythmically (2), pushing the baby down the birth canal and through the cervix. The cervix stretches and sends signals back to the hypothalamus (3). These signals make the hypothalamus release even more oxytocin, which causes the uterus to contract even more, stretching the cervix even further, and so on. Eventually the baby is born, the cervix is no longer stretched, and so it stops sending signals to the hypothalamus.

---

## FROM HAIR COMBING TO SKATEBOARDING

Even the most familiar body movements, such as combing the hair, need a finely tuned feedback system. Before a person starts to comb the hair, he or she must know how far the hand is from the hair. This information is relayed to the brain by sensors in the joints and muscles called proprioceptors. As the person moves his or her hand, these sensors send feedback to the brain. If the hand has moved closer to the hair, the person knows it is going in the right direction and continues until the comb makes contact. In skateboarding, the problem is balance. If the person is leaning too far to one side, impulses from the vestibular apparatus in the inner ear indicate he or she is going to fall. These impulses go to the brain, which sends commands to the muscles. The muscles move the body to correct the imbalance. The vestibular apparatus detects the improvement and relays this information to the brain, which sends modified commands to the muscles. Here the sensor is the vestibular apparatus, the controller is the brain, the effector is the muscles, and the output is the movement of the body to restore balance.

## Feedback in ecosystems

Feedback can help explain how the population size of a species is controlled in an ecosystem (see ECOLOGY AND ECOSYSTEMS). If a population grows too large, there is more food for predators, and thus the predator population also grows. The original population outstrips its food supply, and some individuals starve. Others die of diseases caused by overcrowding. The food supply recovers because the population shrinks, predators become fewer, and the diseases die out. The population recovers and starts to increase. This cycle may be repeated, causing variations in the populations of the species, its predators, and its food supply.

IAN WOOD

**See also:** ECOLOGY AND ECOSYSTEMS; HOMEOSTASIS; HORMONES; INSULIN.

## Further reading:

Johnson, Steven. 2001. *Emergence: The Connected Lives of Ants, Brains, Cities, and Software*. New York: Simon and Schuster.

*Childbirth involves positive feedback. In this system, the error detector is the hypothalamus in the brain, the controller is the pituitary gland, the effector is the oxytocin hormone, which causes output in the form of uterus contractions, and the sensor is the cervix. The escape mechanism is the birth of the baby.*

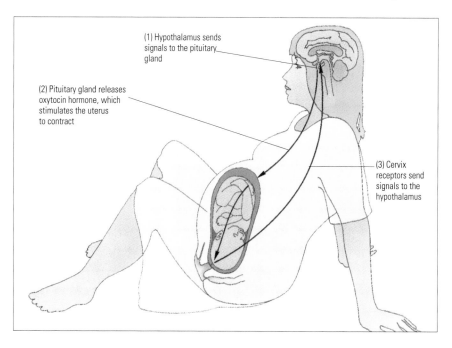

(1) Hypothalamus sends signals to the pituitary gland

(2) Pituitary gland releases oxytocin hormone, which stimulates the uterus to contract

(3) Cervix receptors send signals to the hypothalamus

# INSECTIVORES

**Insectivores are small mammals of the order Insectivora that eat mainly insects**

*Like other insectivores, moles have sensory whiskers that provide information about their environment.*

## CONNECTIONS

● Moles are insectivores that are adapted for digging. Their **HANDS** are broad and turned outward, and their forelimbs are heavy, with large muscles.

● Solenodons and tenrecs live mainly in **ISLAND HABITATS.**

Among the 19 orders of placental mammals, the insectivores are the most primitive. As their name implies, these animals feed mostly on insects, although some eat invertebrates, other small vertebrates, and fruit. Insectivores also tend to be small. One, Savi's pygmy shrew (*Suncus etruscus*) of southern Europe, Africa, and South Asia, is the smallest land-living mammal. It may be as short as 2.5 inches (3.5 cm) and weigh as little as 0.053 ounces (1.5 g).

All insectivores have highly developed senses of smell and touch. They have movable sensory hairs around their mouth, nose, and eyes. These hairs help them locate prey and avoid predators and thus are essential to their survival.

Their pointed teeth are adapted for snaring insects and piercing their hard, shelled bodies. Other common features include a plantigrade stance (when they walk, the entire soles of their feet rest on the ground rather than just the toes) and a relatively small brain with few infolds.

Insectivores include shrews, moles, hedgehogs, tenrecs, solenodons, and golden moles. Although their common names suggest they are insectivores, elephant shrews belong to the order Macroscelidea, and tree shrews belong to the order Scandentia.

## Insectivore evolution

Most Mesozoic mammals (over 65 million years old) were insect eaters, and *Megazostrodon* from the late Triassic period (200 million years ago, MYA) of South Africa was not unlike a shrew. For this reason some scientists think that insectivores evolved before the main radiation of mammals (when the dinosaurs became extinct).

Certainly insectivores are the earliest known placental mammals, ranging from the mid-Cretaceous (about 100 MYA) to recent times. Some insectivores are little changed from their fossil ancestors, and most retain primitive charactersitics, such as a cloaca

### CORE FACTS

■ Insectivores are mammals belonging to the order Insectivora.

■ All insectivores are small, eat mainly insects, and have a keen sense of smell.

■ Insectivores evolved about 100 million years ago during the Cretaceous period.

■ Some insectivores, such as the desmans, are adapted to an aquatic lifestyle; others, such as moles, live underground.

(single opening for the urinary, fecal, and reproductive tracts). Because shrews sometimes have pigmented teeth, they can be recognized in the fossil record as far back as the Oligocene epoch (37 MYA). Fossil hedgehogs are present in Eocene times (58 MYA). They, too, are conspicuous as fossils because of their highly modified forelimbs used for digging. A giant fossil hedgehog, *Deinogalerix*, found in Italy, is about the size of a large rabbit.

## Shrews

More than 300 species of shrews make up the largest family of insectivores, the Soricidae. They live in all parts of the world except Australia, New Zealand, the West Indies and most of South America. Shrews feed mainly on insects, but one, the water shrew, also eats tiny fish and frogs, which it first poisons with venom-laced saliva. It is one of the few venomous mammals. Hunting mainly by night, some species use echolocation to find food.

Shrews are so active that they must eat virtually all the time to provide themselves with the energy they need to stay alive. They can eat as much as their own body weight in food each day.

Shrews possess many adaptations to support this high level of activity: the heart of some shrews beats an amazing 1,200 times a minute, and this rate provides for an exceedingly rapid transport of oxygen and nutrients to and wastes from body cells.

## Moles

Most of the 42 species of true moles live underground in complex systems of burrows. The animals rely mainly on their sense of touch to get around in their dark environment and to find prey such as earthworms and grubs. However, three

### TREE SHREWS

Tree shrews, which look something like squirrels, scurry along branches in the forests of eastern Asia, Borneo, and the Philippines. As their name implies, these animals appear to be insectivores that have adapted to a life above the ground. This notion is bolstered by the fact that tree shrews feed on insects and look not unlike conventional shrews, so the first observers of these animals classified them in the order Insectivora.

On closer examination, scientists discovered characteristics that were similar to those of the Primate order to which such animals as lemurs, tarsiers, monkeys, apes, and humans belong. These characteristics include eye cavities completely surrounded by bone, a complex brain with a large braincase, and other anatomical features of primates. Thus, some scientists have classified tree shrews as primitive primates.

The current view is that tree shrews are sufficiently different from both insectivores and primates to warrant an order of their own, called Scandentia, which comes from the Latin word *scandere*, meaning "to climb." Tree shrews are thought to be most closely related to primates, Dermoptera (flying lemurs), and Chiroptera (bats).

species of true moles, the Pyrenean desman (*Galemys pyrenaicus*), the Russian desman (*Desmana moschata*), and the star-nosed mole (*Condylura cristata*), are adapted for life in water.

Desmans have a flat tail and webbed feet, which they use to maneuver in water. Star-nosed moles have waterproof fur and an array of 22 fleshy projections around their nostrils. These projections help the moles to find prey on the floor of lakes, ponds, and rivers.

## Hedgehogs

Hedgehogs are grouped in one family, although the 20 species can be divided into two subfamilies,

*A tailless tenrec (Tenrec caudata). Tenrecs generally have poor eyesight and rely on their keen senses of smell and hearing to find food in the leafy undergrowth.*

## ELEPHANT SHREWS

Crossing a kangaroo with an elephant and shrinking the result to the size of a rat would produce an elephant shrew. Scientists used to classify the 15 species of elephant shrews with insectivores, but they are now placed in a separate family, Macroscelidea. Elephant shrews have trunklike noses, powerful hind legs, and a long tail, which the animal uses to keep its balance while leaping from place to place.

*The rufous elephant shrew* (Elephantus rufescens). *Despite its common name, the elephant shrew is not an insectivore; it belongs to the order Macroscelidea.*

## A CLOSER LOOK

the spiny hedgehogs and the hairy hedgehogs. The bodies of spiny hedgehogs are covered with spines. When the animal is threatened, powerful muscles in the skin make these spines erect. The hedgehog then rolls into a ball and thus presents a daunting problem for any predator.

Hairy hedgehogs, such as the moon rats of Southeast Asia, do not possess spines. However, they still have an effective defense against predators: two glands near the anus secrete a substance with a foul smell, described as resembling ammonia, rotten onions, garlic, or stale sweat.

### Tenrecs

The most primitive insectivores are the 25 species of tenrecs. Scientists speculate that these animals have survived until the present because many of them have been isolated either on the island of Madagascar or on the nearby Comoro Islands off the east coast of Africa.

Tenrecs produce the largest litters among the mammals: the average litter contains 12 to 15 young. The females possess as many as 24 mammary glands—also a record—and some litters may even exceed this number (a female of one species was found to be carrying 31 embryos).

Tenrecs are warm blooded, but they have difficulty maintaining their body temperature. When the air temperature drops, they become excessively active. This extra activity probably produces enough body heat to maintain a normal body temperature.

### Solenodons

The four species of solenodons are natives to the Caribbean islands of Hispaniola and Cuba. These somewhat large and clumsy nocturnal animals may measure up to 23 inches (58 cm) from the snout to the tip of the tail. Solenodons have trunklike snouts, which they use to search out insects and small animals such as frogs, lizards, and even birds. Some solenodons also eat fruit.

Solenodons get their name from the shape of their second, lower incisor teeth, which are deeply grooved on the inside surface. The Latin word *solenodontidae* means "grooved teeth."

Solenodons have very small litters. Females have two mammary glands and give birth to between one and three young.

### Golden moles

The golden mole family, native to Africa, consists of 19 species. These animals are rarely seen because they spend most of their lives underground. Golden moles are skilled diggers. They have narrow shovel-like hands with four, heavily clawed fingers, attached to muscular forelimbs. These powerful forelimbs can propel a golden mole through 164 feet (50 m) of soil in an hour. At this rate, a golden mole—if it lived in the United States—could dig a tunnel under the Hudson River from New York City to New Jersey in just over a day.

True moles and the golden mole have similar adaptations and ways of life, although they belong to two distinct and separate families. The golden mole is more closely related to the tenrecs than to the true mole. The key difference is that the golden mole has four fingers on each narrow hand, and a true mole has five fingers and broad hands. In addition, the hands of a golden mole are supported by a bony tendon that runs from the elbow to the wrist. No other mammal, including the true mole, has this structure. True moles also have 44 teeth, the largest number found in mammals; most golden moles have 40 teeth—only the five species of the South African golden moles (*Amblysomus*) have 36 teeth.

C. PROUJAN

**See also:** MAMMALS; PRIMATES.

**Further reading:**
MacDonald, David. 1995. *The Encyclopedia of Mammals.* New York: Checkmark Books.
Nowak, R. M. 1999. *Walker's Mammals of the World.* Baltimore: Johns Hopkins University Press.

# INSECTS

**Insects are small invertebrate animals with six legs and three body parts: head, thorax, and abdomen**

*A ladybug (**Coccinella septempunctata**). Both adults and larvae are voracious aphid predators.*

## CONNECTIONS

● The insecticide **DDT** was used extensively in the 1950s and 1960s to control the spread of insects that threatened to destroy **AGRICULTURE** in many areas. Use of natural biological control agents is now increasingly popular.

● Some insects are beneficial to humans; bees, for example, carry out **POLLINATION** of flowers and fruit trees.

A human could not possibly lift 450 times his or her weight or jump 150 times his or her body length. Insects can. For example, fleas can jump enormous distances relative to their size, while ants are capable of lifting great weights in comparison to their own body weight.

Insects are the most numerous class of living animals and inhabit virtually all ecosystems on land and in fresh water, and a few species even live on the oceans. As members of the phylum Arthropoda (from the Latin for "jointed foot"), insects are related to horseshoe crabs, spiders and scorpions, crabs and lobsters, and millipedes and centipedes. The class Insecta comprises two subclasses made up of 30 orders that have species now living (see box page 960).

## Insect anatomy

An adult insect has three body parts: head, thorax, and abdomen. The head bears the antennae, compound or simple eyes (see EYES), and variously adapted mouthparts. The thorax may be further divided into three segments, each of which usually bears a pair of legs. Wings, when present, are on the hind two thoratic segments, which may have small openings, or spiracles, which are connected to internal tubes for respiration (see GILLS AND SPIRACLES). The abdomen also has spiracles on the forward area, while the hindmost segments contain the sex organs and are often adapted for egg laying or, in some

cases, for defense. The abdomen also contains the digestive system, including the Malpighian tubules (long, blind vessels that function primarily as excretory organs).

While insects are related to arachnids (spiders, ticks, and mites), arachnids can be distinguished by having only two body segments: a fused head and thorax with four pairs of legs and an abdomen.

Insects possess an exoskeleton (external skeleton) made of a protein called chitin that surrounds the internal organs and muscles. The tough, relatively inflexible covering of chitin offers protection from predators, provides attachments for internal muscles that enable the insect to move, and inhibits water loss.

## CORE FACTS

■ The class Insecta contains the largest number of species of any group of animals.

■ Two-thirds of all flowering plants depend on insects for pollination; insects are therefore of enormous ecological significance.

■ The great success of insects is shown by their numerous species and extensive geographical distribution, which is related to their ability to occupy most ecological niches.

■ Highly developed social organization has evolved within two insect orders, Isoptera (termites) and Hymenoptera (ants, bees, and wasps).

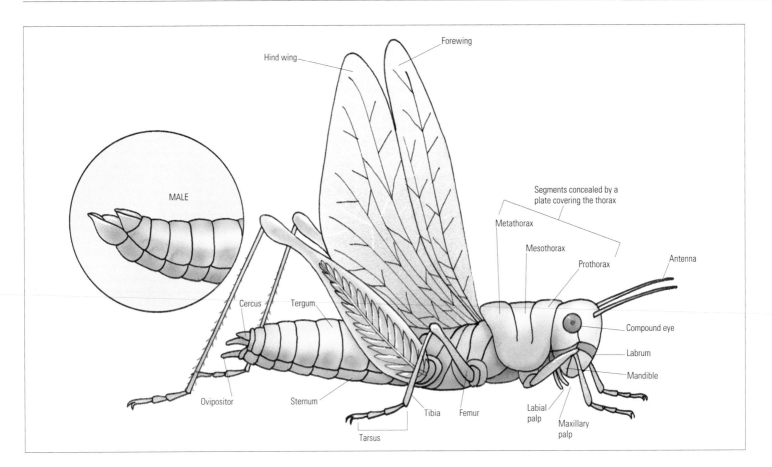

Hind wing — Forewing

MALE

Segments concealed by a plate covering the thorax

Metathorax

Mesothorax

Prothorax

Antenna

Cercus — Tergum

Compound eye

Labrum

Mandible

Ovipositor — Sternum

Tibia — Femur

Labial palp

Maxillary palp

Tarsus

*The female grasshopper, pictured above, shows the basic body structure of an insect, with large hind legs adapted for powerful jumping.*

Adult insects have either one or two pairs of wings. Some groups of insects, such as fleas and lice (see FLEAS; LICE), are flightless, and retain only vestigial wings. Wings have given insects a distinct advantage over many other animals, enabling them to populate areas of the planet that may be too remote for other animals to reach, to escape earthbound predators, and to enlarge their territory rapidly when population pressures require it (see TERRITORY).

## INSECT EVOLUTION

Hundreds of millions of years ago, the ancestors of insects lived in the sea. These early insects were among the first animals to invade the land around 400 million years ago. Paleontologists think that wings evolved soon after, from outgrowths on the thorax. Wings allowed insects to colonize new habitats and move to new areas, and thus, there was an explosion in diversity. With the exception of two wingless insect groups, all modern insects descend from these ancient winged forms that lived during the Devonian period, 375 million years ago.

In the Carboniferous and Permian periods many new groups appeared. Some insects during this time reached enormous sizes—the dragonfly-like *Meganeura*, for example, had a wingspan of almost 3 feet (91 cm). Scientists think higher levels of oxygen in the air led to the evolution of these giants. Around this time, one group of insects evolved in a startling new direction; the young developed a very different body shape from that of the adults, they fed on different foods to avoid competition, and they matured to the adult form via a pupal stage. These insects diversified to form the most successful modern insect orders, including beetles, flies, and moths and butterflies. Following a cataclysmic mass extinction at the end of the Permian, many insect groups disappeared, but the survivors radiated through the Mesozoic. Several groups appeared at this time; ants, for example, diverged from their wasp ancestors around 140 million years ago.

### EVOLUTION

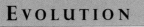

### How many insects are there?

No one knows how many individual insects there are, but more than 900,000 species have been named, and new ones are continuously being added to an ever-growing list.

Insects reproduce in very large numbers, but only a very small percentage of the offspring live to reproduce in the next generation. The fruit fly, *Drosophila*, can produce some 25 generations in one year. While some insect populations can occasionally reach plague proportions, for example, locusts, most populations are usually controlled naturally by parasites and predators. Other insects, birds, reptiles, amphibians, fish, and small mammals prey on insects. In recent years, humans have doused the environment indiscriminately with pesticides to keep insect populations within acceptable limits, the result being severe environmental problems (see PESTICIDES).

### Social insects

Many insects live a solitary existence except when breeding. Others, however, such as ants, bees, wasps (of the order Hymenoptera), and termites (of the order Isoptera), live in colonies of various sizes. The insects within a colony are divided into castes, according to their specific roles within the colony. The ant colony, for example, consists of the queen ant, whose function is to lay eggs; soldier ants that guard the colony against invasion; and workers that locate and retrieve food and look after the queen, eggs, and young.

Each ant remains within a caste throughout its life. A caste is a specialized form of insect that carries out a particular function in the colony. A worker ant cannot adapt to the functions of the soldier ant, for example. The individual is confined to spending its adult life performing a single type of task until it dies.

Termites display some similarities to ants in their colonial life. Some tropical colonies may contain millions of individuals living in huge mounds that can also be cohabited by other insects, small reptiles, and mammals. The greatly enlarged queen termite in her royal chamber serves as a source of eggs to continue the colony's existence and may live many years and thus may produce millions of eggs.

Unlike ants and termites, the common grasshopper is a solitary insect and does not display characteristics that would be attributed to true social behavior, although individuals may live close to one another. However, in some tropical areas huge swarms of locusts, short-horned grasshoppers, migrate across country, decimating vegetation. These swarms may take hours to pass a given spot, measure miles across, and eat all plants in their path. The locusts are not swarming as a colony but as the offspring of a previous generation that laid eggs, which then mostly all hatched. They migrate because they need to find food.

### Insect reproduction and development

Some insects reproduce by laying eggs, depositing them individually or in large clusters. Some insects can reproduce from eggs that have not been fertilized by a male (parthenogenesis). Such unfertilized eggs always produce females.

The young of some insects look like miniature adults (locusts, for example) and shed their exoskeleton periodically as they grow to adult size. Among insects in which the young bear great resemblance to the adults, the change from egg to the various nymphal stages to adult is called incomplete metamorphosis. On the other hand, other insects have newborn that do not resemble the adult at all. These offspring are called larvae (singular, larva). They are wormlike in appearance, and many do not have legs. The larvae may live on plants, under an animal's skin, or in water, preying on smaller forms of life. Many of these larval insects can cause major agricultural damage; others can be beneficial because they prey on harmful insect pests.

At the end of the larval stage, the larva constructs a cell for its change to adult life via an inactive pupal stage. This cell may be a simple hole in the ground or a case constructed of woven fibers or saliva. Many insects spend the winter as a pupa and then emerge the following spring as an adult. This cycle—egg to larva to pupa to adult—is called complete metamorphosis, and butterflies, moths, ants, wasps, bees, and other insect groups develop in this way.

### Color adaptations

Insects adapt to their environment in many ways. Color often conceals insects from predators or prey. Insects that do not have advantageous camouflage may be eaten by predators before they are old enough to reproduce and so do not pass on unfavorable colorings. In this way, the coloring favorable to

## AT RISK

survival is passed on. Other inedible or unpalatable insects are deliberately brightly colored and stand out from their surroundings, as a warning that they are dangerous or toxic to predators. The brightly colored monarch butterfly, for example, makes no effort to conceal itself by camouflage or by hiding. A bird may make the mistake of trying to eat the butterfly but will find it so distasteful that it will release

*Termites, like ants, live in colonies. Some termites, such as those pictured below, build large mounds called termitaria (singular, termitarium), which can reach up to 23 feet (7 m) in height.*

it and learn from the experience. Some butterflies and other insects mimic these warning colorations. Colored like a poisonous species, they are not poisonous themselves.

## Insects and humans

The relationships between insects and humans are many and varied, both beneficial and detrimental. The relationship with honeybees, for example, is mutually beneficial: the bee benefits from the provision of a hive and a source of nectar; humans benefit through bee pollination of fruit trees and flowers and the production of honey.

Other insect species provide an indirect benefit to humans. Certain beetles, for example, prey on other insects that damage human crops or infest livestock. Ladybug beetle adults and larvae are voracious predators of aphids that infest flowers and food crops. These red or orange beetles with black spots can be bought commercially, and their larvae spread over food crops to control pests and thus lower or prevent the need for chemical insecticides.

Control of the Japanese beetle (*Popillia japonica*), an introduced species first found in the United States in 1916, is a good example of biological control. At the time, no one knew the beetle's habits or life cycle, and it became a major pest as its numbers increased and its range of infestation broadened. The larval stage, or grub, lives underground and eats the roots of plants, while the adult lives on plants above ground and consumes the leaves.

Insecticides of the day failed to control the beetle. Then DDT (see DDT) was introduced and farmers began to make inroads against the Japanese beetle. However, DDT proved lethal to more than insects, and it was withdrawn from the market, after which the beetle again became a major agricultural pest. Scientists then discovered that *Bacillus popilliae* bacteria could be used to help control the beetle population. The bacteria attacks the beetle grub in the ground, reproduces inside the insect, and kills it. The bacterial spores remain in the soil, where they can be eaten by other grubs. These bacterial spores are now available commercially. Unlike DDT, they affect only the Japanese beetles and so pose no threat to other insects, animals, or humans.

L. BLASER

**See also:** ANTS; ARTHROPODS; BEETLES; BUTTERFLIES AND MOTHS; CARSON, RACHEL LOUISE; CENTIPEDES AND MILLIPEDES; DDT; DRAGONFLIES AND MAYFLIES; EYES; FLEAS; GILLS AND SPIRACLES; GRASSHOPPERS AND CRICKETS; HEMIPTERA; LICE; PESTICIDES; PREDATION; TERRITORY; WASPS AND BEES.

## Further reading:

Chapman, R. F. 1999. *The Insects: Structure and Function.* Cambridge: Cambridge University Press.
Elzinga, R. J. 1999. *Fundamentals of Entomology.* Upper Saddle River, New Jersey: Prentice Hall.
*Insects and Spiders of the World.* 2003. New York: Marshall Cavendish.

## CLASSIFICATION

The class Insecta consists of 2 subclasses: Apterygota (2 orders) and Pterygota (28 orders). The class used to include 3 other orders: Protura (tiny eyeless animals), Diplura (two-pronged bristletails), and Collembola (springtails). However, many scientists now consider Protura, Diplura, and Collembola to be a separate class because their mouthparts differ from those of true insects.

| ORDER | COMMON NAME |
|---|---|
| **Subclass Apterygota (insects that have never possessed wings during their evolution):** | |
| Archaeognatha ("ancient mouthparts") | Jumping bristletails |
| Thysanura ("finned tail") | Silverfish, bristletails, and firebrats |
| **Subclass Pterygota (insects that have evolved wings):** | |
| Ephemeroptera ("short-lived wings") | Mayflies |
| Odonata ("toothed") | Dragonflies and damselflies |
| Plecoptera ("folded wings") | Stone flies |
| Grylloblattodea ("cricket-roach") | Rock crawlers |
| Orthoptera ("straight winged") | Crickets, grasshoppers, and katydids |
| Phasmida ("phantom") | Stick insects and leaf insects |
| Dermaptera ("skin wings") | Earwigs |
| Mantophasmatodea ("phantom mantid") | Gladiator insects |
| Mantodea (Greek name) | Mantids |
| Blattodea (Greek name) | Cockroaches |
| Embioptera ("lively wings") | Web spinners |
| Isoptera ("equal wings") | Termites |
| Zoraptera ("pure wingless") | Angel insects |
| Psocoptera ("gnawing winged insect") | Book lice |
| Phthiraptera ("wingless lice") | Parasitic lice |
| Hemiptera ("half wing") | True bugs, aphids, cicadas, and leafhoppers |
| Thysanoptera ("fringed wings") | Thrips |
| Megaloptera ("large wings") | Alderflies, dobsonflies, and fish flies |
| Raphidioptera ("needle wings") | Snakeflies |
| Neuroptera ("veined wings") | Lacewings and ant lions |
| Coleoptera ("sheath wings") | Beetles |
| Strepsiptera ("twisted wings") | Stylopids |
| Mecoptera ("long wings") | Scorpion flies |
| Siphonaptera ("wingless siphon") | Fleas |
| Diptera ("two wings") | True flies, mosquitos, and gnats |
| Trichoptera ("hairy wings") | Caddis flies |
| Lepidoptera ("scaly wings") | Butterflies and moths |
| Hymenoptera ("membrane wings") | Bees, wasps, and ants |

Note: Some scientists group Blattodea, Mantodea, and Isoptera as Dictyoptera.

*The tarnished plant bug (Lygus lineolaris) is a serious pest of alfalfa being grown for seed.*

# INSTINCT

**Instinct is the specific inborn behavior possessed by all animal species**

A herring gull newly hatched from its shell is drawn like a magnet to the red dot on its parent's bill. The chick pecks on the dot and thus prompts the parent to regurgitate a piece of partially digested food into its mouth. This behavior is instinctive. No matter that the chick has never seen this behavior before or that its mother has not had a chance to give it a lesson in table manners, every newly hatched herring gull acts the same way.

This attraction to red dots is only one illustration of instinctive behavior. Such instinct is described as innate (inborn); it exists at birth and requires no learning. From the start, instinctive actions are fully functional. They have been shaped by evolution and usually have adaptive benefits (see ADAPTATION).

Usually, such behavior is triggered by a simple stimulus. Consider, for example, what happens when five people of various ages are in a dark room and someone suddenly turns on the light (the stimulus). At first, everyone blinks. Then their pupils constrict, to protect the retina from excess light. Nobody in the room has to think about constricting his or her pupils.

Instincts are related to survival, and many are associated with escape from predators. Young birds who have never seen a snake, for example, know instinctively to avoid the poisonous reptiles. As a scientist who specializes in animal behavior, ethologist Susan Smith demonstrated this instinct by placing birds in an area with various painted wooden rods. The curious birds approached every rod except those with alternating red and yellow rings that mimicked the pattern of the poisonous coral snakes that shared their environment.

## Reflex: The simplest instinct

The simplest instinctive action is the reflex, an automatic response to a simple stimulus, for example the knee-jerk reflex: the doctor's hammer tap on the knee stretches the tendon, stimulating stretch sensors along the muscle fibers. These sensors send impulses along the nerve fibers to the spinal cord and thus triggers another set of impulses that return to the muscle and prompt it to contract sharply. This nervous pathway is called the reflex arc (see REFLEXES).

Reflexes are innate and include not only sharp reactions to pain but also such basic functions as chewing, swallowing, blinking, and standing. They can, however, be modified, as Russian physiologist Ivan Pavlov showed in his experiments with dogs conditioned to salivate (thinking they were going to be fed) to the sound of a bell (see CONDITIONING).

*A newborn herring gull's natural instinct is to peck at a red dot on its mother's beak. It will even peck at a red eraser at the tip of a pencil.*

## CORE FACTS

- Instinctive behavior is inborn and requires no learning.
- The reflex is the simplest instinctive action.
- Fixed action patterns are patterns of movements that are played out in response to a cue. Examples include nest building, food gathering, and escape movements.
- Some instinctive behavior can be modified. An example is when a young galah parrot adopted by a pink cockatoo modifies its call to match that of the cockatoo.
- Avoidance behavior protects against danger and can be stimulated by the sight or smell of danger.
- Darwin first defined instinct in terms of animal behavior.

## CONNECTIONS

- **COURTSHIP** and **MATING** are two natural instincts of most animals and birds.

- Many natural instincts are susceptible to **CONDITIONING**.

- For many birds, **MIGRATION** is a natural instinct during the winter.

*A pink cockatoo (Cacatua leadbeateri). The females of this species chase female galahs (Cacatua roseicapilla) from their shared nests and adopt their chicks. The chicks then modify their instinctive calls when communicating with the cockatoos in the flock.*

## Fixed action patterns

Another type of instinctive behavior is the fixed action pattern (FAP). These are patterns that are played out to completion following the stimulus of a simple cue. Common FAPs include sexual displays, nest building, food gathering, food preparation, attack, and escape movements. Because many of these patterns are unique to individual species, scientists use them in classification.

There are 40 species of fiddler crabs, for example, and each has its own distinctive claw movement. The male in each species waves its enlarged claw in a sexual and aggressive display. Yet, some species wave the claw up, others down, and still others in a circle.

---

## IMPRINTING

Imprinting is an interesting example of a combination of instinct and learning. Young ducks, geese, and chickens will follow the first large, moving object they see on hatching. This behavior is an instinctive response, although they have to learn the shape of the object. Under normal circumstances this will be the mother bird, but chicks and ducklings have been known to become imprinted on a variety of other objects, including humans. The imprinting process is not only important for keeping the young birds under their mothers' care. On reaching adulthood, they direct their sexual behavior toward the same imprinted object.

### A CLOSER LOOK

---

The patterns in FAPs are so firmly established they are always completed once started, even when it is clear that the behavior will fail to produce the desired result. An example occurs when the greylag goose incubates an egg. If the egg is moved a few feet away, the goose stretches her neck in a characteristic manner, tucks the egg under her lower bill, and rolls it back into the nest. If the egg is taken away midway through the process, however, she continues as if she were still pushing it into the nest.

## Instincts that can be modified

The distinction between instinctive and learned behavior blurs in the case of modifiable action patterns. Take the example of the herring gull chicks, who peck on their parents' bills for food. During their first couple of days, they will peck on anything resembling a gull's beak. Pecking angles and speed vary widely from one chick to the next. Within a few days, however, they peck only the bills of their parents, and their pecking becomes consistently fast and accurate. Clearly they have learned to modify their instinctive behavior.

In the case of orphaned galah parrots, calls and flight habits can be altered. The galah parrot (*Cacatua roseicapilla*) and the pink cockatoo (*Cacatua leadbeateri*) live in the Australian eucalyptus forests. Occasionally, a pair from each species will share the same nesting hole. When both females are incubating eggs, the larger cockatoo will banish the galah and is left to incubate the galah's eggs.

The newly hatched galahs cry out for food in the voice typical of other galah chicks, although the sound is decidedly different from that of the cockatoos that share the nest. The galahs also cry much as their own species do when alarmed.

Meanwhile, they have modified their instinctive "contact calls," used to communicate with other members of the flock. The galahs' contact calls are found to be identical to those of the cockatoos. These adopted chicks also mimic the slow, sweeping wing beats of the cockatoos, which are different from the swift beats of their fellow galahs.

Instinctive behavior is controlled by many genes. Mutations in one or more of these genes may affect the behavior of an organism. The courtship ritual of a male fruit fly (*Drosophila*), for example, may be altered by mutations. If females are still attracted to the male, in spite of the new dance, the mutation could be passed down to future generations.

## Instinctive avoidance behavior

An instinct that protects against danger is called avoidance behavior. These instincts stretch far back in evolutionary time. Avoidance behavior is stimulated by the sight or sound of a predator. The eyes of an owl provoke a strong reaction in smaller birds. Even birds raised in captivity respond to a model with painted owl eyes. Some scientists believe that humans' fear of snakes is innate.

Avoidance may be active, as in running, or passive, as in hiding or playing dead. Some reflexes help an animal to avoid danger. Dogs, cats, and other mammals will pull their ears back when threatened; this reflex helps protect their ears from injury during a fight.

An animal that discovers danger often warns others in its species. Birds and mammals typically use warning calls and visual signals. A perching bird who spots an owl will call out to its peers, who respond by forming a mob. Invertebrate species may use chemical signals. Ants who sense danger produce volatile chemicals called terpenes. In low concentrations, terpenes attract more ants. In high concentrations, they cause ants to flee.

Small, slow-moving invertebrates such as beetles would seem to have little chance of escaping from swift vertebrate predators such as birds, but their nervous system has evolved to help them survive. A third or more of the nerve cord running down the length of small invertebrates consists of fibers capable of quickly initiating the flight response.

## Parasites disrupt instinctive patterns

The predictability of instinctive behavior sometimes makes animals easy prey for parasites. The parasitic rove beetle (*Antemeles pubicollis*), for example, lays its eggs in the nest of an ant (*Formica polyctena*). When the beetle larvae hatch, they emit a scent that inspires nurturing in their hosts (see PHEROMONES). The worker ants care for the beetle larvae while the larvae raid the ants' eggs.

Because these beetles disrupt the innate feeding relationship between ants and their young, they are called code breakers. Some code breakers provide a stimulus that is even stronger than that of a species' own offspring, called a supernormal stimulus. These powerful code breakers include several species of birds known as brood parasites. The female in these species stakes out a nest, usually of a smaller species. When the owner briefly leaves the nest, the parasite quickly slips in and lays an egg among the owner's clutch.

After the parasite chick hatches, it provides its adoptive mother with a supernormal stimulus to feed because it is larger and demands more food than her natural offspring. These parasitic chicks sometimes toss others from the nest in their quest for the most food.

In spite of the threat from parasites, the ants' and birds' feeding instinct has survived because the benefits to their offspring outweigh the occasional losses to parasites. Ants that sometimes feed the parasitic beetles still feed their own young 99 percent of the time.

C. WASHAM

**See also:** ADAPTATION; ANIMAL BEHAVIOR; CONDITIONING; LEARNING; PHEROMONES; REFLEXES.

**Further reading:**
Alcock, J. 2001. *Animal Behavior: An Evolutionary Approach.* 7th ed. Sunderland, Mass.: Sinauer Associates.

## THE GREAT ETHOLOGICAL DEBATE

Scientists now readily accept the idea that animal behavior is influenced by a complex combination of hereditary and environmental factors. Yet as recently as the mid-20th century, the notion of combined influences was rejected. European ethologists attributed all behavior to instinct, while their American counterparts attributed it to learning.

English naturalist Charles Darwin first defined instinct in terms of animal behavior in 1859. He saw instincts as inherited reflexes that evolved with other aspects of species.

Later on, French naturalist Henri Fabre also attributed animal behavior to instinct, basing his studies on insects. Fabre, who died in 1915, observed the activities of insects for 40 years and is often called the father of animal behavior. Darwin and Fabre influenced Konrad Lorenz and his fellow European ethologists who fueled the 20th-century debate.

In the late 1930s, Lorenz (pictured below) identified many fixed action patterns that he said were influenced by heredity. Niko Tinbergen, who discovered the herring gulls' pecking instinct, proposed in 1951 that energy for instinctive actions was arranged in a hierarchy. He believed that one activity, such as reproduction, would stimulate several lesser activities, including nest building, courtship, and parental care.

The instinct theory dominated thinking about animal behavior until scientists discovered that many animals, including humans, acted solely for the reward of stimulation, exploring a new environment, or seeing others. U.S. behaviorists, who observed animals in a laboratory setting rather than in the wild, discovered that with appropriate punishment and reward, countless behaviors could be learned. J. B. Watson, a pioneer of the science of behaviorism, suggested that animals were born with a mind that was a blank slate and that all their actions were shaped by experience.

Later, scientists arrived at the current understanding of the subject: some behaviors are indeed innate, yet even those innate patterns may be influenced by environmental factors.

## DISCOVERERS

# INSULIN

**Insulin is a hormone that regulates the amount of glucose and other sugars in the bloodstream**

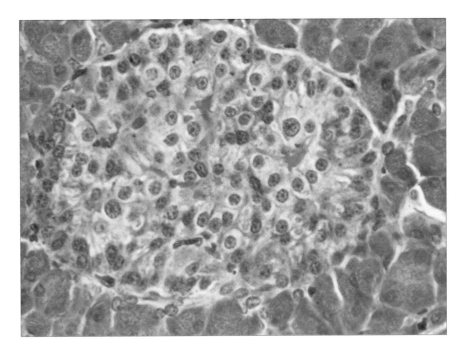

*An islet of Langerhans in the pancreas, containing the insulin-secreting beta cells.*

## CONNECTIONS

● Many **HORMONES**, including estrogen and **EPINEPHRINE**, are produced in the **ENDOCRINE SYSTEM**, which secretes hormones directly into the bloodstream.

● Insulin plays a key role in protein **METABOLISM**, by increasing **PROTEIN** synthesis and decreasing protein breakdown. This mechanism maintains normal tissue growth and repair.

● Insulin also helps control the storage and use of **CARBO-HYDRATES** and fats as energy sources.

Every living cell needs a regular energy supply. For animals, it comes from the food they eat, and they have a storage and retrieval system that enables them to store such fuel and distribute it as required.

The hormone insulin is the key regulator of this system in vertebrates. It controls the amount of fuel (usually glucose or another sugar) circulating in the blood, and influences the rate at which glucose enters the cells, where it is metabolized for energy or stored as animal starch (glycogen).

Insulin is produced by the beta cells of the islets of Langerhans, microscopic islands of endocrine (hormone-producing) tissue scattered throughout the pancreas. Like all endocrine tissue, the islets have a rich blood supply enabling the beta cells to secrete insulin directly into the nearby capillaries.

Insulin reduces blood sugar concentrations when they are too high (such as just after a meal) by stimulating cells to take up glucose from the bloodstream. Beta cells begin working in response to hormones secreted by the small intestine and to signals from nerves activated during digestion even before glucose-rich blood reaches the pancreas as digested food is absorbed from the small intestine. Within minutes, cells throughout the body, especially in the liver and the muscles, are absorbing glucose. As glucose concentrations in the blood return to normal, the beta cells switch off. The hormone glucagon (also secreted by the islets of Langerhans, but this time by the alpha cells) acts antagonistically to insulin. It promotes the breakdown of glucose stores (glycogen) and the release of glucose into the bloodstream when blood sugar concentrations are particularly low. Glucagon also promotes the mobilization of stored proteins as amino acids and the conversion of fats into fatty

acids, glycerol, and ketones. Each of these substances can be metabolized for energy by most tissues when glucose is in short supply.

## Beta cell activity

In young animals, the islets of Langerhans are very small and contain relatively few beta cells. Mature islets make up over 2 percent of pancreatic tissue, and more than 75 percent of this endocrine tissue consists of beta cells.

Insulin consists of two protein chains, one containing 21 amino acids and the other containing 30 amino acids. Proinsulin, the inactive form, which is made in the rough endoplasmic reticulum (protein synthesis system; see CELL BIOLOGY) of the beta cell, is transported to the cell's Golgi complex, activated, producing insulin, and packaged into granules. On appropriate stimulation, the granules are released into the cytoplasm, where they couple with the membrane and empty their contents outside the cell. Insulin diffuses into the capillaries and is carried to its target sites by the bloodstream. Any insulin that is not taken up within 10 minutes is broken down, mostly in the kidneys and liver.

## Fuel supplies

The majority of the insulin reaches the liver, where most of the glucose from the recent meal is absorbed. Under insulin's control, enzymes in the liver cells convert the glucose to glycogen for storage. During fasting, glycogen is metabolized and reconverted to glucose under the influence of glucagon when there is a demand for fuel. This system is an example of two negative-feedback loops—one for insulin and one for glucagon (see HOMEOSTASIS; INFORMATION SCIENCE).

By binding to specialized receptors on cell surfaces, insulin increases the rate at which cells absorb glucose, which fuels all their normal metabolic processes. Muscle cells, for example, either metabolize the glucose immediately or store it as glycogen for future use. Without insulin, plasma concentrations of glucose would have to rise by up to 20 times for muscle cells to get enough glucose by glucose transport proteins in their cell membranes. At normal concentrations, insulin maintains a steady

## CORE FACTS

■ Insulin is a hormone that controls the concentration of glucose in the bloodstream.

■ It is produced by cells in the islets of Langerhans, present in the pancreas.

■ People with Type I, insulin-dependent, diabetes, rely on regular injections of insulin.

■ Insulin was first used to treat diabetes in 1922.

supply of fuel to meet the energy needs of different tissues. Cells can become more, or less, sensitive to insulin. When the hormone is present in high concentrations—when a person eats frequent, sugary meals, for example—the cells become more resistant to the effects of insulin. Regular exercise, however, increases cell sensitivity to insulin. These changes in insulin sensitivity are due to changes in the number or sensitivity of the cells' insulin receptors.

## Diabetes

Type II (insulin-independent) diabetes is caused by low insulin production or a low sensitivity to insulin and may be treated with drugs (see DIABETES).

Patients with Type I (insulin-dependent) diabetes fail to produce insulin and require regular injections of insulin to mimic normal beta cell function. Insulin cannot be taken orally because it is destroyed by acid in the stomach; it can, however, be administered, manually with a syringe and needle or automatically, using minipumps implanted under the skin.

The central component of the insulin molecule is virtually identical in all vertebrates: bovine (cow) insulin (with three different amino acids) and porcine (pig) insulin (with one different amino acid) are good substitutes for human insulin. Indeed, they were used for many years before the advent of genetically engineered human insulin. However, the body's immune system produces antibodies against these foreign insulins, so higher doses may be required.

Human insulin, available since the early 1980s, is produced from porcine insulin, by replacing one amino acid or, more recently, by splicing the genes coding for human insulin onto a single-celled microorganism, such as *E. coli*, to yield vast quantities of pure human insulin (see GENETIC ENGINEERING).

H. BYRT

**See also:** CELL BIOLOGY; DIABETES; GENETIC ENGINEERING; HOMEOSTASIS; INFORMATION SCIENCE; PANCREAS.

**Further reading:**
American Diabetes Association. 2002. *American Diabetes Association Complete Guide to Diabetes.* Alexandria, Virginia.

# DISCOVERING INSULIN

In 1869 German medical student Paul Langerhans first discovered the alpha and beta cells of the islets of Langerhans, which were later named in his honor. Then in 1889 Oskar Minkowski, professor of medicine at Strasbourg, inadvertently demonstrated that the pancreas was an important factor in protecting the body from diabetes when he removed the pancreas of a dog to investigate its role in the digestion of fats. The unfortunate dog developed diabetes as a result. Insulin itself was not inferred to exist until 1917, by an English physiologist, Edward Sharpey-Schafer, and at that time scientists were unable to prove its existence.

Frederick Banting, a Canadian physician, began his work on diabetes in May 1921. After persuading a skeptical professor of physiology at the University of Toronto, John MacLeod, to provide laboratory facilities, experimental animals, and help in the form of a research assistant named Charles Best, Banting set about trying to do what many people had already failed to do: to extract and isolate insulin from pancreatic tissue and show that it could reduce blood sugar concentrations in diabetic animals. He succeeded in 1922, with the help of biochemist John Collip, who was brought in to help with the research.

The first human patient, a 14-year-old diabetic, was treated in 1922. Banting and MacLeod shared the Nobel Prize for physiology or medicine in 1923 for their discovery. Banting then gave half his prize money to Best, and MacLeod gave half his prize money to Collip in recognition of their work.

In 1958 English biochemist Frederick Sanger, working at the University of Cambridge, received the Nobel Prize for chemistry for his work on the amino acid sequence, or primary structure, of insulin.

*Frederick Grant Banting (1891–1941)*

*John James Richard Macleod (1876–1935)*

**DISCOVERERS**

# INTELLIGENCE

**Intelligence is a complex, controversial concept that includes the ability to learn, reason, and understand**

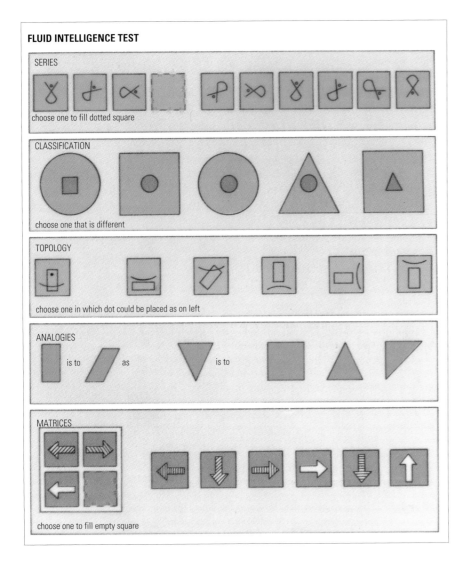

**FLUID INTELLIGENCE TEST**

SERIES
choose one to fill dotted square

CLASSIFICATION
choose one that is different

TOPOLOGY
choose one in which dot could be placed as on left

ANALOGIES
is to     as          is to

MATRICES
choose one to fill empty square

*In the IQ test illustrated above the use of symbols are used rather than words or numbers to eliminate any cultural bias.*

## The history of intelligence and of intelligence testing

The somewhat vague statement that "intelligence is what intelligence tests measure," although unsatisfactory, makes the important point that the evolution of the concept of intelligence has proceeded alongside and even as a function of the evolution of intelligence testing.

The founder of intelligence measurement via the use of tests was the English scientist Sir Francis Galton (1822–1911). Galton tested people's sensitivity to musical pitch and their performance in certain tasks (such as discriminating the weight of objects), skills Galton believed were the rudiments of intelligence. Galton's work was rejected by French psychologist Alfred Binet (1857–1911), who regarded mental skills such as comprehension and reasoning as more appropriate indicators of intelligence. He and fellow psychologist Theodore Simon pioneered the development of the modern intelligence test for school-age children. They proposed that intelligence is a general attribute present in many areas of cognitive function (memory, judgment, reasoning) that develops with age until an individual reaches maturity.

Unlike Galton, who measured attributes and physical skills, Binet and Simon tested individuals' performance in solving problems, remembering, and answering questions. Specifically, Binet and Simon developed a scale for measuring a child's performance in tasks (including drawing, recognizing coins, and making change). Each child's test performance was compared with an average performance level on the same tasks by groups of children of different ages. If the test taker performed the test at a level corresponding to that of older children, he or she was considered to have a mental age exceeding his or her chronological age and was said to have demonstrated above-average intelligence. German psychologist William Stern

An individual may be said to have a "high IQ," but what exactly does this term mean? The concept of intelligence, which originated in the late 1800s, has proved so complex, changeable, and controversial that it still fuels heated debate among psychologists. Intelligence is recognized by most psychologists as being different from instinct and includes the ability to learn and adapt to changes. An individual's central nervous system, as well as socioeconomic and cultural factors, are also thought to play a role in the development of human intelligence.

During what is known as the period of Enlightenment in the 1700s, intelligence was understood as being a specifically human ability to reason and think rationally. The concept of intelligence as something that could be measured by specific tests and precisely defined was not introduced until the 19th century. Since then, investigators have emphasized widely different aspects of intelligence, although most agree that fundamentally it involves perception, learning, memory, reasoning, and problem solving (cognitive processes).

## CONNECTIONS

● Intelligence is thought to involve the processes of perception and **LEARNING** and to be a function of **MEMORY, GENETICS,** and environmental influences.

## CORE FACTS

- Intelligence is influenced by an individual's genetic makeup and socioeconomic and cultural surroundings.
- Most psychologists believe intelligence involves the cognitive processes of perception, learning, memory, reasoning, and problem solving.
- The concept of intelligence has evolved alongside and even as a function of the evolution of intelligence testing.
- The intelligence quotient (IQ) is a person's mental age, as measured by the Simon-Binet intelligence test, divided by that person's chronological age and multiplied by 100.
- Contemporary theories of intelligence include Gardner's theory of multiple intelligences and Sternberg's three factor theory of intelligence.

(1871–1938) expressed this comparison statistically by dividing the mental age obtained using the Simon-Binet test by chronological age, and multiplying the result by 100, the result being the intelligence quotient (IQ). The Simon-Binet test was later adapted in America to become the widely used Stanford-Binet (IQ) test, from which evolved the well known multiple-choice group tests of school performance known as the Scholastic Aptitude Tests (SATs) and Graduate Record Examinations (GREs).

In 1939 David Wechsler developed the Wechsler-Bellevue Scale (later to develop into the Wechsler Adult Intelligence Scale). He challenged the idea that intelligence was a single ability and tested four subcategories: information, comprehension, arithmetic, and vocabulary. His tests indicated that an individual who did well in one category usually did well in the others. This high correlation led English psychologist Charles Spearman (1863–1945) to develop a statistical technique known as factor analysis, which compared the relationship of g and s factors. The g (general intelligence) factor referred to a common factor (influence) believed to underlie the high correlation between an individual's performance in the different subcategories of cognitive tasks. Spearman believed that any particular cognitive task drew on the subject's g factor, as well as on the specific factor (s) that was involved in the particular task at hand.

## Artificial intelligence

Cognitive psychologists believe that intelligence is made up of the ability to mentally represent and use information. In the late 1950s, U.S. psychologists Allen Newell and Herbert A. Simon worked with computer experts to build a computer model of human problem solving that would allow the machine to check each step in its problem-solving process against the desired solution and take steps to bring the program closer to its goal.

The assumption of this model is that humans process information one step at a time. This idea was challenged by other psychologists who believed that human cognitive processes primarily proceed in parallel. Supporting the idea of parallel processing was the fact that the human brain simultaneously handles large amounts of diverse information.

Some biological studies of the brain have contributed to the series-parallel debate. Many psychologists have studied intellectual performance in terms of the different regions of the brain believed to be involved.

The cerebral cortex of the brain is divided into two hemispheres connected by a bundle of nerves called the corpus callosum. The left hemisphere has been found to be superior in verbal and analytical functioning, while the right side is more important in visual and spatial cognition. This division of labor suggests that human intelligence may involve a complex interaction of both hemispheres, which neither the serial nor parallel processing models adequately explain (see BRAIN).

*Albert Einstein (1879–1955), the German-Swiss physicist who formulated the theory of relativity, is regarded by many as a genius. The term* genius *is often applied to an individual whose work shows originality and creativity.*

## WHAT IS GENIUS?

The term *genius*, popularized by the U.S. psychologist Lewis M. Terman, denotes an outstanding intellectual ability, indicated by an IQ score of 140 or above on a standardized intelligence test. The more widely accepted use of the term is taken from the work of 19th-century British scientist Francis Galton, who saw genius as a creative ability of exceptional power, shown by the real achievements of an outstanding individual. For Galton genius involved originality, creativity, and the ability to think and work in areas not previously explored—qualities he characterized as intellect, zeal, and the power of working. In his book *Hereditary Genius* (1869), Galton provided the first clear statistical evidence that extraordinary achievement tends to run in families. Most psychologists now agree that genius, like intelligence, is a function of both hereditary and environmental factors. Often the term *gifted* rather than *genius* is used to describe children who show remarkable intellectual ability.

## A CLOSER LOOK

## Hereditary and environmental aspects of intelligence

The relative roles played by genetic and environmental factors is the most contentious issue surrounding the definition of intelligence. Similarities in intelligence and academic success between family members have been interpreted by many as evidence for a genetic component to intelligence. Nevertheless, most psychologists recognize the complex interaction between genetic and environmental influences that determines the quality of an individual's intelligence.

Many psychologists have attempted to disentangle hereditary and environmental factors by studying twins. Their studies compared the relative intelligences of identical twins (having the same genes) and fraternal twins (genetically no closer than ordinary siblings) to find conclusive evidence for an exclusively genetic component to intelligence. These studies have shown a higher correlation between the performances of identical rather than fraternal twins. Because both types of twins share the same fetal environment and are assumed to be raised in similar familial and social surroundings, many psychologists have interpreted the higher correlation between the IQs of identical twins to be an indicator of the genetic component of intelligence.

There can be no doubt, however, that cultural background and socioeconomic factors play a considerable role in determining intellectual performance. Many studies have indicated that for all children, an enriched educational environment has a dramatically positive impact on IQ, while an impoverished environment has an equally apparent negative effect.

## Are animals intelligent?

Experimental psychologists believe the apparent complexity of human cognition is built from the association of simple elements, and they have demonstrated the existence of associative cognitive processes in many animals other than Homo sapiens. While many psychologists accept this model to explain how invertebrates, birds, and fish behave and learn, they also acknowledge that human behavior and that of animals more closely related to humans (such as primates) is of a more sophisticated order.

Experiments have shown that animals, such as birds and rats, respond to relationships between stimuli varying in size, brightness, or number. Studies have also demonstrated the ability of some animals to learn simple concepts. Mammals in particular are able to master certain tasks that fish cannot. Primates, such as chimpanzees, seem able to learn to use the outcome of one test to predict the outcome of the next. Studies suggest that primates are able to generalize the "win-stay, lose-shift" strategy more readily than many other animals. Although there is little doubt that primates demonstrate cognitive abilities related to those tested on human intelligence tests, the concept of intelligence remains a predominantly human measure.

R. PREISER

See also: BRAIN; COMMUNICATION; CONDITIONING; GENETICS; LEARNING; MEMORY.

### Further reading:

Gardner, H. 2000. *Intelligence Reframed: Multiple Intelligences for the 21st Century*. New York: Basic Books.
Goleman, D. 1995. *Emotional Intelligence: Why It Can Matter More than I.Q. for Character, Health, and Longlife Achievement*. New York: Bantam Books.
Skoyles, John R., and Dorion Sagan. 2002. *Up from Dragons: The Evolution of Human Intelligence*. New York: McGraw-Hill Trade.
Trefil, James S. 1997. *Are We Unique?: A Scientist Explores the Unparalleled Intelligence of the Human Mind*. New York: John Wiley and Sons.

*The chimpanzee, seen fishing here, is able to learn and demonstrate cognitive processes that are more like those of humans than of other animals.*

## THE HEAD START PROGRAM

In 1964 the federal government asked a panel of child-development experts to draw up a program to help communities overcome the handicaps of disadvantaged preschool children. This program became the Head Start program, which began as an eight-week, comprehensive summer program to meet the emotional, social, health, nutritional, and psychological needs of preschool children aged three to six from low-income families. Head Start currently serves over 583,000 children and their families each year in urban and rural areas in all parts of the United States. Head Start children are given the opportunity to interact with other children their own age and are introduced to the concepts of words and numbers, and thus they are exposed to a variety of learning experiences that foster intellectual, social, and emotional growth. Head Start has also created other programs that support children and families as they move through kindergarden and the first three grades of public school. Studies have indicated that Head Start children in preschool score higher than comparable non–Head Start children on achievement tests that measure cognitive ability. The aim is to maintain and enhance these early benefits.

# INVERTEBRATES

*This metallic green beetle is a South American weevil (Lamprocyphus spp.). Its green coloring may act as camouflage.*

Invertebrates are all multicellular animals that do not possess a backbone (vertebral column). This grouping is more a convenience than the recognition of a natural biological relationship. However, a study of invertebrates' structure reveals a steady evolutionary development of increasing complexity, right up to the vertebrates. Invertebrates are classified in more than 30 different phyla, and there is enormous diversity of form and function in these organisms, which range from sponges and flatworms to giant squid, starfish, and butterflies. The greatest variety of invertebrates is found in marine and estuarine environments, but they also inhabit freshwater and terrestrial habitats. Arthropods, mainly insects, are the most successful land animals (see INSECTS).

## Asymmetrical structure

The simplest type of invertebrates are sponges phylum Porifera), which have no specialized tissues or organs. Most lack any symmetry in their body structure, and there is little differentiation in the three layers of cells that make up individuals. A sponge can be forced through a fine mesh, and the individual cells will survive. These cells reaggregate to form a new sponge within a few weeks.

Sponges feed by taking in nutrient-rich water through tiny pores, called ostia. The inner layer of cells has flagella (whiplike protrusions) that circulate the water through a system of channels to a central cavity. As the water passes the cells, small food particles are engulfed and then digested. Gas exchange and excretion take place by simple movement across cell surfaces, which is made easier by the circulation of water in through the ostia and out through a large pore called the osculum.

There is no evidence of sense organs in sponges. They have skeletal parts that are either organic (made of collagen) or inorganic (of silica or calcium carbonate). These hardened elements have left fossil records of sponges from the Cambrian period onward, but their origin is thought to be in the Precambrian, over 570 million years ago.

## Radial symmetry

The phylum Cnidaria (jellyfish, hydras, sea anemones, and corals) and the phylum Ctenophora (comb jellies) have similar body plans. Both have true tissues, a trait that differentiates them from sponges. After development from an embryo, cnidarians and ctenophores have an outer and inner layer of cell tissues, separated by a middle gelatinous layer, the mesoglea. The inner layer of cells is continuous and forms a cavity, or gut. Digestion of food begins in the gut, outside these cells; this digestive process is different from that of sponges, where digestion of food

---

### CORE FACTS

- Invertebrates are multicellular animals without a backbone. They reveal a great deal about evolution.
- There are more than 30 phyla of invertebrates.
- The highest-developed phylum, Chordata, which includes all vertebrates, also contains invertebrates.

---

## CONNECTIONS

● Invertebrates are found in all **BIOMES AND HABITATS** and occupy well-defined niches in the ecosystem.

● The early stages in the development of an animal **EMBRYO**, even a human's, show close similarities to those of invertebrates.

particles occurs only inside the cells themselves. The digested food is then engulfed by the cells lining the gut. Digestion in the gut allows the animals to ingest food that is larger than the individual cells, an important improvement over the cellular digestion of sponges. The gut of cnidarians has only one opening, with food entering and wastes exiting from the same opening. The ctenophores are structurally more complex: they have anal pores, so water and waste substances pass through their bodies and do not exit from the "mouth."

Neither phylum has gas-exchange, excretory, or circulatory systems; they rely on simple exchanges across cell surfaces. They are therefore mostly small organisms whose cells are all within a short distance from available oxygen and nutrients.

Both cnidarians and ctenophores are radially symmetrical: that is, the body parts are organized around a central axis, so any plane that passes through the central axis will divide the body into halves that are near mirror images. Nets of nerve cells coordinate the muscles, but there is no central nervous system. The muscles are the simplest type known in the animal kingdom.

Ctenophores are marine organisms that live in the open ocean from surface waters to depths of at least 10,000 feet (3,000 m). They move through the water by means of eight comblike plates of fused cilia that beat in a coordinated fashion.

## Bilateral symmetry

The phylum Platyhelminthes (flatworms, flukes, and tapeworms) has the simplest body plan of organisms with a bilateral symmetry: that is, they have a right and left half that are basically mirror images of each other. Bilateral symmetry is an important evolutionary development, because it allows animals to move more efficiently while seeking food and mates and to avoid predators. Platyhelminths also differ from the cnidarians and ctenophores in that they have three fully developed tissue layers—the ectoderm (outer), mesoderm (middle) and endoderm (inner).

Platyhelminths are unsegmented worms that are either free living or parasitic. Like the cnidarians, they have a digestive cavity (gut) with only one opening. They do not have a circulatory system to carry oxygen and nutrients throughout the body, so each of their cells must be within diffusion distance of oxygen and nutrients. All flatworms, flukes, and tapeworms are thin animals with a branching gut that allows the passage of nutrients and oxygen to all the cells of their bodies. They have a network of little tubes that end in so-called flame cells, cells lined with cilia that constantly flicker like small flames. The cilia move water and waste products to exit pores in the outer layer of body cells, the epidermis (see EXCRETORY SYSTEMS).

Most platyhelminths have a simple nervous system: a cerebral ganglion (a nerve junction box) in the head and nerve cords running along the body with cross-connections between the nerve cords. Free-living flatworms use sensory pits or protrusions on the side of the head to detect motion, chemicals, and nutrients. These free-living forms live mostly in marine and freshwater habitats, although a few species are terrestrial. Most platyhelminths are parasites of other animals, including humans.

Ribbon worms, in the phylum Nemertina, have a body plan similar to that of flatworms. However, they have a one-way, complete gut, with a mouth

*Cnidarians, such as sea anemones, have specialized stinging structures called nematocysts. Many sea anemones from tropical waters, like this* **Heteractis magnifica,** *have a symbiotic relationship with clownfish* **(Amphiprion spp.),** *which have developed immunity to the sting.*

at one end and an anus at the other, for more efficient digestion of food. They also have a simple, closed circulatory system. Mainly marine organisms, they have a unique feeding mechanism. To capture prey they can shoot out part of their digestive system through their mouth.

## Pseudocoelomates

The basic body plan of all other bilaterally symmetrical invertebrates (pseudocoelomates) differs from that of the platyhelminths and ribbon worms (the so-called solid worms). Pseudocoelomates have a fluid-filled cavity between the outer body wall and the gut. They also have circulatory, excretory, and muscle systems, which allow for larger organisms with more varied methods of locomotion. There are two types of fluid-filled cavities, the pseudocoelom and the true coelom. Both cavities represent a major improvement over the body plan of the solid worms, but in terms of evolutionary success, the development of the true coelom led to more diversity within the invertebrates.

The pseudocoelom is a fluid-filled cavity that develops between the mesoderm and endoderm (middle and inner tissue) layers of organisms. The organs of pseudocoelomates are free within this cavity and are bathed directly in its fluids. The lining of the pseudocoelom provides a place for muscles to attach, improving the locomotion of these animals.

There are nine phyla in the pseudocoelomates. Of these, only the nematodes (phylum Nematoda) contain a large number of species, which are present in all types of habitats. Nematodes are bilaterally symmetrical, round, unsegmented worms. They have longitudinal muscles that extend the length of the body between the epidermis and the pseudocoelom and pull against both the epidermis and the pseudocoelom. The pull of the muscles on the fluid-filled pseuodocoelom creates a pressure, which allows the organism to move along a surface as it pushes against it. This type of arrangement is called a hydrostatic skeleton.

Nematodes have a well-developed body covering called a cuticle. In terrestrial species, the cuticle is very thick and allows nematodes to exist either in dry soils or parasitically in the digestive tracts of host species. There are no circulatory or gas-exchange structures in nematodes; these functions are accomplished by diffusion and transport in the fluids of the pseudocoelom. Because nematodes rely on diffusion to transport oxygen and nutrients within their bodies, they are still restricted in size, and most are microscopic. They have a central nervous system with a cerebral ganglion and longitudinal nerve cords with cross-connections.

## Protostomes

There are two major branches of animals with a coelom—protostomes and deuterostomes. Protostomes ("first mouths") comprise a group of invertebrates in which the mouth develops from the blastopore, the embryonic opening to the external

environment (see EMBRYO). The coelom arises from the mesoderm as the cells divide and move away from one another. The major phyla of the protostomes include the segmented worms (phylum Annelida), the arthropods (phylum Arthropoda), and the mollusks (phylum Mollusca).

The body plan of annelids (such as earthworms) is a long tube (the digestive tract) inside another tube (the coelom), around which are longitudinal and circular muscle layers, which, with the coelom, form a hydrostatic skeleton. In annelids a cerebral ganglion and longitudinal nerve cords form a well developed nervous system. They are segmented, each segment possessing a nerve ganglion that coordinates the muscles of the segment for efficient movement and exterior bristles (setae) that anchor the worm during locomotion. Each segment also contains blood vessels and excretory and reproductive organs. In annelids the segments are internally divided from each other by thin partitions called septa. Segmentation allows an organism to grow larger by repeating the basic plan of the septum over and over again.

Arthropods are one of the most successful groups of invertebrates in terms of the numbers of species and habitats that they occupy. They too are segmented invertebrates, and some arthropods, such as millipedes, have bodies with many segments. In others, such as insects and spiders, the segments are fused together in sections: the head, thorax, and abdomen.

Arthropods have a well-developed central nervous system similar to that of annelids, as well as excretory and respiratory systems. The digestive system is complete, with two openings. The coelom is somewhat reduced, and there is a main body cavity called a hemocoel. The arthropod heart pumps blood into the hemocoel to bathe the internal organs.

The arthropods are distinguished by their jointed appendages and their exterior skeletons. In contrast to the hydrostatic skeleton of annelids, arthropods have a hardened exterior skeleton, called an exoskeleton. The advantage of an exoskeleton is that

*The paddle worm (Phyllodoca lamelligera) is an annelid. Its hydrostatic skeleton allows it to move across the surface of a rock, against which it pushes with an undulating motion.*

it provides strength and protection against predators and dry conditions. However, one drawback to the exoskeleton is that it cannot be expanded, and so it limits the organism's size. Thus, to grow, arthropods must shed their exoskeleton by molting (ecdysis) and replace it with another (see MOLTING).

The phylum Onychophora, wormlike animals with an exoskeleton, is an evolutionary line that connects the annelids and the arthropods.

Mollusks include snails, octopuses, squid, clams, and oysters. Their bodies are unsegmented. Mollusks are bilaterally symmetrical, with a visceral (organ-containing) mass enclosed in a mantle, a thickened fold of tissue that arises from the body wall and forms a space around the visceral mass. In shelled mollusks, the mantle secretes the shell. Within the mantle space, mollusks have either gills or lungs, depending on whether the species is aquatic or terrestrial. The visceral mass contains the digestive system, the excretory and reproductive organs, and an open circulatory system that circulates blood within it.

Mollusks have a coelom, but it is much reduced in size. The remains of the coelom lie near the heart. Mollusks are noted for their muscular foot, which is used in locomotion, and have a developed central nervous system. Cephalopods (octopuses, cuttlefish, and squid) have brains that are larger than those of any other invertebrate.

## Deuterostomes

The second group of coelomate animals is the deuterostomes (meaning "second mouths"). In the embryo of these animals, the anus forms from the blastopore, and the mouth forms from a second opening. The coelom develops from pockets inside the mesodermal gut cavity.

Deuterostomes include two large phyla, Echinodermata and Chordata, and two smaller phyla, Chaetognatha and Hemichordata.

The echinoderms include spiny-skinned organisms, such as starfish, sea urchins, and sand dollars, that have a radial symmetry that repeats itself five times. This type of body plan is unique and develops only at maturity.

Echinoderms have a well developed coelom and a water vascular system composed of a series of complex fluid-filled canals. Most echinoderms have a complete gut, the digestive system ending in an anus, where the waste products of digestion are pumped out. They lack specialized excretory organs. The nervous system is not centralized and is more like a nerve net. Echinoderms have an internal skeleton that is composed of separate plates. They move about on hundreds of hydraulically powered tube-feet (see ECHINODERMS).

The phylum Chordata contains not only invertebrates but the subphylum Vertebrata. Therefore, the deuterostomes as a group include both invertebrate and vertebrate animals.

Chordates have three main distinguishing characteristics. First, they have a single, hollow nerve cord that runs along the back, or dorsal surface, of the animal. Second, they have a flexible rod called a notochord, which forms on the dorsal side of the gut in early embryonic development. The notochord is present at some stage in all chordates, but in vertebrates it is replaced by a vertebral column. The third characteristic is the presence of gill slits at some point in the life cycle.

Among the living chordates, only two groups are invertebrates: the tunicates (sea squirts and their plankton relatives; subphylum Urochordata) and the lancelet (also called amphioxus; subphylum Cephalochordata).

M. GRISWOLD

**See also:** ANNELIDS; ARTHROPODS; CHORDATES; CORALS; ECHINODERMS; EMBRYO; EXCRETORY SYSTEMS; FLATWORMS; INSECTS; JELLYFISH, SEA ANEMONES, AND HYDRAS; MOLLUSKS; MOLTING; NEMATODE WORMS; PLANKTON; SPONGES.

## Further reading:
Margulis, L. and K. V. Schwartz. 1998. *Five Kingdoms: An Illustrated Guide to the Phlya on Earth.* New York: W. H. Freeman.
Wallace, R. L. and W. K. Taylor. 1996. *Invertebrate Zoology: A Laboratory Manual.* 5th ed. New Jersey: Prentice Hall.

*The lancelet resembles a primitive fish but is believed to have diverged from the evolutionary line at an early stage. It has no brain, the notochord extending all the way through the head. It feeds by taking water in through the mouth and trapping particles in a mucous net.*

# IRON

**Iron is a mineral that is required by virtually all living organisms for the transport of oxygen**

Virtually every living organism uses iron, an essential mineral, in its biological processes. Often the iron is present in such tiny amounts that it is known as a trace element.

Iron is best known for its role in helping the blood to transport oxygen through the body. In vertebrates, iron is at the core of the protein hemoglobin, present in red blood cells. Each iron atom can form a reversible chemical bond with an oxygen molecule. This ability provides a convenient mechanism for transporting oxygen around the body.

In the lungs of air-breathing animals, the hemoglobin binds to oxygen from the air, which is present at a high concentration. As oxygenated blood travels through the body's tissues, where oxygen concentrations are lower, it surrenders the oxygen molecules. While in the tissues the blood picks up carbon dioxide molecules produced by the cells. The carbon dioxide is released when the blood returns to the lungs, and the cycle begins again.

Iron is a component of other important organic substances. It is present in myoglobin, an oxygen-binding protein found in muscle tissue that takes oxygen from the blood and stores it for future use.

Hemerythin, another iron-containing oxygen transporter, is found in only a few marine invertebrates. Like hemoglobin, hemerythin has an affinity for oxygen and so can carry this vital gas from the gills to all the cells of the invertebrate.

## Metabolic role

Iron plays a vital role in the metabolic processes of plants, animals, and bacteria. In plants, it is involved in photosynthesis, the process by which green plants use sunlight to produce food. In photosynthesis, chlorophyll in the plant's cells absorbs sunlight and releases electrons. The electrons then proceed through a complex series of reactions, called an electron transfer chain, which use a set of iron-containing enzymes called cytochromes and ferredoxins. The electrons are required to transfer energy for the manufacture of glucose.

Iron also plays a similar role in animal cells and bacteria. For example, iron-containing cytochromes are found in animal cells in the inner membrane of the mitochondrion, the cell organelle that supplies energy from respiration, which requires oxygen.

Iron is also present in leghemoglobin, a protein found in many species of Rhizobium bacteria. Using leghemoglobin, these microorganisms, which infect the roots of legumes and similar plants, take nitrogen from the soil and convert it into a more usable form. Other bacteria, such as *Thiobacillus ferrooxidans*, are able to oxidize iron itself to produce energy. Groups of these bacteria, commonly called iron bacteria, may grow into large masses that can obstruct cast iron water pipes.

## Iron intake

Most adults take in about 15 to 20 milligrams of iron daily. However, only 0.5 to 1.5 milligrams are absorbed into the body, either because the iron in food is present in forms that are not easily absorbed, such as fiber, or because the iron forms insoluble compounds with intestinal secretions.

The iron in red meat is particularly well absorbed by the body. Other plentiful sources of iron include liver, egg yolks, leafy green vegetables, legumes, and whole grains. Many foods, such as breakfast cereals, are fortified with additional iron.

## Iron deficiency

A small amount of iron is lost through excretion, including sweating. Women lose large amounts in their menstrual blood, so it is particularly important that their diets are sufficiently rich in iron.

About 70 percent of the iron in the human body is present in hemoglobin. If there is not enough iron, the hemoglobin content of the red blood cells is low and as a result the oxygen-carrying capacity of the blood is reduced, and iron-deficiency anemia develops. Iron deficiency is the most common cause of anemia. Pregnant women are especially prone to iron-deficiency anemia because the developing fetus uses the mother's stores of iron to make its own hemoglobin and other iron-requiring proteins.

V. KIERNAN

**See also:** ANEMIA; BLOOD; NUTRITION.

## Further reading:
Dan, M. 2000. *The Doctor's Complete Guide to Vitamins and Minerals.* New York: Random House.
Vander, A., J. Sherman, and D. Luciano. 2001. *Human Physiology.* 8th ed. New York: McGraw Hill.

*Red blood cells contain 70 percent of the total amount of iron in the human body.*

## CONNECTIONS

● Sickle-cell anemia is a **HEREDITARY DISEASE** that is particularly prevalent in people of African descent. The red blood cells are distorted and block capillaries, and thus cause oxygen deprivation in tissues and intense pain.

● Iron-containing hemoglobin has an important role in carrying **OXYGEN** around the body.

# ISLAND HABITATS

## Island habitats are areas of habitat that are isolated within another type of habitat

*The Maldives are coral atolls in the Indian Ocean. Many of these islands are still uninhabited because they are isolated from the mainland.*

## CONNECTIONS

● **FLIGHTLESS BIRDS,** such as the kiwi, the moa, and the emu, often live in island habitats, where there are few (if any) predators.

When most people think of an island, they imagine a patch of land in the middle of an ocean. However, in ecological terms, any area of habitat that is isolated in the middle of another habitat can be thought of as an island. To ecologists, an oasis in the middle of the Sahara Desert, a snow-capped mountain peak in the middle of the African savanna, or an ancient freshwater lake system are as much islands as are the coral atolls of the South Pacific.

Geographical islands, whether continental or oceanic, are unusual places because they are isolated. It is difficult for living organisms to reach the islands in the first place, and once they arrive, these organisms themselves become isolated from their relatives that remain on the mainland or in the source population. Islands, therefore, make good "laboratories" for the study of evolution.

Isolation is a key factor, if not the critical factor, in allowing evolutionary change to take place in an island's plant and animal inhabitants (called the biota). The isolated gene pool of these island residents branches off from that of the source population, and as islands are usually separated from one another, each island's biota may be unique.

The evolution of island biotas is also influenced by the ability of living organisms to colonize and spread. This movement requires special adaptations, such as a strong flying ability for birds or the ability of the seeds of plants to withstand long immersion in salt water. These adaptations limit the types of organisms arriving at an island.

With few of their competitors sharing the journey, however, those species that do arrive on an island can evolve at their own pace. Other factors that influence the evolution of island biota are the island's size, its proximity to a potential source of immigrants, its topography (the physical and natural land surface), and its latitude.

### How islands are colonized

Unless creatures are able to fly, oceans may prevent most terrestrial and freshwater biota from reaching islands. Remote islands may be colonized directly by some of the larger and stronger flying animals, particularly migratory birds that are blown off course. Smaller birds, bats, and flying insects may become caught up in strong air currents from which they are unable to break free. These flying visitors, in addition to founding new colonies of their own species, may also serve as the transport mechanism for the eggs or dormant stages of seeds, fruits, spores, or even other animals. Birds may carry seeds in their crop—some seeds, for example, remain viable after up to two weeks in a bird's stomach—or in the mud on their feet. Species that are unable to fly or are too heavy to be carried by air currents and storms may be able to colonize islands by using natural rafts of floating vegetation.

Plants are unable to walk or fly, so most have evolved adaptations for dispersing seeds away from the parent. Seeds that are usually dispersed by the wind, such as orchid seeds, have been known to travel up to 125 miles (200 km). Plants can also colonize an island if a single fertile spore or seed lands and germinates. In contrast, because most animals reproduce sexually, unless a female lands on an island already pregnant, a minimum of two

---

### CORE FACTS

■ Islands are isolated areas of habitat.

■ Organisms that arrive at an island must have adaptations so that they can reach it.

■ New immigrants often find few predators or competitors.

■ New species adapt over time to the new environment and food sources on the island.

■ Until they are well established, island populations are often too small to survive chance catastrophes.

adults, male and female, is required for the successful colonization of the island.

## The variety of island habitats

In general, islands with a greater variety of habitats (usually those that are relatively large) have the potential to accommodate a greater variety of species. Very small islands, for example, are often incapable of holding fresh water and present a relatively harsh environment to most immigrants.

## Problems that face island populations

Life on an island has the distinct advantage that there are usually fewer competitors. Frequently, predatory species are unable to survive on islands because there is insufficient food to support them. Living on islands, however, presents various problems as well.

The small size of populations reaching islands makes them vulnerable to extinction by chance events —early on, when only a few individuals have colonized an island and populations have not had a chance to grow, any small variation in either the birthrate or the natural death rate can wipe out the colonizers. A random change in the gene frequency of a small, isolated population is called genetic drift.

Remote islands are also likely to be colonized by only a few individuals, with the result that the island population will have relatively little genetic variation (see GENETICS). This lack of genetic variation may make island species unable to adapt to changing environmental conditions. If conditions are highly variable, island species may quickly become extinct. In addition, new immigrants to an island already possess adaptations to the mainland and are not yet adapted to island conditions.

The genes possessed by the individuals in the colonizing population also affect the survival of the population. The founder individuals of the colonizing population will have only a small and perhaps nonrepresentative sample of the parent population's gene pool. Subsequent evolution in this population will take a different course from that in the parent population as a result of this limited genetic variation, and a completely new species could evolve. This phenomenon is called the founder effect.

Island populations are particularly vulnerable to catastrophes, such as volcanic eruptions or severe storms, because island inhabitants have little opportunity to leave the area and subsequently return. If on the mainland a volcano erupts and kills all forms of life in a 12-mile (20-km) radius, living organisms from outside this area will slowly recolonize the affected regions. In contrast, if island populations are wiped out by a catastrophe, it may take hundreds or thousands of years for these areas to be recolonized (see ENVIRONMENTAL DISASTERS).

## Reaching a balance

The number of species that an island can support is determined by many factors—the topography or geographic variety of the island, the diversity of habitats, the accessibility to a source of colonists, and the number or diversity of species present at that source. Because island populations are prone to

*An oasis in a desert region. In ecological terms, this isolated habitat counts as an island.*

**On the Galápagos Islands off South America, finches have evolved beaks of different sizes to take advantage of the available food sources.**

missing. Therefore, once early immigrants are established, they face little competition and have the potential to exploit the island's entire range of food sources and habitats. This release from competition allows behavioral changes to take place and also allows the evolution of new species because the particular groups of individuals become specialized enough to eat the new available food sources.

An example of this diversification can be observed by watching the behavior of ants on the Dry Tortuga islands close to the Florida Keys. Only a few species have successfully colonized the island. These include *Paratrechina longicornis*, an ant that on the mainland normally nests in the open in the shelter of large objects. On the Dry Tortugas, this ant also nests in tree trunks and on open soil—environments that on the mainland are occupied by other species of ants.

### Darwin's finches

The best studied example of evolutionary change and diversification is that of Darwin's finches, which live only on the isolated Galápagos Islands off the west coast of South America. These finches were one of Darwin's main pieces of evidence for his theory of natural selection (see NATURAL SELECTION). Scientists think the ancestor finch species that arrived on the Galápagos had a typical small seed-eating bill. Over time, new species have evolved on each island, and their bills reflect the food availability on the different islands in the Galápagos group. On one island, larger-beaked finches can crack open the fruit of the abundant caltrop bush (*Tribulus cistoides*), while on another island, smaller finch species with more delicate beaks process more abundant smaller seeds from a variety of species of plant.

Two "natural" experiments in the Galápagos have allowed scientists to examine evolution in the making. In 1977 the Galápagos suffered a terrible drought, and large, tough seeds were the only food available in the following year. The birds would therefore need larger bills to open the seeds. When scientists measured the average bill size of the most common finch, *Geospiza fortis*, on the islands they discovered there had indeed been an increase in bill size—only birds with larger bills had survived the drought. Birds born during the years following the drought also had larger bills. In 1982 the climate showed an extreme variation in the other direction —the Galápagos had the wettest year for over a century. Small seeds were abundant, and in the following years, birds with smaller bills prospered.

Another good example of diversification can be observed in the Rift Lakes of eastern Africa. These isolated lakes were formed millions of years ago when the African continent began to separate. Their environments are diverse, and they contain a tremendous variety of fish. In Lake Tanganyika alone there are 37 genera and 126 species of fish, while in Lake Malawi there are 20 genera and 196 species. These include predatory fish, plankton feeders, vegetation feeders, and bottom feeders.

extinction, the number of species on an island at any given time represents a balance between the colonization of new species and the extinction of species already on the island. In time, islands should reach a point where the number of species is more or less constant.

Once a species has colonized an island, the arrival of other members of the same species does not increase the number of species present on the island. Hence, the number of new species reaching the island will decrease because more and more of the immigrants will belong to species already present. Conversely, as more and more species colonize the island, there is a greater opportunity for extinctions to occur. The first species to arrive can choose from the variety of habitats and faces no competition from other related species. As time goes by and the island fills up with different species exploiting the various resources on the island, it becomes progressively more difficult for new immigrants to gain a toehold. Also, with a greater number of species on the island, it is more likely that one of them will become extinct. Eventually, the rates of immigration will approximately equal the rates of extinction.

### Evolution on islands

Most species have evolved to deal with a variety of parasites, predators, and competitors. Frequently, however, when a creature arrives on an island, many of its competitors, predators, and parasites are

What is remarkable is that all these fish belong to a single family, the cichlids, the suggestion being that they may have evolved from a single species.

Trees are often missing from island fauna because their seeds are usually much larger and heavier than those of other plants and are much less likely to disperse over long distances. Some plants have adapted to fill this vacant niche. For example, most members of the Rubiaceae family are low shrubs, but on the island of Samoa, this family of plants has produced a tree that is 25 feet (7.5 m) tall.

Released from competition on islands, big animals tend to get smaller, while small animals tend to get bigger. The mechanism for this shift in size remains unclear for many island situations. One theory is that animals change in size to fill the niches that on the mainland are occupied by other species. For example, most monitor lizards are small, but on the island of Komodo in Indonesia, one species of monitor lizard, the Komodo dragon (*Varanus komodoensis*), has grown larger than the species on the mainland because there are no other predators of the same size on Komodo Island. Monitor lizards on the Canary Islands show the same phenomenon; the *Lazerta galloti* lizard on Tenerife Island is much larger than its mainland counterparts.

However, while these animals have grown larger, others have grown smaller. Because small populations have a greater risk of extinction than larger ones, as the size of an animal goes down, the number of individuals of that species that can be supported by resources on the island goes up. Smaller animals with lower food requirements are better equipped to survive with the limited food supplies of an island than are larger animals.

Long-distance dispersal can be a disadvantage to plants and insects on a small island because small seeds and animals can be blown into the oceans. Unsurprisingly, the seeds of many island plants have lost their tufts or wings. Many island insects are also wingless. While it may be relatively simple for a bird with good flying abilities to get to an island, once on the island, those same flying skills may increase the chances that the bird will be blown offshore. Furthermore, one of the major reasons for flight—escape from predators—is of little value if the island has no predators. As a result, it is not uncommon for island birds to become flightless, as was the case with the kiwi, the moa, and the kakapo (a flightless parrot), residents of the islands of New Zealand. While flightlessness may initially have advantages, the introduction of predators, whether cats, rats, or humans, makes extinction of these birds more likely—an example being the dodo of Mauritius, an island in the Indian Ocean. The bird was pushed to extinction by sailors who easily caught them for food (see EXTINCTION).

J. GINSBERG

**See also:** ENVIRONMENTAL DISASTERS; EVOLUTION; EXTINCTION; GENETICS; NATURAL SELECTION; SPECIES.

## Further reading:
MacArthur, R. H., and E. O. Wilson. 2001. *The Theory of Island Biogeography.* Princeton, N.J.: Princeton University Press.
Vitausek, P. J., L. L. Loope, and H. Anderson, eds. 1995. *Islands: Biological Diversity and Ecosystem Function.* Ecological Studies, Vol. 115. New York: Springer Verlag.

*The Komodo dragon (*Varanus komodoensis*), which lives on an island in Indonesia, is much larger than most other lizards.*

# JAWS

**Jaws are hinged mechanisms of bone or cartilage that enable an organism to grasp objects with its mouth**

*Lions have powerful jaws, so they are able to seize prey and tear up meat.*

## CONNECTIONS

● **SHARKS'** jaws are made from **CARTILAGE.**

● Jaws are often used as weapons in **DEFENSE** and to show **AGGRESSION.**

Jaws have transformed the world's ecology. This specialized hinged mechanism of bone or cartilage allows organisms to grasp and manipulate objects. Teeth provide grip so that jaws can reduce food to a manageable size (see TEETH). Organisms with jaws include most fish, amphibians, reptiles, birds (although their jaws are modified into a beak), and mammals. The upper jaw is called a maxilla, and the lower jaw is called a mandible.

## Living without jaws

Many invertebrates survive successfully without jaws, but their lifestyle and food type are limited. Jaw substitutes, which are not made from bone or cartilage, are also common. For example, the throat of the squid (*Sepia* spp.) contains brittle, jaw-like protrusions made of keratin that look very much like an inverted parrot beak.

## Fish

The first fish, in the class Agnatha, were jawless filter feeders. The Agnatha still exist in the form of lampreys and hagfish, which filter feed or feed using suckers. As with modern fish, their gills (located behind the mouth) were supported by a series of paired arches made of cartilage, and it is thought that jaws first evolved from one of these pairs. Around 80 million years after the appearance of jawless fish, during the early Silurian period (438 to 408 million years ago), the first fish with jaws appeared. These were the so-called spiny sharks in the class Acanthodii. Many modern fish possess jaws that are specialized to fit in with their particular lifestyle (see FISH). For example, the long-nosed pike (garpike; *Lepisosteus osseus*), has a long, tubelike jaw that it uses to pry prey from crevices in rocks.

## Amphibians and reptiles

Amphibians evolved from jawed fish, and most have small teeth to help them hold and seize prey. Reptiles have much larger, stronger jaw muscles than amphibians. The lower jaw of the snake, for example, has two halves. Each half moves in turn, so the jaws are flexible, virtually able to dislocate in order to engulf large prey (see SNAKES). Some turtles have an extra adaptation. A serrated broad alveolar shelf (secondary palate) in their upper jaw enables them to crush stems and fruit (see TORTOISES AND TURTLES).

## Birds

Heavy jaws with teeth would slow birds down during flight, so birds' jaws have been replaced by a lighter, highly specialized beak.

The beak has been modified to accommodate different diets. Fish-eating shorebirds that feed on slippery prey have serrated keratin covering their beak, to give them more grip. Spoonbills (*Platalea alba* and *Ajaia ajaia*) have wide, flattened, spoon-shaped jaws to sieve the water for prey.

A bird's skull is composed of four units, each highly flexible. As the beak opens, the upper jaw

## CORE FACTS

■ Jaws are hinged mechanisms made from bone or cartilage.
■ Jaws enable organisms to grip, grind, and chew food.
■ Jaws are thought to have first evolved in primitive fish.
■ Birds' jaws have been replaced by a beak, light enough to enable birds to fly.
■ Herbivorous, carnivorous, and omnivorous mammals have jaws that are adapted to their particular food type.

flexes upward, and the lower jaw expands sideways. This trait is especially useful for a bird such as the brown pelican (*Pelecanus occidentalis*), which has an expandable pouch of skin between each half of the lower jaw, used for storing its catch.

## Mammals

Mammals have a particularly high energy requirement and must obtain and process food efficiently to survive. The jaws of mammals, along with the teeth, muscles, and the digestive system, form a highly specialized feeding unit.

In terms of basic opening and closing, jaw action is fairly straightforward. Paired muscles (one end originating in the ear region and the other end inserting into the top of the lower jaw), contract to open the mouth; gravity closes the mouth, so there is little need for muscle power. Chewing is more complex, and the actual movement depends on the type of food. Three main jaw plans dominate: carnivorous, herbivorous, and omnivorous.

Herbivores (and to some extent omnivores) feed on tough, indigestible plant material, so it is important that food is chewed thoroughly. The jaws of herbivores are perfect for grinding. They close almost directly on top of one another so that all the teeth come into contact simultaneously. The lower jaw moves in a rotating, grinding path relative to the upper jaw, so vegetation can be sliced, cut, and crushed.

An extra adaptation to the herbivorous jaw of some animals, such as sheep and cows, is the diastema. This gap between the large cheek teeth and smaller grazing teeth, moves the cutting apparatus away from the face, creating a snout capable of penetrating narrow openings and reaching close to the ground during grazing.

Carnivores, such as cats, bolt their food, swallowing it whole, or slice it into bite-size chunks. The carnivorous jaw resembles that of a pair of sharp scissors, capable of slicing through flesh in an instant. The back teeth come into contact with the food before the front teeth, and carnivores hold and kill their prey using sharp, highly developed canine teeth. The temporalis and masseter muscles, the well-developed muscles at the side of the head, provide the force required to tear apart the tough flesh.

Omnivores, such as humans, have both carnivorous and herbivorous characteristics. Their teeth can grind and slice. The masseter and temporalis muscles are intermediate in size and have variable mobility so that a human can crunch a carrot, slice through a pastrami sandwich, or chew gum for hours.

I. HOLMES

**See also:** FEEDING; FISH; SNAKES; TEETH; TORTOISES AND TURTLES.

## Further reading:

Bradley, R.M. 1995. *Essentials of Oral Physiology.* St Louis: Mosby Year Book.
Ewer, R. F., and D. Kleiman. 1998. *The Carnivores.* Ithaca, NY: Comstock Publishing Associates.

## DEEP-SEA FISH

Deep-sea fish live in one of the most hostile environments on Earth, impenetrably cold and black except for a few spots of luminous bacterial light. Prey is rare, so when an opportunity arises, a carnivorous fish must seize this chance to feed, however large (or small) the prey is. The jaws of viperfish, such as *Chauliodus* spp., have adapted along with the rest of the skeleton to meet this challenge. Just before the attack, the head is thrown back so that the snout moves through almost 90 degrees. Simultaneously, the gills and structures surrounding the heart are pulled down and back, out of the pathway of the potential food. A huge gape in the jaws is created, and prey that is larger than the fish itself can be scooped up and swallowed, destined to provide energy for weeks.

**A CLOSER LOOK**

*Snakes have flexible jaws, which allow them to eat prey, such as frogs, that are larger than their mouths.*

## AFRICAN HUNTING DOGS

The African hunting dog, *Lycaon pictus*, is notorious for its killing techniques. It is, however, limited by small jaws and weak jaw muscles and has neither the speed nor the bite strength to take prey as cats do. Instead, adult members of the pack hunt cooperatively, chasing and snapping at the heels of the selected zebra or wildebeest over long distances until, exhausted, the prey slows down. The dogs then use their teeth to bite at the stomach and rump of their prey until it falls down.

**A CLOSER LOOK**

# JELLYFISH, SEA ANEMONES, AND HYDRAS

Jellyfish, sea anemones, and hydras are radially symmetrical, tentacled marine invertebrates in the phylum Cnidaria

*Sea anemones, of the class Anthozoa, are flowerlike in appearance and live as polyps throughout their lives.*

Brightly colored, symmetrical, and with waving tentacles, jellyfish, sea anemones, and hydras can be found throughout the world's coastal waters, rocky coasts, and coral formations. Others, including some hydras and hydrozoans, are freshwater animals. Jellyfish, sea anemones, hydras, hydroids, and corals are members of the phylum Cnidaria (also called Coelenterata, from the Greek for "hollow gut"). These invertebrates have evolved into three separate classes based on various adaptations: Scyphozoa (cuplike animals), the jellyfish; Hydrozoa (hydralike animals), the hydras and hydroids; and Anthozoa (flowerlike animals), the sea anemones and corals. There are thought to be about 9,000 living species of cnidarians.

### Cnidarian characteristics

Cnidarians contain special cells called cnidoblasts that help in feeding and defense—a major characteristic that gives the phylum its name. These cells are usually concentrated on the tentacles and on the outside of the animal's body. They contain stinging structures called cnidocysts. The most common cnidocysts are called nematocysts.

During their life cycle, cnidarians live as one of two basic body forms—a polyp or a medusa (plural,

medusae). Some cnidarian colonies contain both types (hydroids). A sea anemone is an example of a polyp—a small, cylindrical sac with a closed end that is attached to a surface and an open end with a mouth; it does not have a medusal stage.

The medusa is a free-swimming umbrella-shaped animal, with the mouth opening underneath; these animals are commonly called jellyfish. Certain hydroids and jellyfish can alternate generations,

## CORE FACTS

■ Cnidarians are divided into three classes: Scyphozoa (jellyfish); Hydrozoa (hydras and hydroids); and Anthozoa (sea anemones and corals).

■ Cnidarians are simple, two-layered creatures with an inner gastrodermis and an outer epidermis; in between is a soft, jellylike mesoglea.

■ During their life cycle, cnidarians live as one of two different body forms – a nonmobile polyp (like the sea anemone) or a free-swimming medusa (like the jellyfish). Sometimes both forms are present, as in hydroid colonies.

■ Jellyfish and anemones have tentacles with special stinging cells (cnidoblasts) for capturing prey and protecting themselves.

passing at some time during their life cycle through both polypoid (asexual) and medusoid (sexual) stages. Others exhibit polymorphism ("many forms"), a phenomenon in which several functionally distinct individuals live within a colony (see DIMOR-PHISM AND POLYMORPHISM). The colony exists because each animal carries out a separate role (for example, feeding or protecting) and contributes to the overall survival of the colony and the species.

The cnidarians do not have organs but are made up of soft tissues. Both polyps and medusae have two layers of cells: an inner gastrodermis (or endoderm) and an outer epidermis (or ectoderm). Between the layers is a soft, gel-like substance called mesoglea. Cnidarians have a simple digestive cavity, called the coelenteron, with one opening, which serves both as mouth and anus, since it is the only way to take in food and get rid of wastes. The coelenteron acts as a gullet, stomach, and intestine.

## Jellyfish (class Scyphozoa)

In the medusa stage there are numerous characteristics that distinguish jellyfish. Most are bell-shaped sacs, while others are saucer shaped or spherical; they can be found in marine and freshwater environments. Some jellyfish have thin tentacles and four to eight frilly "arms," others just have four to eight arms hanging below. The tentacles and arms are responsible for capturing food (mostly fish and crustaceans) and aiding in digestion. The body, tentacles, and arms all have nematocysts that aid in defense and capturing prey.

Unlike other classes of the phylum Cnidaria, jellyfish are not colonial but are made up of a single male or female organism. They are composed mostly of mesoglea, the gel-like, watery substance that gives the organism its name.

## SECONDHAND STINGS

Some sea creatures benefit from the cnidarians, for example, the molluskan nudibranchs (meaning "naked gills"), commonly called sea slugs. They live around intertidal or subtidal coastal areas, and unlike reef-forming cnidarians, they are free moving. One group, the eolids, have appendages, called cerata, over their backs, which act as breathing gills. One type, the striped nudibranch (*Cratena pilata*), found along the eastern coast of the United States, feeds on other animals such as hydroids and sea anemones and uses its many jaws to tear off chunks of tissue. Amazingly, the nudibranchs are not stung by their prey. Instead, the anemone's stinging cells pass right through the digestive tract of the eolid to the tips of the cerata, where they can be used to sting predators and thus add to the defense and protection of the sea slug.

Jellyfish move through water by contracting their body sacs, forcing jets of water diagonally downward. This movement causes a backward and downward thrust and thus keeps the jellyfish upright and propels it forward. As a result, the animal glides easily through the water.

## Hydras and hydroids (class Hydrozoa)

Hydras are solitary, carnivorous polyps found in freshwater lakes, rivers, ponds, and streams, attached to rocks and water plants by a sticky secretion from the animal's base.

The mouth is surrounded by four to eight tentacles. These tentacles contain stinging cells used for defense and for catching food. When an unsuspecting animal, such as a small crustacean or worm, brushes past the hydra's tentacles, it is showered with poisonous, numbing threads that pierce the animal's body. The tentacles then drag the victim to the hydra's mouth.

*The jellyfish (*Aurelia aurita*) seen from above, displays the typical bell-shaped appearance of many jellyfish.*

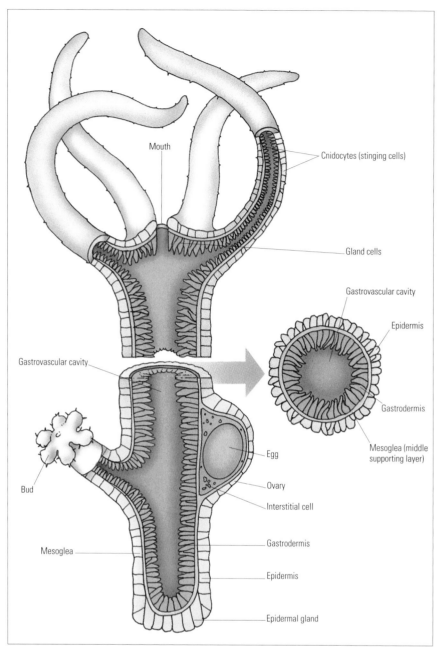

Mouth

Cnidocytes (stinging cells)

Gland cells

Gastrovascular cavity

Epidermis

Gastrovascular cavity

Gastrodermis

Egg

Mesoglea (middle supporting layer)

Ovary

Bud

Interstitial cell

Gastrodermis

Mesoglea

Epidermis

Epidermal gland

*Hydras, as illustrated above, display the two-layered structure common to all cnidarians and the thin mesogleal layer characteristic of members of the class Hydrozoa.*

Hydras reproduce asexually by budding, the process by which a section of the body wall and an extension of the coelenteron develops and eventually separates from the parent. When well fed, hydras can produce new buds once every two days. They can also reproduce sexually, usually during fall and winter, and have special cells containing reproductive organs. Some hydra species are hermaphrodites, in which an individual has both male and female sex cells (see HERMAPHRODITES).

Internally, hydras have a primitive nervous system called a nerve net. Neurons, or nerve cells, are linked together in a network, in which some of the neurons are receptors. If the hydra is touched, a nerve impulse is triggered at the site, and as a result the animal retracts and shrinks away from potential danger. Hydras are also able to regenerate tentacles or repair serious injuries. Even if a hydra is cut into pieces, many of the pieces will regenerate the missing parts to become whole, independent hydras.

Although most hydras are sedentary, living attached to submerged objects, some are capable of being independent. Their movement involves somersaulting head over heels.

Hydroids, the hydra's marine cousins, live in salt water. They usually form small (2 inches, or 5 cm), delicate, bushlike colonies attached to underwater surfaces. Generally, hydroids exhibit polymorphism, but some polyp colonies take the concept one step farther, and each organism within the colony has a certain body function. For example, the Hydractinia colony has feeding polyps (with mouths and long tentacles), protective polyps (with stubby, stinging, nonfeeding tentacles that protect the colony), and reproductive polyps (carrying the medusa buds). As all these different polyps are interconnected, it is difficult to determine where one individual ends and another begins (see DIMORPHISM AND POLYMORPHISM).

## Sea anemones (class Anthozoa)

Unlike certain hydroids and jellyfish that alternate between polyp and medusa stages, a sea anemone

## DIFFERENCES IN JELLYFISH

Different types of jellyfish can be found in different parts of the world:
• The purple jellyfish, found from Cape Cod to Florida, has red dots on its bell. Those of the genus *Beroe* have a yellow tint, because of special algae in their body tissues. The animal's eight digestive cavities also generate natural bioluminescence – the ability to "glow" with a naturally developed light. When the animal's transparent skin is disturbed or perhaps when it wants to attract prey, the spots in the digestive cavity brighten.

• The world's largest jellyfish is the lion's mane jellyfish (*Cyanea capillata*). In one summer, it can grow from a small polyp barely ¹⁄₁₀ inch (0.3 cm) in diameter to 8 feet (2.4 m), although it usually

averages 3 feet (0.9 m). It is found from Maine to Florida, with the largest creatures inhabiting the cooler waters of the north.

• The moon jelly (*Aurelia aurita*) is one of the most common jellyfish along the Atlantic coast and is also found worldwide. It is white, pink, or beige and measures about 1 foot (0.3 m) in diameter. About 250 hairlike tentacles run along the base of the bell; its sting produces a mild burning sensation.

• The cannonball jellyfish (*Stomolophus meleagris*) is found mostly from North Carolina to Florida. It is about 1 foot (0.3 m) in diameter and shaped like half an egg; it has eight arms but no tentacles.

A CLOSER LOOK

stays as an individual polyp all its life. Another difference is the sea anemone's gastrovascular cavity; its central coelentron cavity is divided into several sections, whereas the other cnidarians have a single, open cavity.

Sea anemones have stout, muscular bodies resembling hollow tubes. At the end of the body attached to a surface is a slimy basal disk that allows the anemone to slide slowly across the surface. At the top end is a mouth surrounded by stinging tentacles, which can be extended into long, smooth, fingerlike digits or contracted, so the sea anemone looks like a soft, colorful ball. The tentacles trap food by stinging prey, but the sting is too weak to harm humans.

Sea anemones are the most specialized of the cnidarian polyps. They have a well-developed nerve net and several specialized muscles. Each type of muscle has a particular function: longitudinal muscles pull the mouth dish and tentacles completely inside; a layer of circular muscles help to stretch and elongate the polyp's body during locomotion; and another type of circular muscle contracts just under the mouth, which closes off the anemone and allows it to resist drying out during low tide.

Sea anemones produce identical offspring asexually, by pulling apart into two halves. Tissue fragments left behind (usually as the anemone moves or after an injury) often regenerate and grow into identical adult anemones. The animals can also reproduce sexually by releasing eggs and sperm; the fertilized egg settles onto a surface and grows into a new individual.

Sea anemones are either sessile creatures (that is, they are permanently fixed in one place, not free moving) or they can swim, crawl, or burrow. Most attach themselves to rocks, shells (even to living organisms, such as clams), or submerged human-made objects, such as wharves and wrecks. Most live in tidal pools, between crevices on rocky shores.

Size and features vary greatly: the pink-tipped anemone (*Condylactis gigantea*) lives along the Florida coastline and can grow up to 1 foot (30 cm) in diameter. By contrast, the striped anemone (*Haliplanella luciae*), living along the United States coast from Maine to the Chesapeake Bay (thought to be an immigrant from Japan and Europe), has red or yellow stripes and grows to about ¾ inch (2 cm).

P. BARNES-SVARNEY

**See also:** CORALS; DIMORPHISM AND POLYMORPHISM; HERMAPHRODITES; INVERTEBRATES; OCEAN HABITATS.

**Further reading:**
Castro, Peter, and Michael E. Huber. 2002. *Marine Biology.* New York: McGraw-Hill College Division.
George, T. C. 2001. *Jellies: The Life of Jellyfish.* Brookfield, Conn.: Millbrook Press.
Nybakken, J. W. 2000. *Marine Biology: An Ecological Approach.* 5th ed. New York: Benjamin/Cummings.

## SAILING AWAY

One of the most interesting cases of mistaken identity in the marine world involves two members of the order Siphonophora—the Portuguese man-of-war (*Physalia physalia*) and the by-the-wind sailor (*Velella velella*), both of which resemble jellyfish. They are members of the phylum Cnidaria but are not jellyfish. They are classed as hydrozoans because of the unique way in which polyplike and medusa-like individual organisms coexist to form a colony.

Both species are planktonic (that is, they are suspended in the water and float with its movement), and most are found in the tropics or the subtropics—from Maine to beyond the tip of Florida. Like most hydrozoans, they consist of more than just one organism; they are colonies of many modified medusoid and polypoid individuals. For example, the Portuguese man-of-war is a floating, gas-filled sac with a bluish purple "sail," or crest, on top, which is about 12 inches (30 cm) long. This sail can be pointed at 45 degrees to the wind, allowing the creature to move around in search of food.

The sac is not simply a gas-filled bubble—hanging from the bottom are several types of specialized polyps, medusae, and tentacles. The tentacles, which can measure 60 feet (22 m) long, are responsible for catching food. In this respect, the Portuguese man-of-war is similar to the jellyfish; nematocysts on the tentacles sting the prey, and the tentacles contract to bring it to the feeding polyps and medusae. The powerful nematocysts are also responsible for the painful sting received by human swimmers who get too close; the nematocysts can still sting even when the animal is dead.

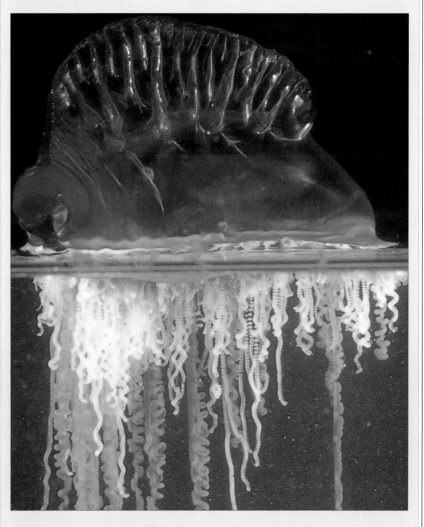

*The Portuguese man-of-war (*Physalia physalia*), although similar in appearance to a jellyfish, is in fact a hydrozoan.*

A CLOSER LOOK

# JENNER, EDWARD

*An illustration of Edward Jenner vaccinating eight-year-old James Phipps in May 1796, using pus from the hand of a dairy maid named Sarah Nelmes.*

## CONNECTIONS

● Active **IMMUNIZATION**, or vaccination, introduces antigens (foreign substances) into the body. In this way, **ANTIBODIES** can be produced against disease-causing organisms.

Edward Jenner was born in Berkeley, Gloucestershire, England, on May 17, 1749. After attending grammar school and being apprenticed to a surgeon for nine years, Jenner went to London in 1770 to study anatomy and surgery as a pupil of English surgeon John Hunter (1728–1793). Hunter was also a great naturalist, and Jenner assisted him in organizing the zoological specimens collected by English naturalist Joseph Banks (1743–1820) during the first voyage of HMS *Endeavour*. In 1773 Jenner returned to Berkeley to work as a medical practitioner, but his interest in natural history continued. In the following years, he observed and documented the parasitic nesting behavior of the cuckoo and presented his findings to the Royal Society, London, in 1787. The following year he was made a Fellow of the Royal Society of London and married Katherine Kingscote, with whom he had four children.

### The smallpox vaccine
Vaccination against smallpox was first introduced to England during the early part of the 18th century (see SMALLPOX). To gain immunity, doctors gave healthy people a mild dose of the disease by inoculating them with matter taken from smallpox pustules. However, there was always a risk of severe infection, and the practice also encouraged the disease to spread.

Jenner realized that some of his patients were already immune to smallpox. Subsequent investigation revealed that these people had previously had cowpox. In 1796 Jenner successfully inoculated an eight-year-old boy using cowpox taken from the arm of a milkmaid. However, the results were considered inconclusive. Undaunted, Jenner gathered data on a further 23 cases, publishing the details in 1798 in a memoir entitled *An Inquiry into the Causes and Effects*

## English doctor Edward Jenner (1749–1823) popularized vaccination as a method of disease prevention

*of the Variolae Vaccinae, a Disease Discovered in Some of the Western Counties of England, Particularly Gloucestershire, and Known by the Name of Cow Pox.* Following its publication, the practice of vaccination spread at astonishing speed. The number of deaths from smallpox in England dropped from over 2,000 a year to around 600 a year. Using cowpox vaccine to control smallpox saved many thousands of lives.

The term *virus* was first used by Jenner to describe the matter that produced cowpox. Jenner also discovered that the lymph fluid necessary to produce the vaccine could be dried in a glass tube and kept for three months. The dried product could be sent all over the world, and there was a real possibility that the disease could be eradicated.

### Later years
In 1802 the British Parliament granted Jenner £30,000 as reimbursement for lost income while researching the smallpox vaccine. He was also awarded honorary degrees from both Oxford (1813) and Harvard. The Royal Jennerian Society was founded in 1803; it provided free vaccinations and a facility to collect the lymph needed to produce the smallpox vaccine. Jenner retired in 1815 and continued with his studies of the natural history of birds. He died on January 26, 1823.

KIM DENNIS-BRYAN

**See also:** SMALLPOX.

**Further reading:**
Marrin, A. 2002. *Dr. Jenner and the Speckled Monster: the Search for the Smallpox Vaccine.* New York: Dutton Books.

## LADY MARY WORTLEY MONTAGUE

Lady Montague (1689–1762) was an early advocate of immunization against smallpox. At that time the vaccine used gave the person being inoculated a mild dose of the disease. As the wife of the British ambassador extraordinary to the Turkish court, she wrote many letters to England, and in one of them she described the inoculation process. Lady Montague had suffered a dose of smallpox, which left her with facial scarring and without eyelashes. She therefore decided to have her children inoculated so that they would not suffer the same fate. Her son was inoculated in 1718, and her daughter three years later. Owing to her influential position in London society, she made it fashionable to be inoculated despite the cost.

**DISCOVERERS**

# KELPS AND SEAWEEDS

**Kelps and seaweeds are advanced, photosynthesizing, multicellular algae, rich in minerals and vitamins**

From large, free-floating rafts to underwater forests, seaweeds dominate large areas of the ocean. The kelps are the largest of the seaweeds and can grow in forests over a hundred feet tall, with many smaller seaweeds growing on their stems.

## Classification

Seaweeds are advanced multicellular algae. There are many thousands of algae in the ocean, mostly invisible, microscopic, single cells that form the base of

---

### CORE FACTS

■ Seaweeds are advanced green, red, or brown algae whose color is determined by the different photosynthetic pigments present.

■ The giant kelp can grow to nearly 150 feet (46 m) and is the fastest growing aquatic organism known—rates of up to 17½ to 18 inches (46 cm) a day have been recorded.

■ Because of the high mineral and vitamin content, over 2 million tons (1.8 million tonnes) of seaweed are harvested annually for human and animal food and as fertilizer.

■ Several important byproducts of seaweed include agar, iodine, soda, and alginates, which are used extensively in the food industry as thickeners, stabilizers, and jelling agents.

---

many food chains on which all animals ultimately survive. They become visible when present in large quantities and can make the water cloudy or create a green film on the surface of mud.

Traditionally, algae were classified in the plant kingdom because they contain chlorophyll and are capable of photosynthesis. However, at the level of single-celled organisms, the boundary between animals and plants is unclear. Recent classifications separate singled-celled blue-green algae (cyano-bacteria) into the kingdom Monera and multicellular algae into the kingdom Protista.

The larger algal species (kelps and seaweeds) occur in three phyla: green (Chlorophyta), red (Rhodophyta), and brown algae (Phaeophyta). The brown algae are some of the most advanced algae and include the kelps and many large seaweeds.

## Seaweed colors

Seaweeds produce sugars by photosynthesis; these sugars are synthesized from water and carbon dioxide, using sunlight as a source of energy. This energy is trapped by chlorophyll, present in all photosynthesizing organisms, and several other closely related pigments. Chlorophyll is the dominant pigment in most plants and algae and gives them their green color. Brown algae contain mainly chlorophyll and a

*A forest of giant kelp, off the coast of California. These kelp can grow to over 100 feet (30 m) long and are the largest seaweeds.*

---

## CONNECTIONS

● Because of their rapid growth rates, seaweeds are thought by some scientists to be a major food source for the future, a rich renewable resource.

● As a food, seaweeds are a rich source of minerals and **VITAMINS**.

brown pigment called fucoxanthin, whereas red algae have large quantities of the red pigment phycoerythrin and the blue pigment phycocyanin. These pigments absorb energy from different wavelengths of light: for example, red pigments best absorb light at the blue end of the spectrum.

The presence of more than one photosynthetic pigment means more efficient energy absorption from the light reaching the organism. This is particularly important for seaweeds growing at considerable depths, because the water reduces the amount of light reaching them. Blue light penetrates water better than red light, so it is important for seaweeds to make the best use of the blue end of the spectrum. Red algae are particularly good at this: those growing at greater depths tend to have higher concentrations of phycoerythrin than those in shallow depths. Red algae can also grow well in shady rock crevices, sheltered from the full force of the waves.

### Structure of seaweeds

There are about 7,000 different types of seaweeds, in varying shapes and sizes—tubes, compressed strips, filaments, flat plates of tissue, or encrustations on rock surfaces. Some species even resemble flowering plants, with stemlike stipes and leaflike fronds, but these are not true stems or leaves. Neither do seaweeds have a vascular system like that of plants to transport nutrients and water to the cells. In seaweeds, all the cells are capable of absorbing fluid and

*This kelp (*Macrocystis *sp.), growing in Snare Island, New Zealand, shows clearly the holdfast points on rock.*

nutrients directly from the surrounding water. In addition, the holdfast at the base may be rootlike, but its only function is to fix the seaweed to a firm surface, rather than to absorb nutrients for nourishment.

Most seaweeds are attached to rocks or stones, at least initially, but some free-floating forms occur where conditions are calm, such as in sheltered inlets. The Sargasso Sea, east of the Caribbean, is surrounded by strong currents from the North Atlantic Ocean but is itself an area of weak currents, low rainfall, and light winds. Here seaweeds, particularly gulfweed (*Sargassum* spp.), form large, free-floating rafts, which support a highly specialized ecosystem that includes some unique species.

Other seaweeds grow in very turbulent conditions and must attach themselves firmly to a surface using their holdfast. The holdfast produces such a powerful glue that the stipe is more likely to break than the holdfast is to separate from the surface to which it is anchored. The fronds are flexible and elastic and usually divided into lobes, or segments, to allow water to flow past easily. They have a slippery texture to prevent rubbing against adjacent fronds and to discourage the buildup of lime on the surface, which would make the frond brittle.

Species growing in the intertidal zone have to cope with considerable turbulence when the tide is in and are frequently exposed to high temperatures, high light intensity, and variations in salinity when the tide is out. Species that grow at higher levels on

the shore are more tolerant of the drying effects of air, as their cells usually have thicker walls that lose water more slowly. Many seaweeds contain water-absorbing alginate compounds that prevent them from drying out. There is usually a clear zonation of seaweeds at different levels of the shore.

## Pacific kelps

The largest seaweeds grow in the Pacific Ocean. The biggest is the giant kelp (*Macrocystis pyrifera*), which grows along the coast from Alaska to California and along the coast of Chile. The fronds can reach 150 feet (46 m) in length and grow in waters as deep as 83 feet (25 m). The kelps may live for five years, but individual fronds usually last for about six months. It is the fastest growing aquatic organism known—growth rates of up to 18 inches (45 cm) a day have been recorded.

Several other large kelps grow along the Pacific coast of America. The bull kelp (*Nereocystis luetkeana*) ranges from Alaska to California. It grows up to 120 feet (36 m) long, even though it rarely survives longer than a year. The rarer elk kelp (*Pelagophycus*) of southern California is also short-lived but manages to reach even greater lengths of up to 130 feet (40 m).

These large kelps form dense underwater forests and provide a sheltered environment for many plants and animals. They are also harvested for various seaweed products, particularly alginates.

## Reproduction

Most brown and green seaweeds have two alternating phases of growth, an asexual, spore-producing phase and a sexually reproducing phase, although there are variations. The spores grow into sexually reproducing (gametophyte) seaweed. After fertilization the resulting zygotes grow into spore-producing (sporophyte) seaweed, and the cycle goes on. Red algae have two sporophyte phases between the gametophyte phase.

Sometimes, the zygote can develop a thickened skin and become a dormant spore (zygospore). This alternation between sexual and asexual reproduction, called alternation of generations, occurs in almost all the less advanced, multicellular plants and algae and provides an advantageous mixture of sexual reproduction and easy spore dispersal.

## Human and animal food

Seaweeds have been used for many centuries by humans as food and fertilizers. Nowadays there are many other uses, and about 2 million tons (1.8 million tonnes) are harvested every year worldwide.

Shen Nong, the father of Chinese medicine, prescribed seaweeds for certain illnesses around 3000 BCE. However, the greatest quantity and variety of seaweeds have been eaten in Japan since 800 CE, and now account for about 10 percent of the Japanese diet. The demand is so great that seaweeds are cultivated on nets in many bays and estuaries. Considerable quantities are also eaten in China and

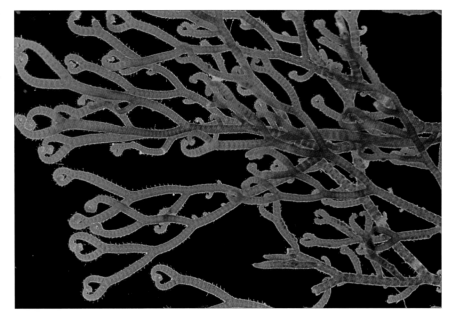

other parts of Southeast Asia. Elsewhere, seaweeds are eaten in many coastal areas and can form a significant part of the diet where the terrain or climates make it difficult to grow terrestrial crops (on islands, for example).

Seaweeds contain a high proportion of carbohydrate and fiber. Some species are rich in protein, but their main value is their high mineral and

*Ceranium shuttle-worthianum, a small red alga. Red algae are best adapted to life in deep water.*

## SEAWEEDS AND THE DINNER TABLE

The use of seaweeds for food has occurred for thousands of years. Some of the species used are the following:

**Brown seaweeds**
- Dabberlocks, alaria (*Alaria esculenta*): eaten in several places around the North Atlantic Ocean; used in stews or eaten raw; high in vitamins B6 and K.
- Kombu, kelp, tangle, oarweed (*Laminaria* spp.): several species eaten in Japan and the United States. Europeans prefer sugar kelp (*Laminaria saccharina*) and tangle or oar weed (*Laminaria digitata*). They are usually cooked in soups.
- Bull kelp (*Nereocystis luetkeana*): one of the large kelps growing on the Pacific coast of North America. It is either pickled or used in candy.

**Green seaweeds**
- Green nori (*Enteromorpha* spp.): sometimes called intestine weeds. In Japan and eastern Asia nori is eaten raw in salads, toasted, or steamed.
- Sea lettuce (*Ulva* spp.): eaten raw in salads, cooked in soups, or sometimes made into tea. All species are rich in iron.

**Red seaweeds**
- Irish moss, carrageen (*Chondrus* spp.): high in vitamin A, this seaweed is eaten in several places along the coast of the North Atlantic Ocean. It is useful in making jellies and as a thickener in soups.
- Nori, laver (*Porphyra* spp.): several species of high-protein nori are eaten in Japan and North America; laver (*Porphyra umbilicalis*) is used in soups and stews in parts of Britain and Ireland.
- Dulse (*Palmaria palmata*): widely used in temperate parts of the Northern Hemisphere, it is eaten raw, cooked, or made into a relish.
- Pepper dulse (*Laurencia pinnatifida*): used in Europe and North America as a condiment and as a substitute for chewing tobacco.
- Hijiki (*Hijikia fusiforme*), wakame (*Undaria pinnatifida*): high in protein, these seaweeds are eaten raw or cooked in Japan and eastern Asia.

vitamin content, including iodine, iron, magnesium, and vitamins A, $B_1$, $B_2$, $B_6$, $B_{12}$, C, and K.

In many coastal areas, seaweeds have been used as animal feed and fertilizers for many centuries, particularly in colder climates, on islands, and where the terrain makes the land difficult to cultivate. The mineral and vitamin content of seaweeds occurs in an easily assimilated organic form and thus makes them a useful supplement to other fodder. Livestock are fed mainly seaweed on some isolated islands: for example, on the Scottish island of Soay, the sheep survive wholly on a seaweed diet; a wall around the island confines them to the shore.

Wet seaweed is bulky and difficult to transport, and it is not usually economical to dry it for animal fodder or fertilizer use. However, there are a few factories that process seaweeds into dried meal or liquid extract, after which it is easier to transport and more practicable for general use.

## Soda

Soda (sodium carbonate, $Na_2CO_3$), a gray-white, odorless, water-soluble powder, was one of the earliest industrial products to be extracted from seaweeds; reports go back to the mid-17th century in France. It was used in the manufacture of glass and soaps. The main species used were brown seaweeds such as kelps (*Laminaria* spp.), wracks (*Fucus* and *Ascophyllum* spp.), and furbelows (*Saccorhiza polystichoides*). The industry waned in the mid-19th century, when soda became more easily available from salt pans and saline mineral deposits.

## Iodine

Iodine is an important chemical used in medicine. It has antiseptic properties and is important in the treatment of thyroid disorders, such as goiter (swelling of the thyroid gland in the neck).

Iodine occurs in seawater in very small amounts (0.01 to 0.07 parts per million) but is accumulated by some seaweeds to concentrations 200 times this amount. Iodine extraction began in the mid-19th century, at the time the extraction of soda began to decline, but became less important in the early 20th century when saltpeter (a naturally occurring form of potassium nitrate, $KNO_3$) was discovered in Chile.

## Agar

Agar is a clear, gelatinous substance derived from *Gelidium* and several other species of red algae. It is used as a vegetarian substitute for gelatin and as a neutral medium for plant and bacterial culture. It is insoluble in cold water but soluble in hot water: a 1 or 2 percent solution sets to form a firm gel that can incorporate any required nutrients. It is also resistant to bacterial liquefaction, a disadvantage of gelatin and other jellies.

## Alginates and carrageenan

In addition to agar, there are several other gelatinous products extracted from seaweeds. The most impor-

### ENERGY

Methanol and other alcohols can be extracted from seaweeds and blended with or used in place of gasoline. The giant kelp is the fastest growing aquatic organism. If it could be harvested economically; it would be a possible renewable energy source. Experiments are being carried out off the Californian coast, where seaweed is grown on nets hanging from small, floating platforms. Seaweed farms of many thousands of acres are being considered. If successful, they could provide a cheap source of seaweeds for energy and other uses.

### SCIENCE AND SOCIETY

tant are the alginates, derived from kelps and wracks, and carrageenan, derived from Irish moss (*Chondrus crispus*). They have many hundreds of uses, particularly in the food industry. As they absorb water quickly, alginates are used for thickening liquids and for stabilizing food to prevent it from liquefying. They are also used to provide a medium for holding solids and oils in the form of pastes and emulsions, for coating food to prevent air from reacting with it, and as jelling agents and waterproof coatings. Alginates are used in substances as different as ice cream, toothpaste, and wax polish.

N. STEWART

**See also:** ALGAE; OCEAN HABITATS; PHOTOSYNTHESIS; PLANT KINGDOM; SHORE HABITATS.

**Further reading:**
Raven, P. H., R. F. Evert, and S. E. Eichhorn. 1999. *Biology of Plants*. 6th ed. New York: W. H. Freeman/Worth Publishers.
Thomas, D. N. 2002. *Seaweeds*. Washington D.C.: Smithsonian Institution Press.

*Humans are not the only mammals to use seaweed. Here a sea otter has wrapped itself in kelp to anchor itself in the water.*

# KIDNEYS

## Kidneys are the specialized organs in most vertebrates that filter the blood and remove metabolic waste products

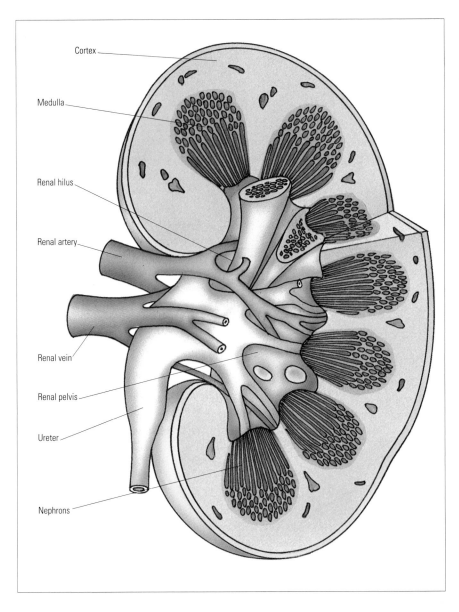

Cortex

Medulla

Renal hilus

Renal artery

Renal vein

Renal pelvis

Ureter

Nephrons

*Waste enters the kidney in the blood, via the renal artery, and leaves through the ureter as urine.*

## CONNECTIONS

● About one-third of people with **DIABETES** develop kidney disease because of damage to the nephrons from high blood-glucose levels. The kidney cannot reabsorb all the glucose, and some spills over into the urine.

More than just mere garbage disposal units, kidneys have an important and vital role in most vertebrates. They are specialized excretory organs that filter out the waste products in the blood. In humans, a remarkable 48 gallons (180 liters) of fluid passes through the kidneys every day. Most of this is fluid reabsorbed back into the bloodstream, except for about 0.4 gallons (1.5 liters), which is excreted as urine. The kidneys also maintain the levels of water and salt in the blood; this function is essential for the survival of all vertebrates (see EXCRETORY SYSTEMS; HOMEOSTASIS).

### Invertebrate excretory organs
Marine invertebrates, such as sponges, do not need specialized excretory structures, as their waste products diffuse out of their bodies straight into the water. However, invertebrates on land have developed structures called nephridial organs to help them conserve water.

In flatworms, the waste products collect in specialized cells, called flame cells, and pass through to the outside of the body through pores. Each segment of an earthworm (phylum Annelida) has a pair of metanephridia that filter out water and glucose from the waste fluid of the body cavities, a concentrated urine being left behind. In crustaceans, fluid from the blood passes into the antennal glands (found at the base of their antennae), where essential nutrients are reabsorbed. Insects and spiders possess Malphigian tubules, which contain cells that transfer salts and wastes into the intestines. Rectal glands reabsorb the salt and water, and the waste product is a semidry paste of uric acid.

### The vertebrate kidney
Humans and other mammals possess two kidneys that lie high up at the back of the abdominal cavity, one on either side of the spine. Each kidney is shaped like a large bean, enclosed by a tough, fibrous capsule and cushioned by a layer of fat.

When a kidney is cut open, one can see the outer cortex, just beneath the capsule, and the medulla, which lies closer to the center of the kidney. The renal artery, supplying blood from the aorta (the main artery from the heart), enters the kidney from above. Collecting ducts in each medulla drain via tubes called ureters into the bladder (the storage vessel for urine). Urine exits the bladder via a single tube, the urethra. Birds and reptiles differ slightly from mammals in that they do not store their urine in a bladder but excrete it directly from their kidneys.

Each kidney contains around 600,000 nephrons, structures that consist of a ball of capillaries called the glomerulus (plural, glomeruli) and long, winding tubules. The number of nephrons is particularly high in birds and mammals, because their high rate of metabolism yields a large amount of waste. The length and precise structure of the nephron is related to how much an animal needs to conserve water, and this need in turn relates to the animal's environment. In humans, in whose environment

### CORE FACTS

■ Kidneys remove waste in most vertebrates; invertebrates have simpler excretory systems.

■ Each kidney contains an outer cortex and an inner medulla and is supplied with blood via the renal artery.

■ Blood is filtered in nephrons, which contain looped tubules and balls of capillaries called glomeruli.

■ Kidneys have an important role in maintaining the salt and water content of the blood.

■ The kidneys produce several hormones, some of which help to maintain blood pressure.

*The sand rat, a desert dweller that needs to conserve fluid, has a high proportion of long nephrons.*

of Henle is particularly long so that it can absorb more water. Lower vertebrates, including marine bony fish, do not possess a loop of Henle, and they are unable to produce concentrated urine, as their kidneys do not absorb very much water. These animals do not need to conserve water because it diffuses easily across their gills.

In birds and mammals, as the filtrate flows around the U-bend of the loop of Henle, water diffuses out into the surrounding tissue, and the filtrate becomes highly concentrated. This process is called the countercurrent multiplication system (see EXCRETORY SYSTEMS). The distal tubule and the collecting ducts are the sites of homeostatic regulation, where, under hormonal control, the final adjustments are made to water, salt, and urea content. The final filtrate, urine, consists mainly of urea or uric acid. These waste products are derived from the breakdown of proteins and contain nitrogen.

water is readily available, most nephrons are short. About 15 percent of bird and mammal species, however, must conserve water more efficiently and thus, their kidneys contain long hephrons.

The various parts of the nephron include the cup-shaped Bowman's capsule, which contains the glomerulus; the proximal tubule (nearest to the capsule); the loop of Henle; the distal tubule (farthest away from the capsule); and the collecting duct. The glomerular capillaries filter the blood so that only molecules below a certain size get through. Plasma—the liquid component of blood—and small molecules are filtered through easily, leaving behind large proteins, red and white blood cells, and fatty acids.

In the proximal tubule, the substances that are essential to the body are reabsorbed. They include glucose (blood sugar), phosphate, amino acids, vitamins, uric acid, bicarbonate, hormones, salt, and water (60 to 80 percent of which is reabsorbed). The main function of the U-shaped loop of Henle, apart from the fine tuning of the filtrate, is the further reabsorption of water. In desert mammals, the loop

## A balancing act

The kidney is able to maintain blood pressure in the glomeruli independent of the overall blood pressure in the renal artery. Thus, the filtration rate in the glomerulus remains constant whether the blood pressure is high (during strenuous exercise, for example,) or low (during sleep, for example). However, the balance can become disrupted if the glomerulus or tubule becomes damaged through injury or kidney disease.

The concentration and volume of the blood is detected by osmotic receptors in the hypothalamus (an area in the center of the brain). If the concentration of the blood is high (that is, if the blood contains very little water), the hypothalamus secretes a hormone called antidiuretic hormone (ADH) that travels along nerves to the pituitary gland, from where it is released into the bloodstream. ADH increases the permeability of the walls of the distal tubules and collecting ducts so that water can be reabsorbed to dilute the blood. Once the adjustment has been made, it is detected by the brain's receptors, and the supply of ADH is shut off. Dilute blood, on the other hand, suppresses ADH release: the tubule walls become impermeable to water, and water is lost as dilute urine. This process is called a negative-feedback mechanism.

## Endocrine function

The kidneys also act as endocrine glands, producing hormones that are discharged directly into the bloodstream. Renin, an enzyme that is released from the kidneys when the blood pressure falls, acts on a protein in the blood to produce a hormone called angiotensin. Angiotensin constricts the small arteries in the body and thus increases the blood pressure back to normal. The renin-angiotensin system also raises blood pressure by stimulating the kidney's cortex to release aldosterone, a hormone that acts on the tubules to promote the reabsorption of sodium and the excretion of potassium. The kidneys also produce prostaglandins. One of

## MONITORING CHANGES

Fluid samples taken from various segments along the nephron of the kidney have allowed scientists to study the many changes that occur in the filtrate composition as it passes from the glomerulus, along the tubules, to the ureter. In one technique—micropuncture—the tubule is compressed just beyond the sampling site, and a small volume of filtrate is drawn out, using a micropipette, so that it can be analyzed.

**A CLOSER LOOK**

# RENAL BLOOD SUPPLY

The kidneys have a rich blood supply, to enable them to filter the blood, and to provide their cells with nutrients. Each glomerular tuft represents a tiny branch of the renal artery. The afferent arteriole enters the glomerulus, forming a knot of around 50 capillaries, each of which is in close contact with the membrane lining the capsule. A hydrostatic pressure (the pressure exerted by the fluid itself) drives the filtrate into and through the tubule. The efferent arteriole leads away from the glomerulus, dividing again to form the peritubular capillaries, which surround the tubule and collecting duct. Capillaries also run alongside the loop of Henle; they are called the vasa recta. All the capillaries rejoin to form a larger venule, which eventually runs into the main renal vein.

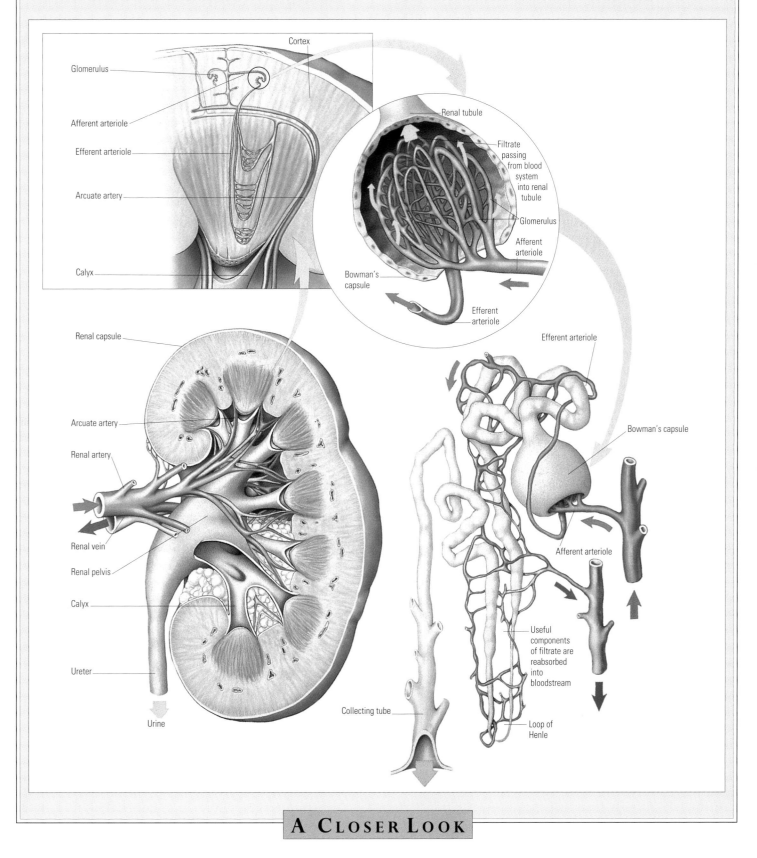

Cortex
Glomerulus
Afferent arteriole
Efferent arteriole
Arcuate artery
Calyx

Renal tubule
Filtrate passing from blood system into renal tubule
Glomerulus
Afferent arteriole
Bowman's capsule
Efferent arteriole

Renal capsule
Arcuate artery
Renal artery
Renal vein
Renal pelvis
Calyx
Ureter
Urine

Efferent arteriole
Bowman's capsule
Afferent arteriole
Useful components of filtrate are reabsorbed into bloodstream
Collecting tube
Loop of Henle

## A CLOSER LOOK

# KIDNEY FAILURE

Only one normal kidney is needed for good health, so kidney failure is only life threatening if it affects both kidneys. There are two types of kidney failure: acute (developing suddenly) and chronic (developing over months or years).

Acute kidney failure may occur for several reasons, including very low blood pressure (hypotension), a decrease in the blood flow to the kidneys (perhaps from dehydration, hemorrhage, or extensive burns), damage to the kidney, or the obstruction of urine flow. The main symptom of acute kidney failure is a decrease in urine production, although symptoms of the underlying cause may also develop. Kidney function usually returns to normal once the underlying cause has been discovered and treated.

Chronic kidney failure can be caused by kidney disease. People with chronic kidney failure tend to produce large quantities of urine, as either their damaged glomeruli allow more fluid to filter through or the reabsorption of water in the tubules is impaired. Symptoms of chronic kidney failure include weight loss, itching, headaches, and if severe, eventual collapse, coma, and death. Mild chronic renal failure often needs no treatment, providing the patient drinks plenty of fluid. If the chronic renal failure is severe, a life-threatening condition known as end-stage renal failure develops.

When the kidneys are damaged, their functions must be maintained so that waste products are still removed from the body and the chemical balance of the blood is maintained. Replacement therapy includes organ transplant (see TRANSPLANTS) or dialysis, a technique that involves filtering the blood through a semipermeable membrane (see LIFE SUPPORT). Without such artificial kidney dialysis, toxic wastes build up in the blood and tissues and cannot be filtered by the damaged kidneys. This condition is called uremia, meaning "urine in the blood," and is eventually fatal. In acute kidney failure, dialysis will be temporary, until the blood pressure, blood volume, and urine flow are back to normal. In chronic kidney failure, dialysis is likely to be long term, and many patients learn to perform the procedure at home.

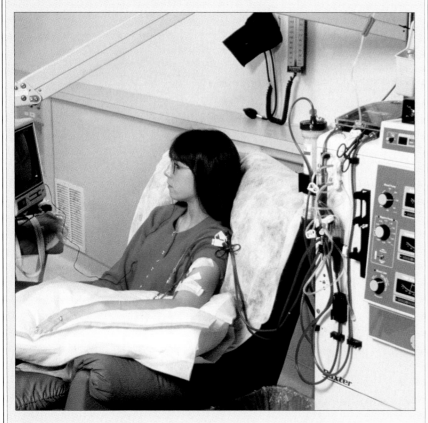

*Dialysis involves using an artificial kidney machine to remove waste products and fluid from the blood.*

## A CLOSER LOOK

the functions of these hormones is to act on the kidney to regulate the renal blood flow. Some prostaglandins cause arteries to constrict; others cause them to dilate. The kidneys also produce a hormone called erythropoietin in response to oxygen starvation; it acts on stem (precursor) cells in the bone marrow to make more red blood cells.

## Embryonic development

In primitive fish – known as cyclostomes – as well as in fish and amphibian larvae, rudimentary kidney organs develop from the series of body segments (somites) that occur early in embryonic development. Stalks protruding from the segments develop into a single nephrotome, which has a uriniferous (urine drainage) tubule.

In higher vertebrates, the kidney arises from a succession of structures. Tubules derived from cells of the embryonic nephrogenic (kidney-forming) cord form a Bowman's capsule at one end, which is supplied with a blood vessel from the branching aorta. The other end of the tubule leads to the mesonephric, or Wolffian, duct, a collecting channel that completes the adult form of the fish and amphibian kidneys.

In reptiles and birds, an intermediate structure (the mesonephros, from which the final kidney is derived) functions until hatching. In mammals, the role of the mesonephros is variable. It is responsible for producing urine in the fetal pig until birth and yet is only rudimentary in rodents.

In human embryos, the mesonephros produces urine between gestational weeks 5 and 12 and eventually degenerates to form the ureteric bud, which grows toward the nephrogenic cells. As the two tissues interact, the ureteric bud branches out into collecting ducts, and renal tubules begin to combine from the nephrogenic cells at the duct tips. The Bowman's capsule appears at an early stage, and as nephron formation proceeds, many tiny arterioles reach out from the renal artery, forming capillaries. The growing tubule elongates to form the loop of Henle and produces urine (and thus maintains homeostasis) well before birth. The guinea pig and human fetus have their full complement of nephrons at birth; in a newborn rat, nephrogenesis continues for a few days. Urine from mammalian fetal kidneys is the major component of amniotic fluid, the fluid surrounding the fetus.

E. SAREWITZ

**See also:** EXCRETORY SYSTEMS; HOMEOSTASIS; LIFE SUPPORT; TRANSPLANTS.

## Further reading:
Callaghan, C. A., and B. M. Brenner. 2000. *The Kidney at a Glance*. Boston: Blackwell Scientific.
Grenberg, A., A. K. Cheung, and T. Coffman. 2001. *Primer on Kidney Diseases*. 3rd ed. New York: Academic Press.
Koeppen, B. M., and B. A. Stanton. 2001. *Renal Physiology*. 3rd ed. St Louis: Mosby Publishers.

# KREBS CYCLE

**Krebs cycle is the central biochemical process that harnesses energy from food to be used by cells**

*Strenuous exercise needs immediately available energy. Krebs cycle helps provide ATP, which supplies the energy.*

## CONNECTIONS

● **CARBOHYDRATES** are important **ENERGY** stores.

● Krebs cycle is an important part of **CELL BIOLOGY** and **ATP PRODUCTION**.

● **BIOCHEMISTRY** is the study of chemical processes in living organisms.

All living organisms require energy to live. At a cellular level, small organic molecules are constantly being organized into polymers (large chains of molecules) such as proteins and DNA (deoxyribonucleic acid, the genetic material). In addition, substances are pumped across membranes, and cells are continually moving, changing shape, growing, repairing, and reproducing (see CELL BIOLOGY). To perform these tasks, there must be an input of fuel, which comes from eating plants, animals, and other organisms. How does the body change the chemical energy present in the food eaten into a form it can use to fuel its cellular processes?

## ATP and its production

Adenosine triphosphate (ATP) is the fuel that powers cellular work and drives all biochemical processes within the body. It is generated from glucose during cellular respiration. Respiration consists of three metabolic processes: glycolysis, Krebs cycle (sometimes called the citric acid cycle or the tricarboxylic acid cycle), and electron transport/oxidative phosphorylation (see CARBOHYDRATES; ENERGY; METABOLISM). Glycolysis and Krebs cycle are the pathways that break down glucose into organic fuels. The enzymes required for glycolysis are in the cytosol, the fluid inside cells, while Krebs cycle and the electron transport enzymes are present inside the cell organelles called mitochondria.

During glycolysis, each molecule of glucose is broken down into two molecules of pyruvate. The pyruvate then crosses the double membrane of mitochondria into the matrix (the central zone of the mitochondria), where it is converted to a compound called acetyl coenzyme A (acetyl CoA) and carbon dioxide by the link reaction (see page 994). Acetyl CoA then enters Krebs cycle by joining with oxaloacetate to form citrate. Then in a series of metabolic steps, two carbon atoms from the citrate are oxidized to form carbon dioxide. The electrons derived from these reactions are carried to a series of proteins in the mitochondrial membrane that make up a multicomponent electron transport chain.

The electrons carried through this transport system eventually join with oxygen to produce water. Before this final step, the free energy derived from the electron transport reactions is used to make small, easy-to-use molecules of ATP by the oxidative phosphorylation process. Respiration cashes in the large amount of energy banked in glucose. For each molecule of glucose broken down by glycolysis, Krebs cycle, and electron transport, 38 molecules of ATP are manufactured.

## Accessible fuel

ATP has a triphosphate tail containing three negatively charged phosphate groups. This tail is the key to the molecules' energy-releasing abilities. The tail is the

---

**CORE FACTS**

■ Krebs cycle, also called the citric acid cycle or tricarboxylic acid, is the central process at the heart of the body's energy production.

■ Krebs cycle was first worked out by German-British scientist Hans Krebs. The cycle releases electrons from compounds derived from glucose. These electrons are used to make ATP—the body's fuel.

■ Krebs cycle takes place inside mitochondria, tiny power plants present in almost all living cells.

chemical equivalent of a loaded spring. The three closely packed, negatively charged phosphate groups form an unstable energy store because the negative charges repel each other. The cell harnesses this energy using enzymes that transfer phosphate groups from ATP to other compounds. ATP is converted to ADP (adenosine diphosphate), energy is released as the phosphate group is removed, and ADP is rapidly recycled back to ATP. A working muscle cell recycles ATP at a rate of 10 million molecules per second.

## The link reaction

Krebs cycle is fed by glycolysis. Glycolysis releases less than a quarter of the chemical energy stored in glucose; the rest remains locked in two molecules of pyruvate. In the presence of oxygen, pyruvate enters a mitochondrion and is converted to acetyl CoA by the link reaction, a three-step process that strips the pyruvate of its acetyl group ($CH_3CO$) and transfers it to a coenzyme (CoA), forming acetyl CoA. (A coenzyme supports a specific enzyme.) Without the coenzyme, the enzyme cannot perform its function.

The first step in this process is the removal of pyruvate's carboxyl group, which is released as a molecule of carbon dioxide, $CO_2$. In step two, the remaining two-carbon fragment is oxidized to form acetate. An enzyme then transfers the removed electrons to $NAD^+$, and energy is stored in the form of NADH. In the final step, coenzyme A, a sulfur-containing compound derived from vitamin B, is attached to the acetate by an extremely unstable sulfur bond, and thus, the acetyl group is very reactive. The chemical product of the link reaction, acetyl CoA, is now fed into Krebs cycle.

## HANS KREBS

Hans Adolf Krebs (1900–1981) was a German-born British biochemist who was the first to discover the citric acid cycle, now called Krebs cycle. His achievement was honored in 1953, when he was awarded the Noble Prize for chemistry. Like many scientists, however, Krebs owed much of his success to earlier researchers. In the early 1930s scientists knew from conducting experiments on minced muscle tissue that citrate, α-ketoglutarate, succinate, and malate were rapidly oxidized during respiration. Scientists had also discovered that stopping the oxidation of succinate to fumarate also stopped cellular respiration. This finding suggested that succinate played an important role in cellular metabolism. In 1935 Hungarian scientist Albert Szent-Gyorgi found that the rate of oxidation during respiration could be rapidly accelerated by adding small amounts of succinate, fumarate, malate, or oxaloacetate to muscle tissue, the indication being that these substances were directly involved in the respiration reactions. Szent-Gyorgi also discovered that one substance could be converted to another, in the following sequence:

succinate ⟶ fumarate ⟶ malate ⟶ oxaloacetate

At a similar time, Carl Martins and Franz Knoop demonstrated that citrate (citric acid) could be oxidized to α-ketoglutarate via cisaconitate and isocitrate.

At the University of Freiburg (1932), Krebs and fellow researcher Kurt Henseleit had already discovered the urea cycle, a series of chemical reactions in which ammonia and carbon dioxide are converted to the much less toxic urea.

In 1933 Krebs was forced to leave Nazi Germany for England, where he continued his research at the University of Cambridge and at Sheffield University. Armed with the idea of a cycle and a number of pieces of the puzzle, Hans Krebs set about investigating respiration. He conducted experiments on minced pigeon breast muscle, which has a very high rate of respiration. Krebs showed that in the presence of a substance that inhibits the oxidation of succinate to fumarate, succinate could be formed from added fumarate, malate, or oxaloacetate. The inhibitor acted like a blockage behind which succinate accumulated. Since the inhibitor also prevented the direct formation of succinate from fumarate, it was clear that the reaction had gone in a circle. Krebs then showed that pyruvate and oxaloacetate could be combined by enzymes; a discovery that enabled him to close the circle and explain how pyruvate was metabolized. Finally, he demonstrated that the rates of each reaction were rapid enough to account for the rapid rate of respiration. By 1937 Krebs had uncovered the cycle that is central to nearly all metabolic processes and the source of two-thirds of the food-derived energy in higher organisms.

### DISCOVERERS

# KREBS CYCLE IN DETAIL

**Step 1** The cycle begins with acetyl CoA, generated from pyruvate by the link reaction. Acetyl CoA and oxaloacetate react in the presence of water to form citrate (or citric acid). This reaction is catalyzed by the enzyme citrate synthase. In this reaction, the acetyl group ($CH_3CO$) from the two-carbon acetyl CoA is added to the four-carbon oxaloacetate to form citrate, which has six-carbons. CoA is then free to prime another two-carbon fragment derived from pyruvate. Water gives up hydrogen to CoA, while oxygen is used to form citrate and is combined as a hydroxyl group (OH).

**Step 2** Citrate is now converted to its isomer isocitrate by the enzyme aconitase. Isomers are made up of exactly the same molecule types and have the same number of each molecule, but the arrangement of the molecules is different. In citrate the hydroxyl group (OH) is attached to the third carbon in the chain, but in isocitrate it is moved to the fourth carbon. Aconitase moves the hydroxyl group by removing water from the molecule, forming cis-aconitate. It then adds water back again to form isocitrate.

**Step 3** Isocitrate is now converted to $\alpha$-ketoglutarate by the enzyme isocitrate dehydrogenase. Isocitrate is oxidized to the intermediate oxalosuccinate, reducing a molecule of $NAD^+$ to NADH and releasing a free hydrogen ion ($H^+$). Carbon dioxide ($CO_2$) is then released to give the five-carbon $\alpha$-ketoglutarate.

**Step 4** The forth step is a little more complicated; $\alpha$-ketoglutarate is catalyzed by a multienzyme complex (similar to that which converts pyruvate to acetyl CoA) to form succinyl CoA. The enzyme $\alpha$-ketoglutarate dehydrogenase causes $\alpha$-ketoglutarate to release a further molecule of carbon dioxide ($CO_2$). At the same time, CoA gives up hydrogen to a second $NAD^+$ to form NADH, and another free hydrogen ion is released ($H^+$). The CoA now combines with the $\alpha$-ketoglutarate residue (by an unstable sulphur bond) to form succinyl CoA.

**Step 5** CoA is now released from succinyl CoA, forming succinate. The enzyme that catalyses this reaction is succinyl-CoA synthetase. CoA is displaced by a phosphate group, which is then transferred to

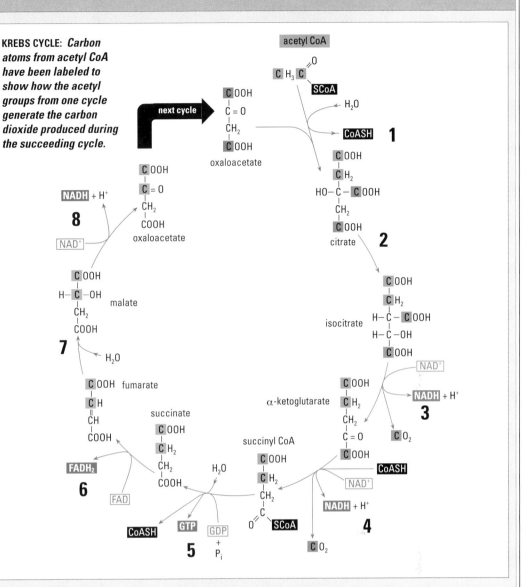

**KREBS CYCLE:** *Carbon atoms from acetyl CoA have been labeled to show how the acetyl groups from one cycle generate the carbon dioxide produced during the succeeding cycle.*

GDP (guanosine diphosphate) to form GTP (guanosine triphosphate). It should be noted that the high-energy sulphur bond is transferred to a molecule of GDP, which takes up another phosphate group, the result being high-energy GTP. Substrate level phosphorylation occurs at this step because ATP is formed when GTP donates a phosphate group to ADP.

**Step 6** Next succinate is converted to fumarate by the enzyme succinate dehydrogenase. Succinate is oxidized to fumarate, and two freed hydrogen atoms reduce the coenzyme FAD to $FADH_2$

**Step 7** The enzyme fumarase now adds water to fumarate to form malate. The bonds in the substrate are rearranged during this step owing to the addition of a water molecule.

**Step 8** The last oxidative step converts malate to oxaloacetate with the help of the enzyme malate dehydrogenase. At the same time, $NAD^+$ is reduced to NADH, and another free hydrogen ion ($H^+$) is released.

**Step 9** The oxaloacetate then reenters the cycle at step 1.

*Ice hockey players use large amounts of energy. Working muscle cells recycle ATP, the energy-supplying molecule, at a rate of 10 million molecules per second.*

## Krebs cycle

Krebs cycle is the central "gear wheel" of the metabolic machine. The second of the major stages in ATP production, it is named for German scientist Hans Krebs (1900–1981), who discovered it. Krebs cycle is fueled by acetyl CoA and passes through a series of eight steps, converting one substance to another and giving up high-energy electrons and carbon dioxide along the way. Specific enzymes within the mitochondrial matrix catalyze each stage. The product of the last step in the cycle (oxaloacetate) then reenters at step 1, and the cycle begins again (see the diagram on page 995).

The circular sequence of Krebs cycle means that energy is released gradually in stages rather than in a sudden burst. Energy released during Krebs cycle is conserved for ATP generation. Krebs cycle generates high-energy electrons, which are required by the final stage of respiration to transform ADP to ATP.

## MITOCHONDRIA

Mitochondria (singular, mitochondrion) are present in virtually all eukaryotic cells. They are the "power plants" that convert energy into a form the cell can use. Mitochondria are the sites of cellular respiration; they extract energy from sugars, fats, and other fuels with the help of oxygen to create an energy store in the form of ATP. There are often hundreds or even thousands of mitochondria within the cytoplasm of a cell. The greatest numbers of mitochondria are found in cells that require a large amount of energy, such as muscle cells. Mitochondria are about the size of a bacterium. They are oval and have a double membrane. The outer membrane is smooth and easily permeable to sugar molecules, such as glucose, while the inner membrane is ruffled with infoldings called cristae. Krebs cycle occurs in the matrix, while the electron-transport chain takes place on the large surface area provided by the cristae. The matrix contains a mixture of hundreds of different enzymes, including all those required for Krebs cycle. A membrane complex from the inner membrane, called ATP synthase, catalyzes the synthesis of ATP in the matrix. Mitochondria contain their own ribosomes and carry their own genomes, which are similar to those present in bacteria. Mitochondria can grow and reproduce on their own within the cell. This ability has led some scientists to believe that mitochondria (like chloroplasts) may have evolved from prokaryotes that lived symbiotically inside larger cells.

## Redox reactions

How does the breakdown of glucose build up the energy for ATP production? The answer is based on the transfer of electrons. The relocation of electrons releases the energy stored in food molecules, and this energy is used to manufacture ATP.

During respiration, electrons are transferred from one reactant to another. These electron transfer reactions are called oxidation-reduction (redox) reactions: one substance is reduced (gains electrons), and another is oxidized (loses electrons). A substance that causes the reduction of another substance (and is oxidized itself) is called a reducing agent, while a substance that causes another substance to be oxidized (and is reduced itself) is called an oxidizing agent.

Some of the steps in glycolysis and Krebs cycle are redox reactions, in which dehydrogenase enzymes transfer electrons from the breakdown products of glucose to the electron carrier nicotinamide adenine dinucleotide ($NAD^+$) to form NADH. $NAD^+$ is therefore an oxidizing agent.

NADH carries electrons from glycolysis and Krebs cycle to the electron transport chain. $FADH_2$, a reduced form of flavin adenine dinucleotide (FAD), also carries electrons from Krebs cycle to the electron transport chain.

## Phosphorylation

The electron transport chain accepts electrons from the products of the first two stages. Electrons are passed from one carrier to another, and as they pass along the chain, hydrogen ions are pumped across the inner mitochondrial membrane, producing a concentration gradient. The flow of hydrogen back through the membrane is believed to be the driving force for ATP production, much like water turning a waterwheel. The enzyme ATP synthase uses the ion flow to convert ADP to ATP. The returning hydrogen ions combine with oxygen to form water.

This mode of ATP production is called oxidative phosphorylation because it is governed by redox reactions that transfer electrons from food to oxygen. ATP is produced in large amounts by the electron transport chain. Smaller amounts of ATP are formed by substrate phosphorylation from some of the reactions in glycolysis and Krebs cycle. However, 90 percent of ATP is produced by oxidative phosphorylation.

The sum total of the reactions in Krebs cycle can be expressed as follows:

$$\text{Acetyl CoA} + 3H_2O + 3NAD^+ + FAD + ADP + P_i \rightarrow 2CO_2 + 3NADH + FADH_2 + \text{CoA-SH} + ATP$$

T. JACKSON

**See also:** CARBOHYDRATES; CELL BIOLOGY; ENERGY; METABOLISM.

## Further reading:

Nelson, D. L., and M. M. Cox. 2000. *Lehninger's Principles of Biochemistry*. 3rd ed. New York: Worth Publishing.

# LACTATION

**Lactation is the formation and secretion of milk for the nourishment of offspring**

*The female snow leopard (Panthera uncia), seen above suckling two cubs, passes on immunological resistance while feeding her young.*

## CONNECTIONS

● **HORMONES** play an important part in controlling the beginning and duration of lactation.

● The virus that causes **AIDS** can be transmitted through breast-feeding if the mother is infected.

Although lactation (the ability to secrete milk) is generally associated with mammals, a variety of organisms produce fluids to nourish their young. Bees and wasps, for example, produce new queens by providing select larvae with royal jelly, a fluid rich in sugar and protein. In some elasmobranches (sharklike fishes), part of the ovary secretes a fluid, often called uterine milk, that nourishes the young in utero. Although these substances are not strictly milk, they are nourishing fluids that feed offspring. However, there are two species of birds that do produce milk. Pigeons and flamingos, both male and female, are able to produce milk in their crops (called crop milk). The milk is the only food intake of the young hatchlings for the first few days of life.

In mammals, milk is produced by specialized mammary glands, the breasts, and the transfer of this fluid from mother to infant is a defining characteristic of this group. The milk glands deliver their milk through an equally specialized structure—a teat, or nipple—that allows the infant to suckle.

### The mammary gland

Both the number and position of the mammary glands and the external shape of the teats differ among species. Most mammals have somewhere between two and eight teats; however, the mouse opossum (*Marmosa* spp.) has up to 19 teats.

Mammals without teats belong to a primitive mammalian group, the monotremes, which includes the duckbill platypus (*Ornithorhynchus anatinus*). In these mammals, the milk-producing glands are not ducted together to open into a central nipple: instead milk is licked or sucked from tufts of hair situated above the mammary glands. In humans and many other mammals, the teat is prominent; in rats and mice, it is nearly flat. The internal structure of the gland, however, is

---

### CORE FACTS

■ Lactation is predominantly a mammalian characteristic, but other animals may also produce similar milklike fluids.

■ Mammalian milk is produced by specialized mammary glands (breasts) and is delivered to offspring via a teat, or nipple.

■ Mammalian milk serves two purposes: the provision of food and water for the developing young and the transmission of the mother's immunological resistance (antibodies).

similar in most species and is composed of a system of milk-producing tissue, ducts, and supporting tissue.

## The dual purpose of mammalian milk

Milk has two functions: it provides offspring with water and an easily digested and concentrated food, which promotes rapid growth, and it also provides protection for the young from certain diseases. The antibody immunoglobulin A (IgA; see ANTIBODIES; IMMUNE SYSTEMS) is produced by the breast and acts mostly against intestinal microorganisms and antigens. This antibody is able to pass through the digestive tract to the intestine of the infant. Cells and other immunogenic molecules are also passed to the offspring through the milk.

## Milk production and suckling

In most mammals, milk production begins in the last trimester of pregnancy (see PREGNANCY AND BIRTH). The epithelium (outer cell layer) of the ducts is stimulated by increased levels of the hormones estradiol and progesterone (produced mainly by the placenta) to develop into alveoli capable of secreting milk. However, progesterone also inhibits milk secretion. Following birth, the placenta is ejected, thus removing its inhibitory effect on the brain's pituitary gland. The pituitary secretes large amounts of the hormone prolactin to stimulate the breast to produce milk.

Prolactin and growth hormone are produced in the mother at low levels prior to birth and before suckling. As the suckling action of the infant empties the glands in the breast of milk, the pituitary gland is stimulated to increase its production of prolactin and growth hormone; in turn, the production of milk by the glands is increased. Hence milk production is a positive-feedback loop (see INFORMATION SCIENCE), in which more suckling leads to more milk, which in turn leads to more suckling.

Depending on the species, milk is delivered by two routes. In the first, suckling releases milk directly into the mouth of the infant. In the second, the milk must drop, or be let down, a process called the milk ejection reflex. In this case, suckling stimulates nerves in the teat, or nipple, which send signals through the spinal cord to an area of the the brain called the hypothalamus, which triggers the release into the bloodstream of the hormone oxytocin, which stimulates contraction of special cells in the mammary gland. These contractions create pressure in the gland, and the milk ejects out through the teat when the infant sucks on it.

Suckling frequency and the method of milk transfer vary widely. Some marine mammals suckle a few times a week and receive gallons of milk each time; rodents may nurse their young up to 80 times a day. Even within species, the rate at which an infant suckles will decline through the period of lactation. In the horse, for example, peak lactation occurs in the first six or eight weeks, with the infant suckling for three or four minutes each hour. From about two months weaning begins, and both suckling frequency and duration decline until at approximately seven to nine

---

# MILK'S VARIABLE COMPOSITION

The composition of milk varies both within and between species. For a short period after birth, the mother produces colostrum, a fluid high in antibodies and critical to early immunity in the offspring. Thereafter, a milk rich in fats, sugars, and proteins is produced. The most familiar milk to humans, cows' milk, is usually about 85 percent water, 3 percent protein, 3 percent fat, and 9 percent milk sugar (lactose). Even cows' milk varies widely, with the milk of some cattle breeds producing twice this amount of fat. Milk quality also changes throughout the period of lactation, with the proportion of solids (fat and protein) declining through time. A female kangaroo is remarkable in that she will often be suckling young at very different stages of development and will therefore be producing milk of different compositions from different teats.

Differences in composition, in particular the concentration of fat and protein, often reflect the environment and ecology of the species involved. In many species of seals, the female nurses on breeding beaches or ice floes and has only a short period in which to raise her young. Females will nurse for a relatively short period of time, usually 20 to 40 days, in the hooded seal (*Cystophora cristata*), as little as four days. During this period, the seal pup must grow adequately to survive in the ocean; it increases in length but also acquires a thick insulating layer of fat that both protects it from cold water and provides a buffer of energy, which it needs while it learns to feed in the ocean. Seal milk is therefore very rich; 36 percent fat, 15 percent protein, and only 40 percent water. During lactation, a female seal may lose 30 to 50 percent of her body weight, and her pup may double its weight. In contrast, many desert animals produce dilute milk. Camel milk, for example, is watery, since young camels frequently get all their water from their mother's milk, and has 1 to 2 percent fat. As the water requirements of a lactating camel can therefore double, the animal must remain near a water supply.

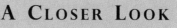

## A CLOSER LOOK

months, the young foal is completely weaned, that is, able to take food other than its mother's milk.

J. GINSBERG

**See also**: ANTIBODIES; HORMONES; IMMUNE SYSTEMS; INFORMATION SCIENCE; MAMMALS; PREGNANCY AND BIRTH.

## Further reading:

Riordan, J. and K. G. Auerbach, eds. 1999. *Breastfeeding and Human Lactation.* Sudbury, Mass.: Jones and Bartlett Publishers.

*The farm pig has a large number of teats that run from the lower abdomen to the upper chest.*

# LAKES AND PONDS

**Lakes and ponds are open areas of standing or slow-moving water entirely surrounded by land**

Lakes are relatively large bodies of water occupying inland basins, either naturally occurring or artificially made; they are usually sufficiently deep that sunlight cannot reach the bottom. They may be fresh water or contain concentrations of dissolved minerals, such as salt or soda. The physical boundary, the sides and bottom of the lake, is called the lake basin.

Most large lake basins present in the temperate zone were formed by the scraping and gouging action of massive glaciers that appeared during the ice ages of the Pleistocene epoch, which ended some 10,000 years ago. In other areas, lake basins and catchment areas have been shaped by earthquakes, landslides, volcanic activity, natural dams,

erosion, the impact of meteorites, and human activities such as quarrying, mining, and dam building.

Ponds are smaller bodies of water, usually shallow enough for sunlight to penetrate to the bottom. Many ponds have been created by human activity, but natural ponds can be formed by glacial action, slow-moving streams, by sinkholes, and by the thawing of permafrost in tundra regions. In contrast to most lakes, ponds are usually able to support a variety of plant and animal life from shore to shore. Being smaller and shallower, ponds have a relatively short life and may last anywhere from only a few years or decades to several hundred years before they become filled in with plant life. This process is called succession. Some ponds may be seasonal, appearing and disappearing with wet and dry seasons.

Lakes and ponds differ from moving bodies of water, such as streams and rivers, in two important ways. First, lakes and ponds lack any strong directional flow of water; second, the quieter waters of lakes and ponds support large colonies of plant and animal plankton. These organisms multiply in large numbers and thus provide a rich source of nutrients that support other plants and animals (see RIVERS AND STREAMS).

*Lakes and ponds often freeze over when the temperature drops to freezing point or below; the result is temperature differences between the water at the surface and the water at the bottom.*

## CONNECTIONS

● **ALGAE, FISH,** and **FROGS AND TOADS** are just some of the animals that live in lakes and ponds.

● Many plants and animals living in lakes and ponds enter a state of **DORMANCY** during droughts.

### CORE FACTS

- Freshwater lakes make up only 0.0009 percent of Earth's water by volume but represent 98 percent of surface water available for human use.
- Lake waters are divided into littoral, limnetic, and profundal zones.
- In winter in temperate zones, the bottom water of lakes and ponds is warmer than that at the surface.

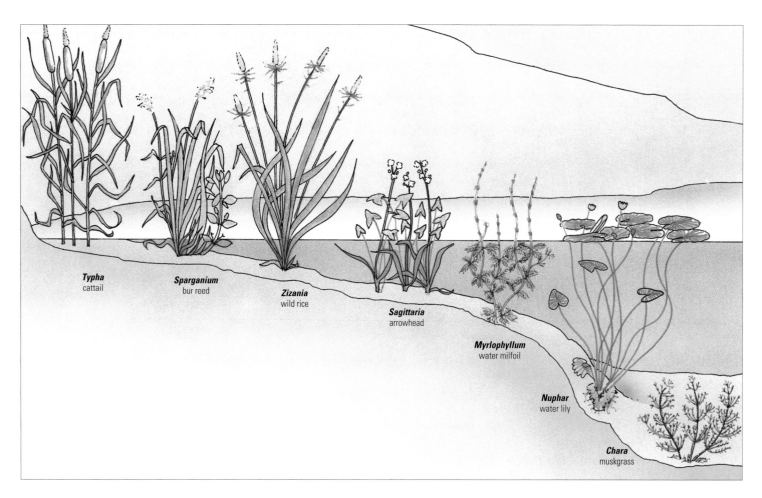

Typha
cattail

Sparganium
bur reed

Zizania
wild rice

Sagittaria
arrowhead

Myrlophyllum
water milfoil

Nuphar
water lily

Chara
muskgrass

*The diagram above shows some of the typical species of plants that grow in the littoral zone of lakes and ponds.*

## Lakes and ponds in the environment

All lakes and ponds play a vital role in their surrounding environment. Water enters these basins and depressions from rainfall, ice, groundwater, soil moisture, and drainage from land (called runoff). Lakes and ponds store the water, return some moisture to the atmosphere through evaporation, and in the case of many lakes, pass water on toward the sea. Between its arrival and departure, water influences the surrounding area by affecting local climate, causing flooding or erosion, and supporting a wide range of plant and animal life. As water moves through lakes and ponds, it acquires organic and inorganic materials from the surrounding land and, carrying them through the ecosystem enriches other land and waters.

## Productivity and zones of lakes and ponds

The productivity of lakes and ponds (the amount of animal and plant life they support) depends on several factors: their geology, depth, water density, pH, the amount of sunlight available, oxygen and carbon dioxide levels, minerals, and nutrients available. Lakes or ponds in which the supply of nutrients is low are called oligotrophic (from the Greek *oligo*, meaning "little" and *trophic*, "food") bodies of water. Those with a rich mix of nutrients are called eutrophic (from the Greek *eu*, meaning "good" or "well").

Generally, shallow lakes and ponds are more productive per unit area than deeper lakes in the same ecosystem. In shallow water, organic matter is broken down and recirculated for use more quickly. The waters also receive more sunlight for photosynthesis, a factor that speeds up both decomposition and the reproduction of plankton and other, larger plants. With a greater abundance of food, shallow lakes and ponds often support large, varied populations of fish and birds.

Most lakes and ponds contain three communities, or zones, with differing conditions and inhabitants. From the shoreline to open water is the littoral (from the Latin *litoralis*, meaning "of the shore"), or shallow-water zone, where light penetrates to the bottom. The limnetic (from the Greek *limne*, meaning "pools" or "marshes") zone is the layer of open water free from both the sides and bottom of a lake or large pond. This zone is open to light penetration and absorption of oxygen. The profundal (from the Latin *profundus*, meaning "deep" or "vast") zone is the bottom of the lake or pond, which is usually covered by layers of fine, thick mud, in which animals may live. There is little light or oxygen at this level.

• **Littoral zone:** Plants commonly present in the littoral zone include cattails, reeds, pond weeds, and water lilies. Living in shallow waters near the shoreline, these large plants receive abundant sunlight, oxygen, and nutrients. They also help to create a habitat for other organisms by providing an area of quiet water where fine mud settles and more fragile organisms can live without being battered by waves. Reed beds and pond weed provide food, shelter, and breeding grounds for aquatic birds, reptiles, insects, amphibians, shallow-water fish, crustaceans, snails, and mollusks. Some fish, such as the stickleback (*Gasterosteus aculeatus*), spend their entire life in the littoral zone, while others, such as the pike (*Esox lucius*), feed in the limnetic zone but lay their eggs among the vegetation in the quieter littoral waters. No rooted land plants can grow beyond the littoral zone because of the greater water depth.

• **Limnetic zone:** Because even the smallest living organisms tend to sink in fresh water, plants and animals that live in the limnetic zone must have some type of flotation device or be kept suspended by water turbulence. Microscopic planktonic organisms can swim but are at the mercy of waves, currents, and eddies, which can overpower their ability to direct their own movements. Fish are powerful swimmers and most also have swim bladders to keep them afloat and to reduce the amount of energy required to counteract gravity (see FISH). Other active swimmers may include frogs, turtles, muskrats, otters, beavers, crocodiles, and hippopotamuses.

Prey and predator species have developed different adaptations to living in open water where there is literally nowhere to hide. Some prey, such as crustaceans of the genus *Daphnia*, have evolved nearly transparent bodies to make it difficult for predators to spot them. Other prey species hide in the darker depths of the water during the day, rising only at night to feed on plankton. Fish that commonly live in the limnetic zone are insect-eating fish, including trout (*Salmo trutta*) and their relatives. This zone also supports insect-eating birds such as grebes, pelicans, and terns, which dive for their prey or catch it close to the surface. Birds may also use open water as a refuge from land predators (see WATERBIRDS AND WADERS).

• **Profundal zone:** Very few ponds have a profundal zone. Most organisms living on the bottom of a lake or burrowing into it survive primarily from nourishment that falls from the limnetic zone above and by being able to withstand low oxygen and light levels. Several species of algae live here, sharing the zone with numerous smaller animals such as nematode worms and ostracods (small crustaceans).

The larger animals present here are mainly worms, the larvae of chironomid flies (midges), and mollusks. The prolific chironomids are a major food source for other animals and serve as a vital link in the food webs of nearly every lake ecosystem. Mollusks and mussels are also important inhabitants of the profundal zone and are often the largest members to feed directly on algae. Because of the low oxygen content of this zone, many of the worms, such as those of the order Oligochaete, have red blood cells that help trap oxygen. Other animals adapt to the lack of oxygen by decreasing their respiratory and metabolic rates. Fish that feed in these gloomy depths do not find their prey by sight. Many have evolved sensory barbels, or whiskers, around their mouth, to taste and feel for their prey. Carp and catfish are among the most common fish present in this zone.

## POLLUTION AND LAKES

Industrial waste, human sewage, and the drainage of commercial fertilizers, pesticides, and herbicides from farmland have threatened the survival of many lakes and ponds. These forms of pollution add nutrients to the water, primarily nitrogen and phosphorus, which encourage the rapid growth of algae. These algal blooms, as they are called (see the picture below), set off a chain of events in the lake or pond ecosystem called eutrophication, or accelerated productivity. As algae multiply, they use up oxygen during the night stage of photosynthesis. Oxygen is also required to decompose algae when they die. As the level of oxygen falls, fish and other animals suffocate. Bacteria decomposing the algae release phosphorus back into the water, which in turn feeds more algae. As sedimentation fills the basin, large plants begin to smother the remaining open water. The resulting wetland dries out, and woody shrubs invade, until eventually the lake or pond disappears.

Other chemicals also threaten life in lakes and ponds. Silicates, ingredients of some detergents, can damage diatoms and algae whose cell walls contain silica. Acid rain can affect the pH of a body of water until it approaches the acidity of lemon juice (see ACID RAIN). The more acidic a lake or pond becomes, the less able it is to support life.

Biological Oxygen Demand (BOD), as a measurement of the level of oxygen in a body of water and the demand on this oxygen by organisms in that water, enables environmental protection agencies to determine the health of the water. The information provided by this measurement helps to show whether pollution is taking place. By determining whether pollution is taking place, efforts can be made to control and legislate against it by local state and federal governments.

## AT RISK

## CITIES BY LAKES

Since the earliest days of human civilization, people have built cities near large bodies of water. Lakes and their connecting rivers provide vital transportation routes to and from the sea and from one section of a country to another. On the Great Lakes in the American Midwest, for example, barges, steamships, and freighters carry raw materials, farm produce, and finished goods to and from the cities along their shores.

Lakes also serve as sources of irrigation water for surrounding farmland. In many countries, particularly hot countries such as Egypt and Pakistan, rivers feeding into lakes have been dammed and artificial lakes created to supply water for millions of acres of desert land. Some of these storage reservoirs can also be used to supply hydroelectric power for cities. Lakes are also popular as recreational areas, and they often support a thriving industry of summer and winter water sports.

One of the most famous cities by a lake in North America is Salt Lake City, set on the shores of the Great Salt Lake in the Utah desert. This city, founded by the Church of Jesus Christ of Latter-day Saints, or Mormons, in 1847, overlooks the largest lake in the western United States. Although Salt Lake's waters are fed by freshwater streams, the lake has no outlet, and evaporation leaves salt and other minerals behind. In dry years, the saline content of the lake may reach 16 to 27 percent. No fish can live in the salty water but a species of briny shrimp survives quite well. The lake supplies salt and other minerals to the city and surrounding communities and generates considerable tourist revenue.

## A CLOSER LOOK

### Seasonal changes in lakes and ponds

Seasonal cycles bring distinct changes in growing conditions in lakes and pond. Most lakes and some deeper ponds develop temperature differences between the surface and the bottom. In summer, the surface water is warmer and therefore less dense, the result being so-called thermal stratification, in which the cooler, denser water remains at the bottom. The sharp temperature change between the two layers is called the thermocline. For temperate zone lakes, the windier weather in fall and spring combined with changing temperatures mixes the layers from top to bottom. These conditions distribute nutrients, oxygen, and detritus throughout the zones and increase the productivity of the waters. Lakes in tropical regions, where there is little seasonal change in temperature, seldom show this level of mixing.

Lakes in climates where temperature variations are more extreme often freeze over during the winter and by doing so create inverse stratification. Water is at its most dense at 39 °F (4 °C) but as it cools and becomes ice at 32 °F (0 °C), it becomes less dense. As ice forms on the surface of the lake, the warmer, denser water that is just below freezing point moves to the bottom of the lake. Most organisms move to the deeper, warmer layers to survive the winter, but with little light or oxygen reaching these depths and with the temperature at only 39 °F (4 °C), some plants and animals do not survive.

Ponds are particularly sensitive to seasonal changes. During rainy seasons, they may overflow their boundaries and so create temporary wetlands and provide breeding grounds for amphibians, birds, small mammals, and fish. In summer or during dry seasons, they may shrink significantly or even disappear. The plant and animal life of ponds often become dormant to survive droughts.

L. S. BAUGH

**See also:** ACID RAIN; RIVERS AND STREAMS; WATERBIRDS AND WADERS.

**Further reading:**
Bronmark, C., and L. A. Hanssin. 1998. *The Biology of Lakes and Ponds (Biology of Habitats).* Oxford: Oxford University Press.
Wetzel, R. G. 2001. *Limnology: Lake and River Ecosystems.* London and New York: Academic Press.

*The stickleback (Gasterosteus aculeatus) is a species of fish that spends its entire life in the littoral zone.*

# LARVAE AND PUPAE

**Larvae and pupae are the stages of development that some animals go through to reach adulthood**

Looking at a delicate and beautifully colored butterfly, it is hard to imagine that it was once a caterpillar. In fact, the caterpillar is the butterfly's larva. A larva (plural, larvae) is a juvenile, free-living, sexually immature animal that often bears no resemblance to the adult it will become. Various kinds of larvae include caterpillars (butterflies and moths), grubs (beetles and bees), maggots (flies), wrigglers (mosquitoes), tadpoles (frogs and toads), and trochophores (free-swimming larvae common to several groups of invertebrate sea dwellers).

The extent of the change that the larvae must undergo to become adults and the amount of time they devote to it varies enormously. In many species, the process may take months or years, and the juvenile and adult may be so totally unlike that scientists have often failed to recognize that they are even related.

## CORE FACTS

- Larvae are young animals that often bear no resemblance to their adult form. They may eat different food and live in a different habitat from the adults.
- In complete metamorphosis, the larvae transform into pupae, in which the adult organs develop.
- In incomplete metamorphosis, the larvae molt several times over, until the wings and reproductive organs reach adult size.

A larval stage follows hatching and precedes adulthood. Larvae spend most of their time eating, which enables a species to restrict the growth and development energy expenditures to the larval (and later, pupal) stages of the life cycle and to devote the energy for locomotion and mating to the adult stage. In all insects, for example, only the adults have functional wings, increasing the opportunities to find a mate and suitable sites for egg laying.

Larvae and the adult usually eat different food and so avoid competition for the same food. They also often live in a different habitat. Most insects are selective about where they live and very particular about what they eat. Thus, many different species can live without competition in a small area, such as on a single plant or on a single animal.

Many species are highly specialized, with adaptations that allow them to gain access to food resources that would otherwise be inaccessible. The adult monarch butterfly, for example, lays between 100 and 500 eggs on the underside of the leaves of a milkweed plant, the only plant that her offspring will eat. Some larvae, such as those of the dragonfly, are opportunistic hunters and feed on worms, tadpoles, other insects, and even fish. The larvae of members of the Rhiphiphoridae beetle family are parasitic and live inside wasps, although the adults feed on flowers.

Because larvae do not possess wings, they are vulnerable to predators. To protect themselves from

*Caterpillars feed only on particular foods and thus, butterflies lay their eggs directly onto their young's food source.*

## CONNECTIONS

- Most larvae are extremely vulnerable to **PREDATION**, as they are unable to move rapidly. Some caterpillars use **CAMOUFLAGE AND MIMICRY** to avoid being seen.

- Molting and **METAMORPHOSIS** are under the control of **HORMONES**.

predation, many caterpillars are camouflaged or are covered with irritating hairs or sharp spines. Others are poisonous or distasteful to eat.

Some larvae are aquatic. They include members of the subfamily of mosquitoes called Culicinae, which includes the northern house mosquito (*Culex pipiens*) and the carriers of malaria (*Anopheles* spp.). The larvae of culicine mosquitoes hatch from a floating, boatlike egg mass deposited on the water's surface. By whipping its body in S-shaped curves, a newly hatched larva swims to the surface to reach air. Aquatic mosquito larvae generally feed on algae and microorganisms.

The mosquito larva hangs at the surface of the water, held in place by the surface tension on the hairs that surround the openings to a siphon (which takes in oxygen). The siphon tube is attached to one of the larva's rear segments and points upward. At the tip of the tube are the openings of two main tracheal (breathing tube) branches. The air that is held within the tracheae makes the end of the body sufficiently buoyant to keep the tube pointed upward. A single larva can filter up to a third of a gallon (1.5 l) of water a day, while remaining motionless at the water's surface.

The surface of water does not provide the culicines with good hiding places. Complete immobility would therefore be risky. When danger looms, the larva sinks beneath the surface and can swim away rapidly if required.

## METAMORPHOSIS

The major changes that a larva goes through during its transformation into an adult are called metamorphosis (from the Greek words *meta*, meaning "over" and *morph*, "form"). There are two major types of metamorphoses—complete and incomplete—which differ in the number and type of stages (see METAMORPHOSIS). The number of larval stages ranges from 33 in some stone flies (over a period of one or more years) to only 5 in more advanced insects (over one season).

### Incomplete metamorphosis

Incomplete metamorphosis involves three stages: egg, larva (sometimes called a nymph), and adult. In some insects, the larvae resemble the adults but do not have all the adult body parts. These larvae go through a series of molts (a process in which they shed their skin; see MOLTING).

Grasshoppers are examples of species that undergo incomplete metamorphosis. Female grasshoppers lay their eggs in the ground, where they hatch into nymphs in the spring. The tiny nymph has no wings or reproductive organs, feeds on plants, and expands inside its hard covering (chitin) until it becomes too small. The animal then molts, an activity that is repeated several times until the wings and reproductive organs develop and reach adult size.

Before every molt, a new skin is laid down beneath the old one. As the nymph tries to grow inside the old skin, it eventually cracks and is shed. The new skin beneath it is soft and loose, allowing the nymph to increase in size before the skin hardens.

Amphibians, such as frogs, toads, newts, and salamanders, also have a three-stage metamorphosis. Depending on the species, the number of eggs laid can vary between two or three and several thousand. The tiny, dark eggs are contained in a protective gel-like substance. After one to three weeks, the eggs hatch, releasing a tadpole that has a round head, small tail, and no eyes or mouth.

For a few days after hatching, the tadpole remains in contact with the gel, or hangs onto a branch of a nearby water plant. During those few days, the eyes and mouth form, the tail gets bigger, and on the outside of the body, gills grow to enable the tadpole to obtain oxygen from the water. Once these features are in place, the tadpole, with a side-to-side motion of its tail, can move away from its support. In frogs and toads, the back legs and then the front legs appear, the tail gradually disappears, and the animal starts to look more and more like the adult; in newts and salamanders, the tail remains. The larval stage usually lasts for two or three months.

## Complete metamorphosis

Complete metamorphosis has four stages—egg, larva, pupa, and adult—and involves dramatic changes. About 90 percent of all insects undergo complete metamorphosis. Among them are butterflies, moths, bees, wasps, ants, beetles, and flies. Interestingly, as these larvae increase in size after hatching, several groups of cells do not increase in cell number but simply become larger. When the larvae are sufficiently grown, they shed their skin in a process called ecdysis, with most insects undergoing from 4 to 12 molts.

Inadequate nourishment may prolong the larval stage and increase the number of molts, postponing adulthood. Even when conditions are favorable, many insects stop growing for a time, a period called diapause. For example, many mosquitoes lay their eggs in late spring or early summer. The eggs lie inactive through the summer, autumn, and winter and hatch the following spring. Diapause prevents the insect from hatching too early and protects it from extreme temperatures. It also ensures that the adults all appear at about the same time for mating.

The larva continues to grow and shed its skin several times and with the last molt transforms into a pupa. Often, when ready to pupate, the larva stops eating and leaves the food site.

Many marine animals also undergo metamorphosis. Many of these species, such as sea urchins (*Echinoidea*), have tiny, free-swimming larvae that live as plankton for a while before turning into adults. Some of these adults are free swimming (medusae), sedentary, or bottom living.

## The hormones that start and stop change

Three main hormones are thought to control the development of metamorphosis in insects. By stimulating glands just behind the head, a chemical called brain hormone controls production of a second hormone, called ecdysone.

Ecdysone stimulates molting and the development of adult characteristics and also influences the action of specific genes (chemical blueprints that determine the final adult form). The effect of brain hormone and ecdysone are offset by a third hormone, juvenile hormone, which actively promotes the retention of larval characteristics. As long as juvenile hormone remains active, each molt results in a larger larva, without reaching pupation. When the amount of juvenile hormone declines, ecdysone signals the onset of the change to the pupa.

## Pupae

From the outside, a pupa (from the Latin word for "doll") looks inactive, with a hard shell and sometimes a silken covering (cocoon). However, inside, the pupa is full of activity as the changes associated with becoming an adult take place.

*During the pupal stage, larval tissues are broken down and gradually rebuilt into the organs needed for adulthood.*

## PERMANENT LARVAE

Sometimes the changes from larva to pupa to adult are not completed, and the characteristics of the juvenile are retained by the adult. This phenomenon is known by many names—pedogenesis (also spelled paedogenesis), pedomorphosis, neoteny, or fetalization. It is present in some worms, including the burrowing acorn worm (phylum Hemichordata).

The term *pedogenesis* also refers to an occasional form of reproduction among larvae of certain species of gall midges (small flies whose larvae make bumps and swellings on trees and other plants). Normally, adult gall midges, males and females, come together to mate but some of the larvae of the females have reproductive cells within their bodies.

The females produce several very large virgin eggs. Each egg hatches into a transparent larva, which contains a daughter larva inside it. When fully developed, these larvae devour the parent as they make their way free. In turn, this new generation is devoured by the larvae within their own bodies.

Several generations of larvae may continue in this fashion without ever "growing up" or being involved in mating with the opposite sex. Each hatch is made up of individuals of the same sex. Two populations of both sexes begin to build up under the bark of the tree where the first eggs were laid.

At some point, a generation is produced in which the larvae mature conventionally and develop into pupae. In time, these mature adult gall midges take wing and mate with the opposite sex. Then the cycle begins again.

*The burrowing acorn worm (Hemichordata), shown above, may be the permanent larval stage of an echinoderm such as a sea star.*

## A CLOSER LOOK

A variety of factors, including environmental conditions such as drought or prolonged frost, can postpone the pupal stage. The pupal stage may also be postponed by an animal's introduction into a new niche where food is plentiful or predators are absent. Pressure to prolong the larval stage may even ultimately result in the elimination of the pupal stage (see the box above).

When pupating, many larvae search out a site where they will be undisturbed. In butterflies, for example, the caterpillar often finds a sheltered place such as a fence or tree. There it makes a tiny silk pad from which to hang upside down.

When a butterfly's pupa (the chrysalis) is mature, the future butterfly can often be seen through the chrysalis's transparent skin. In temperate climates, the chrysalis usually passes the winter in this stage. With the arrival of spring, the chrysalis splits open and a butterfly crawls out.

The new butterfly's wings consist of soft-folded membranes between fluid-filled veins, which rapidly expand. Once the wings have been pumped up to their full size, the fluid dries, and the wings stiffen ready for flight. The caterpillar's mouthparts, suited to chewing, have been lost and replaced with a tube suited to siphoning fluids (mostly nectar). Moths undergo a similar transformation.

Unlike the larva of the butterfly or moth, a honeybee larva is unable to take care of itself. The queen honeybee lays approximately 2,000 rice-shaped eggs a day in cells of the honeycomb. The eggs hatch in a few days. The larva, which looks like a small maggot, is fed by a worker bee up to 1,300 times a day. When the larva becomes as large as the cell in which it is growing, a worker seals off the cell with a wax covering, and the larva develops into a pupa, which goes through dramatic changes for about two weeks. When fully developed into an adult, it breaks the wax seal and emerges.

Although pupae differ enormously in size, shape, and other details, almost all appear passive and immobile. Because of its immobility, the pupal stage is often referred to as the resting stage. The pupa, however, seethes with internal activity.

Adult organs that began development in the larval stage continue to develop during the pupal stage. Many small centers of cell growth, called rudiments or buds, also continue to develop. In a process called histolysis, larval tissue breaks down into many loose cells or is consumed by cells called phagocytes. Around the various organs and buds, cells form into tissues, and the tissues combine into adult organs.

When the external conditions are right, the adult emerges. Adults escape from their pupal cases by several means: by cutting their way out using jaws or sharp spines; by secreting a liquid that dissolves the covering; or by puffing up their body and putting pressure on the shell.

Not all pupae are immobile. The cuculine pupa, for example, which floats at the surface of the water, appears inactive, and the pupal case is almost transparent, enabling the pupa to detect light. If exposed to sudden light or otherwise disturbed, the comma-shaped pupa swims down under the surface of the water with a tumbling motion until danger passes (hence its common name, tumbler).

In some insects, the transition from an aquatic larval and pupal stage to a terrestrial flying adult has its difficulties—if the adult emerges underwater it may die. Blackflies get around this problem by inflating with air shortly before the adult emerges, so that when the pupal case splits, the adult fly can rise to the surface surrounded by an air bubble.

M. DICANIO

**See also:** BUTTERFLIES AND MOTHS; FLIES; FROGS AND TOADS; INSECTS; METAMORPHOSIS; MOLTING.

**Further reading:**
Romoser, W. S., and J. R. Stoffolano. 1998. *The Science of Entomology*. 4th ed. Boston: WCB/McGraw Hill.

# INDEX